Managing Business Processes

Managing Business Processes
BPR and Beyond

Colin Armistead and Philip Rowland

JOHN WILEY & SONS
Chichester · New York · Brisbane · Toronto · Singapore

Other Wiley Editorial Offices

John Wiley & Sons, Inc., 605 Third Avenue,
New York, NY 10158-0012, USA

Jacaranda Wiley Ltd, 33 Park Road, Milton,
Queensland 4064, Australia

John Wiley & Sons (Canada) Ltd, 22 Worcester Road,
Rexdale, Ontario M9W 1L1, Canada

John Wiley & Sons (Asia) Pte Ltd, 2 Clementi Loop #02-01,
Jin Xing Distripark, Singapore 129809

Library of Congress Cataloging-in-Publication Data

Managing business processes : BPR and beyond / edited by Colin
    Armistead and Philip Rowland.
        p.   cm.
    Includes bibliographical references (p.   )
    ISBN 0-471-95490-X (cloth : alk. paper)
    1. Reengineering (Management)   I. Armistead, Colin G.
II. Rowland, A. P. (A. Philip), 1951–   .
HD58.87.M365   1996
658.4--dc20   96–14573
                                                            CIP

British Library Cataloguing in Publication Data

A catalogue record for this book is available from the British Library

ISBN 0-471-95490-X

Typeset in 10/12 pt Times by Mathematical Composition Setters Ltd, Salisbury, Wiltshire.
Printed and bound in Great Britain by Biddles Ltd, Guildford and King's Lynn
This book is printed on acid-free paper responsibly manufactured from sustainable forestation,
for which at least two trees are planted for each one used for paper production.

Contents

Contributors

COLIN ARMISTEAD
Colin Armistead is Professor of Operations Strategy and Management and Head of the Strategy, Operations and Decision Making Department in the Bournemouth University Business School, UK. He also holds the Royal Mail Chair of Business Performance Improvement. Previously Colin was Head of the Operations and Project Management Group at Cranfield School of Management. He has been a champion of the establishment of Operations Management within the syllabus of Business and Management courses in the UK through his work with the Operations Management Association. He is also a Director of the Institute of Business Process Re-engineering. Colin's contribution is recognised through his research, publications, conference speaking and consultancy. Recent publications include *Customer Service and Support* (Financial Times, Pitman) and *Inspired Customer Service*, (Kogan Page).

PHILIP ROWLAND
Philip Rowland has extensive experience of business process management and re-engineering within industry and as an academic. As a manager in a large automotive company he worked extensively on improving processes. Following an MBA at Cranfield he stayed on to become a Teaching Fellow in Operations Management specialising in re-engineering. Philip has continued his association with Cranfield as a Visiting Fellow after taking up work as a full time consultant. He is co-author of *The Essence of Business Process Re-engineering* (Prentice Hall).

VALERIE BENCE
Valerie Bence is a Research Officer working with the Cranfield Centre for Logistics and Transportation at Cranfield School of Management, UK. Her main areas of interest are environmental impact within supply chains, BPR in the National Health Service, international logistics and the promotion and development of case writing.

CLIFF BOWMAN
Dr Cliff Bowman is Senior Lecturer in Strategic Management, Cranfield School of Management, UK. He has been engaged in management development since 1979 after a career in Shell and the UK Civil Aviation Authority. He is the author of a number of texts on strategic management including *Strategic Management* (Macmillan) and *The Essence of Strategic Management* (Prentice Hall). His research interests include competitive strategy, organisation structures for sustainable advantage and the strategy process in top management teams.

GRAHAM CLARK
Graham Clark is a Senior Lecturer in Operations Management, Cranfield School of Management, UK. Before Cranfield he had 15 years' industrial experience as a development engineer and then in production management. Since joining Cranfield he has taught on a wide range of courses and was Director of the Executive MBA programme between 1992 and 1995. He is co-author of two books on services management and has research interests in service quality, customer service and support and operations strategy. He is Director of Cranfield's Service Operations Research Club.

JAMES COOPER
Professor James Cooper is the Director of the Cranfield Centre for Logistics and Transportation and Excel Logistics Fellow at Cranfield School of Management, UK. He is an authority on international logistics, strategy and operations. His involvement in the field began when he joined the distribution division of Kodak, following graduation in economics at Nottingham University. He has participated in DRIVE programmes for the European Community and has been a participant in an influential report, *Reconfiguring European Logistics Systems* in 1993. Professor Cooper has written widely and taught at Universities around the world. He is the UK representative on an OECD expert group on advanced logistics and communications and specialist advisor to the European Committee at the House of Lords.

MARTIN DAVIES
Martin Davies is an ESRC Teaching Fellow in Information Systems at the Cranfield School of Management, UK. His work involves the development and application of techniques for use by people dealing with complex policy and organisational problems. These techniques enable an integrated view of managerial activity, problem solving and organisational improvements. His career prior to joining Cranfield spans 15 years' varied work in operations and product management, large projects management, business development and general management, mainly within the defence industry and government sectors.

CHRIS EDWARDS
Chris Edwards is Professor of Management Information Systems, Cranfield School of Management, UK. Chris worked in industry for twelve years involved in developing business systems. During that time he qualified as a chartered management accountant and hence tended to specialise in financial information systems. He joined the Scottish Business School as a lecturer in 1971. After receiving a PhD he moved to Carnegie-Mellon University, Pittsburgh, USA, and then to a Chair of Management Information Systems at Cranfield. He is particularly interested in IT-enabled business change. During 1994 he conducted seminars on Process Re-design in nine countries and three continents.

ALAN HARRISON
Alan Harrison is Excel Fellow in Automotive Logistics at Cranfield School of Management, UK. Prior to becoming an academic Alan was in manufacturing management at Proctor and Gamble and with GEC, where he was Head of Manufacturing at two product companies. He joined the Operations Management Group at Warwick Business School and was there for nine years before moving to Cranfield. Alan is author of *Just-in Time Manufacturing in Perspective* (Prentice Hall) and a co-author of *Operations Management* (Pitman). His research work focuses on enablers and inhibitors in the flow of materials in different operational contexts. His research examines both the technical and social aspects of implementing business processes in service and manufacturing contexts.

MARTIN HILB
Professor Martin Hilb is the Director of the Institute for Leadership and Human Resource Management and Professor of Business Administration at the University of St Gallen in Switzerland. He is also Adjunct Professor of International Human Resource Management at the University of Dallas Texas, USA. Professor Hilb has extensive business experience with the Nestlé Corporation and Buhler Engineering in Switzerland and the Martin Corporation in Germany. He was also Director of Human Resources and Administration for Central and Northern Europe, Africa and the Middle East for the Schering-Plough Corporation. Professor Hilb is a extensive writer and consultant in his field. His research interests are in the Business Strategies of American and Japanese Multinational Companies, International Personnel Policies and Practices and Strategic Human Resource Management.

GRAHAM HUTTON
Graham Hutton is an Executive Director of the Strategic Planning Society. Graham worked for ten years in the Civil Service with a background spanning analysis and programming on Burrough's mainframes, computerisation of paper-based financial systems, project management, procurement, information systems

strategies and internal Civil Service consultancy. As a consultant he worked for over fifty public sector organisations. Graham was employed by CCTA (Central Computer and Telecoms Agency) to be responsible for their BPR advice.

SYLVIE JACKSON

Sylvie Jackson is Quality and Business Process Director for Purchasing and Logistics Services in the Post Office. Her responsibilities include ISO 9002, Total Quality and Benchmarking and she has been leading a team re-engineering the whole of the Post Office Supply Chain. She has been developing methodologies and frameworks for managing the supply chain as a process rather than a set of discrete functions,. Sylvie is a Director of the Institute of Business Process Re-engineering and a member of the Editorial Board of *Focus on Change*. She is a regular speaker at conferences on business process re-engineering.

ALAN KIRKHAM

Alan Kirkham was appointed Managing Director of Mitel Telcom in January 1994. He has worked in the telecommunications business for 30 years. The last nine years have been with Mitel Telecommunications Ltd in the UK, where he has held several positions in the Marketing and Sales groups prior to his appointment as Vice President Sales and Service for Europe, Middle East and Africa. Before joining Mitel, Alan spent 14 years in the Australia/Asia Pacific region where he was Divisional Manager for ITT Business Systems. Alan first entered the industry as an engineer in 1961, specialising in the design and support of line transmission and wireless equipment.

JAMES LYNCH

Professor Lynch was educated at Oxford and after obtaining his first degree he spent several years in a range of senior marketing appointments with the American Multinational Proctor and Gamble Corporation. Subsequently he held board-level appointments, as Marketing Director and Managing Director, in the UK textile industry. He entered academic life in the 1970s and became a senior faculty member at the University of Bradford Management Centre. He was appointed to the Yorkshire Bank Chair of Marketing and Strategic Management at Leeds University in 1991. He is a founder-professor of the Leeds University Keyworth Institute, a multi-disciplinary body devoted to research across traditional functional divisions. Professor Lynch has published extensively in the fields of marketing strategy and competitiveness and also acts in a consultative capacity to several major organisations both in the UK and overseas.

JOE PEPPARD

Joe Peppard is a Lecturer in Operations Management at the School of Business Studies, Trinity College Dublin, Ireland, and a Senior Research Fellow at the

Information Systems Research Centre, Cranfield School of Management, UK. His research interests are wide-ranging and include the areas of information systems strategy, business re-engineering, executive information systems, IS management in global enterprises, electronic commerce and how information technology is shaping new organisational structures and reconfiguring industries.

SUSAN SEGAL-HORN

Susan Segal-Horn is Head of the Centre for Strategy and Policy and Senior Lecturer in Strategic Management at the Open University School of Management, UK, where she is responsible for international business strategy. She is also a Visiting Fellow in Strategic Management at Cranfield School of Management. Her research focuses on strategy in international service industries, particularly international growth and globalisation issues, on which she is regular speaker at international conferences. She also acts as a consultant and facilitator for strategy workshops with a range of commercial organisations and professional service firms. Susan is the author of *The Challenges of International Business* (Kogan Page).

PAULA STANLEY

Paula Stanley is a Research Associate in the Department of Education, University of Cambridge. She is currently a member of a research team funded by the Anglia and Oxford Postgraduate Medical and Dental Education Committee, examining the training of doctors in hospitals. Before this appointment in 1995, Paula was a Research Officer in the Operations Management Group at Cranfield School of Management where she worked on projects for the Services Research Centre and the Public Sector Management Group. She is co-author of a number of articles and reports arising from this research.

KEITH WARD

Professor Ward is Visiting Professor of Financial Strategy at Cranfield School of Management, UK. He studied economics at Cambridge and then qualified as both a chartered accountant and a cost and management accountant. He has worked in the City and abroad as a consultant, and held senior financial positions in manufacturing and trading companies (the last being as Group Financial Director of Sterling International). Keith joined the Cranfield School of Management and progressed to Head of the Finance and Accounting Group and Director of the Research Centre for Competitive Performance. His research interests are primarily in the fields of financial strategy, strategic management accounting, and accounting in marketing activities. He is author of *Corporate Finance Strategy* and *Strategic Management Accounting for Financial Decisions*. He has also published numerous articles and has edited and contributed to several other books.

Preface

Two years ago when we started the project to bring this book together there was much debate in academic circles about Business Process Re-engineering. Was it something new? Where was it positioned relative to other approaches for improving performance? Did information systems/information technology own the area? It became evident to us with our strong interest in operations management that many of the features of BPR, described in the earlier articles and books, we had already seen happening in factories. So was BPR simply about the transfer of learning from manufacturing into service factories of banks and insurance companies?

We felt that there was more to BPR than this. As we attended academic conferences we found an interest in discussing BPR across many of the traditional functional disciplines, although, at these events much of the early discussion was still about whether there was anything new in the subject.

We were convinced that the area which was called Business Process Re-engineering did have something more to it. Large companies who had adopted Total Quality Management as the vehicle for improving their business were increasingly taking a process-based view of their organisation. Accepting the process paradigm for the organisation immediately drew in all the traditional business disciplines, so BPR could not be regarded as the sole preserve of one functional discipline. Companies were also looking for radical improvements in performance over short time periods, something which TQM continuous improvement programmes were not delivering.

So the picture which we see emerging is of companies adopting the process paradigm for the high-level architecture for their organisation. Improvements in performance result from a combination of business process re-engineering and continuous improvement, at various process levels involving differing degrees of scale and scope. Most importantly these programmes drive towards managing organisations in a different way. Here the issue for many is getting the balance between managing by process in contrast to managing by function.

This book aims to address the issues raised by these changes. It is intended to give an account of BPR as seen from the traditional discipline areas, as we feel there is knowledge which can be used synergistically in an interdisciplinary way. So we have a series of contributions written by discipline experts including a comprehensive piece on business dynamics. We tie these perspectives into the process-based paradigm and show how this idea has developed and the approaches which are being taken to manage by process. Of course, there are problems in ensuring success, as many organisations have found. Our aim is to address the problems rather than to try to present generic solutions. We do, however, include an appendix to help you to understand the approach to managing BPR projects.

The book is divided into five main parts, introduction, business processes, "operating" functions, "enabling" functions and case studies. While we have tried to give the book a reasonably logical flow, you will find value in using the index and going directly to parts of most interest. We would suggest using the chapters at the start of each part to gain a flavour of the more detailed chapters which follow.

The cases in the book should help you to understand the problems which do arise. We have tried to guide the reader to use them to investigate general and specific issues. We also encourage you to use them in a comparative way.

One of the areas we have chosen not to attempt to cover is that of New Product Development. Clearly this activity is crucial, but we believe that there is significant literature on the subject, particularly in the manufacturing domain in the form of books on simultaneous and concurrent engineering which is a process-based methodology.

We hope you will find the book an exciting and useful guide to exploring the world of processes.

ACKNOWLEDGEMENTS

We are indebted to all the contributors who have enabled us to achieve the scope we intended. We would also like to thank the companies we visited, students on our courses and researchers, who have all helped us to understand this developing field. We are especially grateful to Carol Armistead for her forbearance, sustenance, assistance and support. Finally, we thank Kate and the Dog without whom this book would never have been completed.

Colin Armistead and Philip Rowland
1996

_____ Part One

Setting the Scene

_____ Chapter 1

Introduction

Colin Armistead and Philip Rowland

IMPROVING CORPORATE PERFORMANCE

The recession of the early 1990s, like others before it, gave rise to a large
number of management cure-all philosophies, adherence to which, the
soothsayers said, would save the day. Looking back, however, it is difficult to
remember any of these corporate elixirs of life, except one – *re-engineering*.
The name captured the imagination and created a whole new movement just as
quality had done some years earlier. Various gurus preached the re-engineering
message urging companies to take a "journey into the unknown" and that is
exactly what many have done. While significant improvements have been made
in many cases, companies are increasingly finding that having oriented
themselves to processes during a re-engineering project they now find
themselves with problems in understanding how this new organisational form
should be managed.

At the heart of the re-engineering philosophy, as far as one exists, is that each
and every action in the company's business processes should add value and thus
contribute to corporate performance. To re-engineer is to improve performance
by stripping out of the processes every action that does not add value and
rethinking those that do to add more value. Managing these "end-to-end"
processes cuts across the traditional, function-based management structures and
must often be undertaken with considerably fewer managers than were present

before the re-engineering project. To meet this challenge every aspect of the organisation, including the supporting structures, systems and culture as well as the processes, must be completely rethought. The function-based organisation which has endured so long is increasingly being questioned and in its place an aspiration to managing along process lines is gaining acceptance, although many questions remain to be answered as to how this can be achieved.

In recognition of the increasing importance of processes, modern quality frameworks such as the European Foundation Quality Award place a high premium on an organisation's ability to manage processes as an integrated part of its structure. Figure 1.1 shows the EFQA model and the place of processes in it.

Quality has often been associated with continuous improvement, often of a more incremental kind than process re-engineering advocates. While we acknowledge that there are important differences between the two in terms of aspiration levels and difficulty of implementation we also believe that the two approaches can co-exist. Continuous improvement should be a feature of any organisation, though the degree of improvement in some time periods will be higher than in others. Re-engineering is one approach to bringing about step changes in performance but it should not act against a culture of continuous improvement, indeed it should seek to foster it where it was not previously in place. Another allied area of confusion is that people sometimes equate the differences between the two approaches in terms of the scale of changes required and from that infer which delivers most benefit. While we would certainly agree that re-engineering and a shift to managing processes requires considerably greater change than more incremental improvement method-ologies we would also point out that change does not equal improvement. In some situations an organisation may in fact get more benefit from an incremental approach than a radical leap and do so with considerably less risk, albeit that the need for subsequent improvements may then lead that organisa-tion to search for more radical solutions of a re-engineering kind.

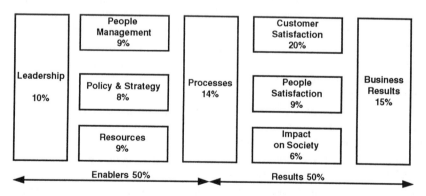

Figure 1.1   European Foundation of Quality Management model

Other planks of the process-based philosophy have roots in those other management philosophies which it overshadowed in the early 1990s, most notably those promoting time-based competition and integrated logistics. Other roots extend much further back, however, and include what many will remember as Organisation and Methods, Just-In-Time manufacturing and Activity Based Costing. Sceptics have pointed to the mixed heritage of re-engineering and process management, claiming it offers nothing new. Like all great innovations, however, re-engineering does offer something new by combining tried and trusted techniques that have an intuitive appeal to many grounded in more mature philosophies.

BREAKING THE MOULD

Perhaps re-engineering's greatest success is in provoking senior management into searching for radically different ways of doing business and considering the unthinkable. By taking a "clean sheet" approach and designing the organisation from scratch many aspects of the existing organisation which have evolved over many years look increasingly inappropriate or in some cases downright damaging.

While senior management may have felt energised by re-engineering's message, actually implementing its creed can be very difficult. Management cannot have all the answers and, having ensured that the strategic direction they wish to follow is clear, executives must find ways to empower the workforce to search for a better way of getting there. This in itself breaks the mould for many who have previously always told or been told what to do. They must not only find a better way but also often take responsibility for the process on an on-going basis. Managers must become leaders, motivating, coaching and listening to staff while staff must become managers taking on greater responsibility for the work that they do and being given the requisite authority to make changes without an overly bureaucratic second-guessing by others. These changes are among the hardest for people to make. The most important quality for leaders, for example, is to inspire others to follow them. This is in contrast to the traditional qualities sought in managers whose orientation is to those above them in the hierarchy.

FUNCTIONS UNDER THREAT OR THE CHANCE TO MAKE A DIFFERENCE?

With interest in processes never greater it is hardly surprising that many whose careers have been spent working in or studying the functional disciplines that have underpinned business for so long feel a little insecure. And so they should.

Functional agendas have set the pace of business life and academic study for too long and business is now receiving a much-needed shake-up in how it views the role of every part of its organisation. "Starting over", as re-engineering is often called, means exactly that. Gone is the safe, lofty place that many functional heads have enjoyed in the organisation; instead there is a desperate need to understand the value-added that each contributes to the processes that deliver service and product to the customer. Even the traditional hiding place of many managers, the mystic art of decision making, is increasingly thought of as a process like any other with speed and value-added the most important qualities. The functional "towers" in the organisation which have required the careful packaging and repackaging of information by many "levels" are now being torn down as process thinking spreads across the organisation without concern for functional or layer boundaries. There is a problem with the erosion of these functions, however, and the advantages of functions should not be forgotten. They provide many features which, if absent, would severely inhibit a company's competitiveness:

- Centres of expertise in which knowledge and expertise in vital business skills can flourish
- Means of collecting and disseminating information from outside the company which can be internalised and used to add value
- Opportunities for those within the business to advance without sacrificing professional growth

Perhaps one of the greatest challenges of process re-engineering and management is to generate an organisation in which functions can co-exist in harmony with processes as the primary means by which business is conducted. This book seeks to help in that challenge by providing inputs from academics in the traditional functions as well as real-world case studies from people involved in re-engineering within their companies.

Chapter 2

Mitel Telecom Business Process Re-engineering: Notes from the Leading Edge

Alan Kirkham

INTRODUCTION

As managing director of Mitel Telecom Limited (part of the global Canada-based corporation), Alan Kirkham leads a team of 1000 staff and has responsibilities for activity in Europe, the Middle East and Africa. He has over 30 years, experience in the telecommunications industry, including 14 years in the Asia-Pacific region with ITT, and has been with Mitel since 1984.

In this case study he describes his company's previous unsuccessful attempt at business process re-engineering and analyses both the mistakes and the lessons learned. The case study also details the bold, new, fast-track BPR strategy which is now being implemented throughout Mitel's UK operation.

THE EARLY ATTEMPT

At Mitel Telecom we know we're at the leading edge of business process re-engineering. We see eminent sense in the Chinese proverb "It is very dangerous to try and leap a chasm in two bounds", and we have set a course to move from being a hierarchical functional-based organisation into a process-focused, process-oriented business in what is effectively one giant leap.

We know that other organisations are taking smaller steps in the same direction. The principles are the same, it's just that we are moving further and faster. It's a situation where there are no rules and no precedents. Tactics and strategies are being devised as the process unfurls. It's an exciting time, a demanding time – the greatest challenge of my career. Exactly why Mitel have elected to move at such a pace will become clear as you read through this chapter.

By way of introduction, I would like to take you through Mitel's first attempt at BPR which, while a failure, provided important lessons which were quickly incorporated into our current strategy.

Mitel's corporate circumstance at the beginning of 1992 was pretty dire in that British Telecom had announced their intention of selling off its controlling interest. A full year had elapsed and there was no sign of a new owner and Mitel was rapidly earning the reputation of being orphaned. There were constant question marks about our future in terms of both ownership and survival. Investment community confidence fell and the share value was driven down.

This, in turn, dented the confidence of our own customers and we had to invest an enormous amount of management time in persuading them to stay loyal. In addition, the recession was upon us; Mitel's cash reserves started to dwindle and things began to look pretty sick.

We concluded that a very different approach would be needed if our business was to be turned round. Early in 1992, we were introduced to the concept of business re-engineering; defined to us as radical re-thinking of the way business is done so as to gain dramatic improvements in costs, quality and customer satisfaction. We were already aiming to drive costs down while improving customer satisfaction through the application of TQM principles. However, business process re-engineering seemed to offer something beyond TQM. So, on the basis of what I must confess was a rather thin business case, we were sufficiently motivated, partly I suspect by fear, to ask seven senior managers to form a team – the Project Front End team – with a 12-month window to investigate and analyse how Mitel did its business. The team would also formulate a different way for Mitel to do business or, at least, investigate the application of business re-engineering concepts to existing processes. By always sitting in the customer's seat, the team would look back into the business so that if we were doing anything which didn't add value to the customer we would question whether we should be doing it at all.

All the customer touching elements were analysed; from the identification of a prospective customer right through to delivering a full solution to that customer and providing continuing account management support. It became clear that our processes were badly fragmented and that attention was being directed towards inventing new "glue" to keep things together. We had a functional organisation with each function diligently applying the concepts and tools of quality improvement. Every time a process was adjusted, it was so complicated that problems were generated both upstream and downstream.

In addition to analysing the problems the team came up with some brand-new ideas about how we interface with the customer and what the customer actually expected from us. From interviews with key customers we estimated that there were significant benefits in following the recommendation which indicated that, at the end of a 12-month re-engineering period, a 50% improvement in customer satisfaction and a £1 million saving in costs were achievable.

The team was disconnected from the business in April 1992, and by November of that year had tabled their recommendations to senior management. These were accepted and Process Owners were identified for each of three key front-end processes.

The first process was the business selling cycle; identifying prospective customers and then selling in Mitel products and services. Input was prospective customers and output was a clean, technically correct order. The second process was order fulfilment, covering everything from the receipt of the clean order to achieving a happy customer with a delivered product and service. The third front-end process covered customer retention and development; applying account management to all existing customers to make sure they benefited from Mitel technology and gained competitive advantage in their own marketplace.

Once these processes were developed, the Process Owners had three months to restructure their part of the business. We took the Head of Sales, Head of Customer Services, Head of Finance and the Head of Logistics and asked them to put together these processes and develop an understanding of what we did and how we did it. This left us with very little time as we wanted to open the doors for business in this new way four months later on 1 April 1993.

ANALYSING THE FAILURE

The Process Owners went on to identify the resource requirements featured in our processes. People were shuffled round in the organisation so that we had the right people in the right processes. This was not done in a consistent way but by directive because there was no time to engage in long debates about who would be best in which process. Employees were asked for a level of trust, after which the managers simply made decisions on who should do what and where.

When we opened for business, we had integrated some of the key functions; for example, Customer Services and Sales had become an integrated group, as had Logistics and part of Customer Services. Group Finance was "marbled" into the organisation and so on.

Three months later, when we performed an audit to assess how well we had implemented the Project Front End recommendations, we found that we had all joined hands and jumped down a big black hole together and that there had been a total misunderstanding of what was meant by BPR. Basically, we had created three functions of the same type as the processes. We had a Business Selling Cycle organisation where people had built a wall around themselves and were actively protecting their own environment and resources. The same was true of Order Fulfilment and Customer Retention and Development.

Why did we fail? Well, first, we did things with indecent haste, with no detailed planning – we really shouldn't have attempted such a major change in culture and company structure over a four-month time frame. Second, we operated a controlled and directed environment, simply telling people that their roles in life had changed. They would be doing a different job on Monday morning and that was that! Third, the senior management group we pulled out to undertake Project Front End were sent back to their old jobs or something roughly the same. We now understand that the people doing the background work and tabling the recommendations should also implement the plan. We also failed to recognise the importance of changes in mindset. People were pulled out of various functions, but they were then allowed to create new functions in their new positions. We made no attempt to remove the functional barriers, we just allowed different ones to be created – probably more than we had before.

Fortunately, most of these problems and mistakes were identified within a few weeks – although not before some of our staff had voted with their feet! We managed to limit the damage, calling a halt to the process and attempting to stabilise the business by continuing for the rest of 1993 as a hybrid of functional and process orientation. For those nine months, we debated endlessly the various scenarios, the background of the failure and what we needed to do to succeed the second time round. I think we all realised that a second chance would be all we would get. There would be no third chance, and even trying it the second time was going to be difficult. I must say, however, that the overall vision expressed by the team was right and many of the recommendations they put on the table are still referred to today.

THE SECOND APPROACH

Bearing in mind the lessons learned from our first attempt, my management team set about creating a much more sophisticated multi-faceted plan – the one we are successfully pursuing today. The new approach involves the development of a business plan which identifies clear goals for the organisation, namely, doubling the revenue and trebling the profits of Mitel over a three-year period. Mitel Telecom Ltd is being fully supported by the Mitel Corporation as a pilot for BPR. Our president, Dr John Millard, will be observing our progress and looking to create a model to apply to the rest of the corporation – leading eventually to the whole of the corporation becoming process orientated.

We started the new approach by taking another hard look at the business we were in and, in particular, we tried to understand the consequences of staying with the current mindset. The conclusion was that "business as usual" was a recipe for rapid disaster. There were significant pressures on our business; our market was flat, we had increasing competition from major multinationals, continuing price compression and commoditisation of our products. We simply couldn't afford to stand still.

Prior to our first BPR attempt, we had interviewed two or three customers to gauge opinion. However, for the relaunch, we consulted with a large number of customers across a wide spectrum of business – from financial centres in the City to small manufacturers in Newcastle upon Tyne.

We found customer perceptions enlightening and perhaps not too surprising. Mitel was considered to be a very difficult company to do business with. We were seen as very tough – if customers placed an order with us, we had certain processes and procedures where every "i" had to be dotted and "t" crossed prior to acceptance. It was an administrative jungle of our own creation and it caused delays in product shipment and reduced the levels of customer satisfaction. Customers also told us that our culture was out of sync with their own. They wanted to see people on their premises who were authorised to deliver the agreed service and to sort out problems.

We had, for example, what we call an escalation process where, if the service engineer discovered a problem outside his experience, it would move through several tiers of management before ending up on the designer's desk. Now we are developing a process which empowers the engineer to contact the source of knowledge directly. This solves the customer's problem very quickly and instead of being a one-day process it's a one-minute process!

The research also showed some positive perceptions of Mitel on which we are building. Customers considered our products to be excellent and were very positive about choosing Mitel as a partner in their business.

THE NEW STRATEGY

We developed a three-part strategy to achieve our objectives. Part One targets diversification by products and by markets; new products into existing markets and existing products into new markets and new products into new markets. The second element – process orientation – meant that people would focus upon processes – what they have to do to service customer requirements. People would not be thinking in terms of function. This change would increase our flexibility and allow us to deploy resources throughout the business to areas where they would bring optimal benefit to our customers. The third element of our strategy was to gain a competitive advantage through our people. This involved developing the skills of our people so that they can effectively evolve with the business. With a new, carefully managed culture and the right people in the right jobs, empowered individuals would be making decisions much closer to the customer.

We have made a point of telling our people that these are not Mitel's ideas in isolation. They have been developed through benchmarking exercises and choosing what we believe are "best in class" business practices from around the world.

You must talk straight to your people if you are to remove the fear of change and are to get them on board. Everyone was told about our corporate objectives and the dramatic growth that was expected. Staff were told that we were trying to drive cost out of the business, but, more importantly, trying to grow the business at a fairly respectable rate. They were told that although we can't offer jobs for life to anybody, we can offer a lifetime employment opportunity to people who are prepared and willing to acquire the new skills needed by the business. For example, all Mitel employees have put their CV on their PC and have been told that if in six months they can't add some significant new skills to that CV they should start asking themselves questions. If by the end of 12 months, they have not developed some new skills, they could be in real difficulty. Quite simply, people have to acquire new and varied skills if they are to evolve with the business. People who stand still will find themselves stranded.

Understanding

The creation of a learning organisation is crucial to the success of the business – with the emphasis on "understanding" rather than "training". Everybody has to have a thirst for knowledge and understanding so they can take on broader, multi-faceted jobs rather than a narrow, strictly functional role.

Every employee has seen a video programme on empowerment which was supported by a presentation on empowerment in Mitel. The more extrovert and ambitious people have grasped the empowerment message very quickly and started to change the way they think and work. We now have an empowerment team which has developed a complete training module so that we can introduce the whole culture of empowerment throughout the organisation through formal and informal training and coaching sessions.

THE CURRENT SITUATION

There is now no doubt that Mitel is moving confidently from a functional and hierarchical structure to one which is project-based, team-based and process-oriented. The formal structure has been taken away altogether. We can have people using various processes at different times; they could even be using one process in the morning and another in the afternoon. People are free to float around in the business and it is now impossible to draw an organisation chart with comfortable lines of control. Instead, we have a organism chart which shows resources fed around the business to the various processes in the business.

The original Project Front End team produced process maps for the whole of the front end of our business. The exercise showed 66 parallel and serial processes which could turn a prospective customer into a satisfied customer once we had applied business re-engineering principles. We then found out that those 66 processes could be reduced to 27 – of which six were brand-new processes. There were a lot of things Mitel did which did not add value to the customer. For example, we found that one person who had been a regular receiver of special quality awards for achieving zero defects on a regular basis was not, in fact, adding any value to the business at all – and that job was closed down.

Flat Management

One of the key elements of process orientation is the flattening of the hierarchy. We are taking managers away from managing people so that they can manage processes. Effectively, we are turning the organisation upside down. We had a ratio of managers to staff of around one to seven in the UK business, and over 100 managers at our headquarters. Already, we've taken 50 of those managers out of the business and have redeployed them in roles that do not involve the management of people. We need the skills, energy, experience and leadership abilities of those managers to drive some of the re-engineering projects elsewhere in the business.

However, many of those managers have the greatest trouble when it comes to changing mindsets. That's quite understandable. They are being asked to abandon the professional practices built up over many years in the industry. For example, some of them on Friday were managing a team of 30 people and measured their importance in terms of the number of people they controlled, the size of their financial budgets and so on. On Monday morning, that manager could be part of a team of five playing a subservient role to the team leader – and the team leader may not have been a manager before! It's a complete change of circumstances. It's very difficult for the managers to accept that the move is a career progression. They have to realise that they don't own any resources, but that as a team, they are responsible for the effective deployment of resources.

We've also done away with job descriptions because they tend to be functionally written. We're working towards "person descriptions" detailing the sort of skills and experience we need in the business. We need a way to reward people on the basis of the skills they bring to the organisation and the individual contributions they may make. At the moment, we are asking employees to trust that we will come up with processes that work.

I've asked everyone to think of themselves as "business entrepreneurs". In our product development process – called "Sprint" – we have taken people right out of the business, with no "back filling", and surprise, the business hasn't collapsed! In fact, products come to market faster, which gives us a real competitive advantage.

I said earlier that we had turned the organisation upside down. This means that my role of Managing Director has disappeared altogether and I have become Chief Coach, reporting to my management team which consists of Process Champions who, in turn, report to their own process teams. We have changed names from the original Process Owners to Process Champions and have impressed upon the managers that their job is to be coach and mentor to the employees but not to direct and control them at all. They simply have to set the direction in which we want to take the business, lay down some business objectives for that process and ask the people they coach how best to use the process to achieve the stated objectives.

Planning matrices (see Figure 2.1) have been produced to show the skills required in each of the five core processes and the Champion for each of those processes. The Champion is responsible and accountable for the performance of the process and for any re-engineering focused on that process. Process Champions are the only people with full authority in the business and it is important to note that individual Process Champions own no resources whatsoever. They simply identify resource requirements for their process and work with the team to make sure that the total resources of the business are deployed into the area which will deliver the best value to our customers.

The other side of the Matrix – what we would have previously called "functions" – is now divided into Skill Centres or areas of competence and we have identified someone in each of those areas of competence as the Skills Champion. Their job is to identify the skill requirements for each process. For example, for the sales process skills they would talk to the Process Champions and develop an understanding of the way their business requirements would evolve. Then the Skills Champion would deliver training and development programmes into the sales process to make sure that the right people evolve and develop to meet the business needs of Sales. This "skills delivery" happens with each of the other processes – Marketing, Customer Services, R&D and so on.

The top edge of the Matrix assembles all the skills – Sales, Marketing, Customer Services, R&D, Statutory Finance, General Finance, Manufacturing, Purchasing, Logistics and so on – and forms a comb interface which matches the corporate comb edge. By keeping the skills definitions the same as the corporate functional definitions we can ensure that the whole plan knits together.

SUBJECT: **RESOURCE PLANNING**

SKILLS

PROCESS	WHO	Carl Sales	Chris Customer Services	Tim Marketing	Tony Engineering	Alan Logistics	Alan Finance	Ed HR	Chris IS	Tony Legal	Nick TQM	Steve Facilities	Steve Manufacturing	John G&A
Business Selling Cycle	Bob	●	●	●		○	○	○	◉	◉	◉	○	○	○
Order Fulfilment	Paul	●	●	○		●	●	○	◉	◉	◉	●	○	○
Customer Retention & Development	Cliff	●	●	●	○	○	○	○	◉	◉	◉	○	○	○
Strategy Planning & Support	Ken	○	○	●	●	◉	◉	◉	●	○	●	○	○	○
Product Development	Stewart	●	●	●	◉	◉	◉	◉	◉	◉	◉	○	○	○

KEY: SKILLS LINKAGES

● Major
◉ Strong
○ General

Figure 2.1   Mitel planning matrix

Communications

Of course, successful implementation of BPR depends heavily on effective communication within the business from the very earliest stages and we have developed a comprehensive communications strategy to that end. Our first move was to bring all our managers together in a day-long seminar where we concentrated on the key elements of the business plan – so that everybody, from the shopfloor to the finance department could articulate to a customer or a supplier, the general thrust of our business. Basically, the five crucial elements were:

- Business as usual is not an option
- Revenue will be doubled in three years
- Profits will be trebled in three years
- The route to achieving those objectives is through Business Process Re-engineering.
- We have a three-part strategy of diversification, process orientation and competitive advantage through people.

The five basics were developed further through a series of workshops where we created a Mitel definition of empowerment and examined how it could be achieved. There was no imposition. We showed the management some generic forms of empowerment and how they operate in various enterprises. They were then asked to continue meetings to devise training modules to develop a common language and understanding both for people being empowered and for those doing the empowering. We also conducted various employee surveys which told us that we were good at communicating both laterally through the organisation and down into the organisation, but we had our fingers in our ears when it came to feedback.

There was a lot of room for improvement. We developed a communication strategy for staff which identified the key messages, and the appropriate media to convey those messages throughout the business. The exercise reinforced the processes for communicating between the various teams and provided the staff with smooth communication channels back into the organisation. These channels were "looped" so that when we received a suggestion, for, say, affecting continuous improvement in some way, that suggestion would be presented to the appropriate team for consideration.

The Team Structure

Teams were important right from the start. We invited all managers to contribute their experiences to a process orientation team which looked at the challenge of process orientating across the whole business. A second team looked at communication strategy and attempted to identify the important issues which needed to be communicated to the staff and communicated back to management. A third team looked at empowerment and the general education and development requirements within Mitel. The emphasis is on "education" rather than "training" because it's vital that people understand why the changes are taking place.

The teams have continued to meet and develop their own strategies with the management simply supporting them. There has been a senior manager on each team, but not as team leader. We make no attempt to lay any rules down. They are empowered! In all cases, the teams have come up with creative, interesting and very practical objectives and recommendations, many of which we are now implementing.

Mitel is now a team-based organisation. It's all about keeping all the right skills together with responsibility and accountability for completing a specific task. The team is fully in control. We have around 40 quality action teams with probably four or five people in each team meeting at intervals of between a week and a month (Box 2.1). Each quality action team is focusing on a specific

---

Box 2.1 Quality action teams for panel

Information Systems	New Product Introductions
Process Orientation	Empowerment
Internal Communication	Performance Management
TQM	Operations Team
Strategy review	Installation
Maintenance	Upgrades
DOA	Manufacturing Yield
Overdue Receivables	Remote Maintenance and Diagnostics
Block wiring	ESD and Housekeeping
Education	Health and Safety
Recycling	Hot Room Elimination
Repair Performance	Static Control
WIP Accuracy	Fastman Implementation
Portable Appliance Test	Pull Project Team
Materials Process	Bulletin Board
Workforce Management	Service Management System
Employee Expenses	General Ledger Close
Strategy Planning and Support	Problem Escalation
Sub-contract Service	Packing Pull Project
Duty management	Purchasing Invoices
Order Lead Time	Stock Availability
Complete Delivery	Time to Answer

problem or set of problems and applying corrective actions to remove those problems permanently. Almost all the teams have skills drawn from a variety of different functional groups. We invite customers and suppliers to join our teams and they make a valuable contribution while experiencing the process of change first-hand. We also have a very close relationship with the Mitel Users Association, a totally independent body sponsored by the Mitel user community. Every element of our business strategy has been shared with them and they have access to any individual within the Mitel organisation worldwide.

There is a good amount of interaction between teams. If a team is looking at a particular process while another team is looking at sub-processes and the main process changes, clearly the sub-process is likely to change at the same time. Consequently, all teams have to be conscious of what's going on within other teams and we have encouraged regular contacts and inter-team visits.

THE CURRENT POSITION

We now have a common understanding and knowledge of process orientation throughout our business and have achieved a common sense of purpose. A bonus plan is now operating to make sure everybody in the management team is focused on exactly the same objectives. So no-one has anything to lose or gain by freeing or expanding or taking on additional resources. Individuals are now responding to empowerment and taking decisions which previously would have been taken at a much more senior level. We don't want people who blindly follow existing rules, we want people who are prepared to break rules and make new rules to try and do things differently. If I say to someone "I'd like you to be in Washington in an hour and a half" – I don't want people to answer "it can't be done" automatically. NASA might have the answer! I don't want people rejecting ideas before checking thoroughly whether the technology is available to make it happen. Everybody has been told to feel confident in making decisions on behalf of the business; providing those decisions are made in the interest of the customer. No-one is going to get criticised for making wrong decisions, providing the motivation is right. However, we are still struggling to change the minds of management. People in non-managerial positions are excited by the prospect of working in teams and it's only the management mindset that needs to be continually coached into a new way of thinking.

I firmly believe that if we want significant gains for our business and our customers we have to be prepared to work rapidly towards BPR, identifying and analysing the risks and doing our best to avoid problems. We're very much aware that as we move forward, we are burning bridges and cannot easily move back.

We've stripped away all the bureaucracy and the formal organisation and abandoned the traditional ways of doing things. We have 4000 documents in our documentation control centre and I can almost guarantee that 90% will not match our requirements. We have over 900 processes documented and nearly all of them are obsolete or not being used but are simply there to satisfy the requirements of BS 5750 accreditation. Our aim is to strip all those out of the business and throw them away, replacing them with processes that work.

I think that BSI may have to review the way they assess organisations, but I think that BSI and other government agencies recognise the tremendous benefits of a process-orientated world and won't inhibit companies from taking that route. BS 5750 doesn't mean you are a quality organisation; it's simply a milestone on the way to quality. The same is true for Investors in People, another third-party award. It's important, but only as a milestone on the journey.

THE FUTURE

The whole BPR exercise for me is about driving customer satisfaction upwards. We are on a growth path, and expect to do more with less people. Growth will enable us to reabsorb staff back into the system. I need all the resources of the business to help support this growth, so it's not a matter of driving costs out of the business but about developing the business without allowing costs to grow.

We are a member of many benchmarking clubs in the IT and other industries where various people get together and try to understand how to approach business problems and opportunities and discuss processes that have been developed to support them. Mitel is involved in benchmarking with a diverse range of organisations including Digital, Hewlett-Packard, ICL, Milliken, Sony, Hilton International and Brent Council.

But as I said at the beginning, we are moving further and faster along the BPR route than any other business in the UK and we are having to invent as we move forward. There are problems, of course. But we are working to overcome them. We don't, for example, have HR programmes in place to support the model we're creating for our business. The performance-evaluation systems and reward programmes we use for the majority of the staff simply do not fit the model, so we're having to change all our HR practices to support our new way of doing business.

You will not walk into Mitel today and see a process-oriented company. But you will see lots of evidence of process orientation and lots of team work. There's still a great deal to be done, but there is no doubt that we are making tremendous progress at every level. Positive changes have already been made and the motivation and commitment of both management and employees becomes stronger with each passing day.

We want to make sure that Mitel itself becomes a model for the innovative deployment of information technology. We plan, for example, to abandon our purpose-built demonstration rooms and use the whole business to demonstrate our capabilities and services.

We've consumed an enormous amount of literature and spent several hundred hours of senior management time throwing ideas at the wall during the last 12 months. We have talked to a lot of businesses that made a start on this path and to those that are considering it. We've taken what we believe are the best management practices from the various businesses and have constructed our own plan.

BPR will give Mitel the flexibility it needs to develop innovative new products and services and to bring them rapidly to market. That flexibility is essential for our success. In Europe, Mitel have around a thousand employees. We compete with people like Plessey Siemens, who may have 390 000 employees, Ericsson who may have 70 000, Alcatel who may have 200 000 not to mention BT. Our smaller size and new, lean customer-oriented structure gives us a fantastic opportunity to drive our advantage home – gaining an important competitive edge from our ability to meet customers' needs in the shortest possible time.

Chapter 3

Business Process Re-engineering – A Public Sector View

Graham Hutton

INTRODUCTION

Like many other developed economies the public sector in the UK has been and will be faced with considerable change. Currently the public sector is undertaking major change in response to the New Public Management initiative. It is responding to a number of aspects such as customer orientation (Citizens' Charter), opening the internal market to the private sector (Market Testing and Compulsory Competitive Tendering), expecting more from less, reduced levels of financial input (capping, budget reduction, etc.) and Fundamental Expenditure Reviews.

Organisations could consider BPR as a response to these initiatives. The aim would be to achieve an organisation that is customer focused; run at an acceptable cost; and aims to ensure its activities add value to the customer's requirements.

The Public Sector can be considered as having four major strands: central government (the Civil Service) consisting of departments, next-step (executive) agencies and non-departmental public bodies; local government consisting of local authorities, local education and the emergency services; the national health service (rapidly becoming made up of separate trusts); and utilities some

Table 3.1   UK Public Spending (£ billion)

	1992/3	1985/6	1978/9
Social Security	79.7	43.5	17.0
Health	41.1	20.7	9.2
Education	32.2	17.0	9.1
Defence	23.6	18.2	7.6
Government Debt Interest	17.9	17.9	7.4
Law and Order	14.2	6.6	2.6
Environmental Services	9.0	4.5	2.7
Housing	6.2	4.1	4.5
Other	34.5	22.9	11.9
Total	269	161	75

of which are in the private sector. Leaving aside the utilities the public sector is still considerably big business as Table 3.1 shows.

In business terms the Department of Social Security alone handles more money each year than BP, ICI and BT put together and operates a money transfer system on a larger scale than any clearing bank.

THE TRANSFORMATION OF THE PUBLIC SECTOR

Over the last fifteen years there has been a re-engineering of public administration falling into two strands, privatisation and changing the bureaucracy. This started with selling companies or shares in companies such as British Petroleum, Amersham International, Rolls-Royce, Rover Group, British Steel, British Aerospace, International Computers Limited and Inmos. It continued with the privatisation of utilities such as Associated British Ports, British Airways, British Airports Authority (including Gatwick and Heathrow), British Telecommunications, British Gas, British Road Services, the regional water companies and regional electricity companies. The public sector interest is being ensured by statutory regulators as well as the introduction of competition when deemed appropriate.

The second strand was to change the bureaucracy. This was tackled by the break-up of government departments into next-step or executive agencies – making business areas independent and responsible for their own administration; the break-up of the National Health Service by the introduction of trusts and an internal market; and the break-up of local government education by allowing schools to become independent. Local government reform is continuing with the introduction of more unitary authorities. With regard to central government there are currently approximately 530 000 civil servants (April 1995). Seventy per cent of these staff are in executive agencies and the aim is to have 90% in agencies. The 10% left in departments will be policy makers. Agencies will deliver specific services, answer to a chief executive, publish annual reports and accounts and be run as a business. Some may face privatisation.

Competition has been introduced into the public sector by compulsory competitive tendering in local government and market testing in central government. Market testing is comparing the in-house service provider against external suppliers. In identifying activities for market testing departments and agencies need to:

- Confirm whether it needs to be performed. If not it should cease
- Confirm whether it is a suitable candidate for privatisation, and, if so, act accordingly
- Where government wishes to retain control consider competition. Agency status should be considered if it is not an agency already
- For policy or management reasons an in-house bid might not be considered. Outsourcing will then be the appropriate way forward
- Market testing will be considered after the above.

Increased standards for the citizen/customer have been introduced by way of charters. The "Citizens' Charter" was an initiative which the Prime Minister introduced in 1991. There are a number of similar initiatives in other OECD countries. Its purpose is to ensure that public sector services are based on quality, choice, standards and value to the end user – the citizen. At the beginning of May 1995 38 charters were in operation from rail services to tax administration. Each has standards, targets and entitlements.

Another initiative to transform government is the private sector finance initiative (PFI) where private capital and expertise is brought in to build and run a service. Current projects are mainly in transportation such as toll bridges, toll roads, the Channel Tunnel and rail connections to the Channel Tunnel. Other initiatives are being considered. For example, it is unlikely the government would fund any new technology infrastructure and would look to the private sector to build and possibly run such an initiative. The recently announced National Insurance Recording System 2 and the National Road-works database are good examples of this.

Besides all the above the government also endorses Business Process Re-engineering in the latest White Paper on the future of the Civil Service. The public sector is responding to the above initiatives. Many central government departments, executive agencies, non-departmental public bodies, NHS trusts, local authorities, police forces and publicly owned utilities are using BPR to change the way they operate and becoming customer-focused organisations.

CCTA published an overview of the subject in May 1994 called *BPR in the Public Sector*. CCTA (Central Computer and Telecommunications Agency) is part of the Cabinet Office's Office of Public Service and is at the centre of the

Civil Service. CCTA's mission is to help the public services successfully acquire and use information systems to meet their business needs. As such, CCTA is responsible for developing best-practice advice on appropriate issues. These issues have in the past included advice and guidance on Information Systems strategies. The impact on these by initiatives such as BPR meant that CCTA needs to explain the subject to allow organisations to assess their response.

ISSUES FOR A BPR EXERCISE IN THE PUBLIC SECTOR

There are a number of characteristics of public sector organisations which have a bearing on BPR or any change-management exercise.

Rigid Hierarchies

The very nature of rigid hierarchical organisational structures militates against any change to looser, flatter structures aimed at delivering a more flexible service delivery. Many managers' positions are dependent on the number of staff working for them. Most people will resist changes that affect their status.

Culture

The public sector culture has traditionally stressed such values as continuity, predictability and fairness rather than change and innovation. This culture is more suited to process improvement and simplification, rather than more radical BPR approaches. The public accountability requires that the culture of much of the public sector is risk-averse by comparison with the private sector.

Crossing Boundaries

Many departments/agencies will have difficulty in re-engineering processes that extend beyond their organisational boundaries because authority is shared among a number of stakeholders. This could militate against the application of BPR. The tendency towards fragmentation of larger departments into a collection of distinct units of varying status, and each with its own objectives, may complicate the task of coordination.

Change of Direction

Changes in policy direction can be sudden and dramatic. In some BPR exercises, especially those that involve the time-consuming documentation of existing processes, a legitimate question could be: will a change in direction occur before there has been time to implement? Solutions adopted may need to be sufficiently flexible to cope with quite different political circumstances.

Other Initiatives

A market-testing project could give rise to difficulties for those wishing to undertake BPR. If an organisation were to undertake market testing without a market-testing strategy, clearly linked to its IS and business strategies, then the outcome of market testing could have serious long-term ramifications for the organisation. Dividing business areas into small units to market test, for whatever reason, will exacerbate problems as this may lead to a function being set "in concrete'. For example, microfiche production has been outsourced as a result of a market test. However, a BPR exercise might have recommended that this function was no longer necessary, or should be continued for an interim period only, or was integral to a business process. Each of these results would have affected the suitability for market testing of that function. Ideally, therefore, BPR exercises should precede market testing so that flexible service contracts are set up to reflect the true need of the parent organisation.

Consequences for Others

BPR undertaken in one business area might have unprecedented consequences for another business area. An example of this might be that if all benefit payments were automated the effect on post offices throughout the UK, many of which are in rural areas, would be significant.

Unrealistic Promises

Some people can get to the point of regarding BPR as a panacea and may make unrealistic promises about the timescales within which change can be achieved. In such cases, those at the top only really commit to the outcomes of re-engineering rather than to the change process itself. Although the outcome is important, understanding and managing the change process, including risks, itself must be given due consideration.

Communication with Staff

As with any programme that brings about change, convincing and managing staff is critical to success. Often the ostensible reasons for BPR may not be believed. People may suspect that "headcount reduction" or "cost cutting" is really what an exercise is all about. If this is the true purpose then be open and honest about it and do not pretend otherwise. If success is to be achieved, corporate attitudes and behaviours may have to change, preferably through positive encouragement.

Internal Focus

Some organisations may focus on internal processes and functions rather than externally on "what represents value for the customer".

Methods and Approaches

There may be a prolonged documentation of existing processes rather than thinking innovatively about alternatives. This may be caused by the use of over-elaborate methodologies. Building sophisticated process models can seem more "interesting" to the specialist than delivering a viable range of options.

WHERE BPR CAN BE USED IN THE PUBLIC SECTOR

BPR can be utilised in a single business area, across a whole department or agency and across multiple departments/agencies. Naturally, the levels of expected benefits from a successful BPR exercise will increase with the complexity of the BPR exercise as may the risk, difficulty and cost.

BPR is particularly relevant in those areas which involve extensive contact with the public, with record keeping and/or claims processing following customer contact or involving financial transactions. This is because the statutory basis, authorisation or rationale of many of these services will often specify the outcome sought, but allows the organisation concerned considerable freedom to determine *how* the service/outcome is to be achieved. These are areas where the basic business transactions are similar, so giving scope for a repeatable process. The work is usually of a relatively routine nature and the amount of discretion to take decisions can justifiably be limited. Specifying the process could increase the flow of work and reduce variation. Where each case is likely to have a unique solution, such as in policy work, specifying a standard process will not be appropriate. Business processes that are routine, repetitive, for instance, lend themselves to the application of transaction processing-based IT systems and all these are candidates for BPR.

Organisations must respond to the pressures for change and the comparative "health" of the organisation and its processes. How much does the organisation need to change and what is its capability for change? The "health check" might be established by analyses such as SWOT (strengths, weaknesses, opportunities and threats) and PEST (political, economic, social and technological). Thus, if the objectives to be met are improved customer service and improved value for money, the organisation must set itself to be the market leader in terms of quality of service and cost effectiveness. On the other hand, if an organisation were driven by a ministerial requirement to be the best of its kind in the European Union, then its transformation requirements would be driven by international benchmarks.

BPR is intended to deliver real and significant change in terms of the costs and quality of its service as perceived by its stakeholders (especially customers). Whether this means a fundamental change in the structure and nature of the organisation will depend on the circumstances of the organisation. Some departments might need to consider legislative change. To be more prescriptive at the outset would be to see BPR as a solution chasing a problem. BPR is instead the means through which possible solutions to serious or potentially serious challenges can be identified. These may have emerged as a result of the change agents themselves or have been recognised through business analysis.

CRITICAL SUCCESS FACTORS IN THE PUBLIC SECTOR

A number of critical success factors (CSF) can be applied to a BPR exercise. A CSF is an element that, if missing, is likely to lead to the failure of a project. Ensuring that the CSF requirements are fulfilled might be considered an organisational prerequisite for a BPR exercise.

- The desire to change the status quo – a willingness to rethink all aspects of the business and challenge fundamental assumptions that underpin the organisation to create a customer-focused organisation.
- Sustained commitment, patience and active involvement at the highest level – throughout the project.
- Clear and consistent strategic focus and long-term vision shared across the organisation – be clear about the purpose and reason for undertaking the exercise.
- Demanding goals – out of reach but not out of sight.
- Ensure good planning and management and be willing and able to allocate appropriate resources and time to the exercise.
- Continuous dialogue with stakeholders to determine their requirements and understand priorities and trade-offs including the involvement of all staff through sensitive two-way communication.
- Continuous measurement of performance/benchmarking.

CONCLUSIONS

Change is not necessarily easy and cultural change for the public sector is perhaps greater than that required of other sectors. However, change is now seen by many in the public sector as a constant and it is unlikely to change under future administrations. There seems to be a trend in all OECD countries to look for savings in the cost of public administration. Public sector organisations might find that their best way forward in response to this trend will be to consider radical change programmes such as BPR. Many of the issues and CSFs that need to be considered are the "soft" issues. For those in the public sector this means convincing staff, ministers, customers and other stakeholders of the necessity for, and advantage of, change. Staff are a crucial part of most public sector organisations, they may have to suffer a big upheaval in their work environment; ministers need convincing that the programme is worth while and merits the long time scale (often two years); customers want things to be right first time, they have often had bad experience of dealing with government, such as long delays and queues. Other stakeholders could include HM Treasury, the National Audit Office and Trusts. Each group of people affected by the proposed changes needs to know exactly the part they can play in that change.

ACKNOWLEDGEMENTS

Much of this chapter is taken from CCTA's *BPR in the Public Sector* with the kind permission of the publisher, HMSO.

_____ Part Two

Business Processes

Chapter 4

Processes: Not New Phenomena

Colin Armistead and Philip Rowland

WHAT WILL YOU FIND IN THIS CHAPTER?

The concept of processes is, of course, not new. In this chapter we will review the themes which seem to us to be important as we consider a new approach to managing by process and the effect the changes have on people in organisations. You will be aware that many of the chapters giving a discipline perspective also contain other information about processes which you should bear in mind. Specifically in this chapter we will:

- Examine some of the key lessons from the past
- Discuss the strategic fit of processes
- Summarise the characteristics of processes.

INTRODUCTION

Are business processes a new phenomena? Clearly not, the word process is an integral part of our language. The terms management processes and production process have long been common place in many sectors of the economy. The dictionary definition (Collins, 1986) of the word is captured in a number of different meanings, including (a) a series of actions or proceedings used in making, manufacturing, or achieving something, (b) Progress, course, (c) A natural or involuntary operation or series of changes. Perhaps the spirit of an organisational process is best captured in the first definition – a series of actions used in achieving something. Described in this simple way processes have been an integral part of all enterprises and essentially describe the way any endeavour is successfully completed. We can see processes in the historical context of organisations being the series of activities which were carried out to achieve goals of making, moving or caretaking. When enterprises were small a group of individuals were the people who were essentially involved in all activities or were in close proximity to each other. In a craft workshop all those concerned with the manufacturing process worked together on the complete making of carts, shoes, or printing even when they might have independent but complementary skills. In this manufacturing context the concept of a "labour process" was introduced by Marx.

As enterprises grew they started to assume the organisational structure commonplace for most of this century in which the individual activities necessary to make products or to move things remained mainly the same. However, scale and size increased and philosophy of Scientific Management (Taylor, 1967) drove the division of work into separate entities each devoted to making part of the product and providing the administrative surround. Each part of the divided enterprise continued to operate a process but more within its own boundaries which often by choice became isolated from the external environment (Thompson, 1967). Over a period of time the functional hierarchical structures of organisations arose, each with its own rituals, language, skills, and separate aspirations which affected the way in which processes were conceived, operated, controlled and developed.

LESSONS FROM THE PAST?

Writers on organisations have dealt with processes both explicitly and implicitly in their examination of the structure of organisations, and the way people in organisations make sense of their situation and react to the external environment. There are some messages from these sources which are relevant to those trying to make sense of the changes associated with business process re-engineering as they search for ways to increase organisational performance:

- Organisations are complex with many variables which impinge on performance. Handy (1985) suggests there are more than sixty so the ability to predict outcomes is difficult.
- Order and effectiveness come from structure which governs either bureaucracies (Weber, 1947) or the more specific aspects of production (Woodward, 1965).
- The integration of functional activities is vital in areas where success can

only be achieved through the efforts of more than one function, product development for example (Lawrence and Lorsch, 1967).

- Organisations are influenced by factors of organisational structure and functions, the composition of groups and individuals personality and behaviour (Pugh and Hickson, 1989). A scheme for analysing structure includes *specialisation* of functions and roles, *standardisation* of procedures, *formalisation* of documentation, *centralisation* of authority and *configuration* of roles.

- There is no one organisational structure which will work in all circumstances but five types recur (Mintzberg, 1983). Structure is driven by focus on one of five aspects of organisations which emerge from observing what managers do rather than what they say they do. The five areas of focus identified by Mintzberg are the *strategic apex*, a *technostructure*, an *operating core*, the *middle line*, and *support staff*. The five resulting structures are:

  − *Simple Structure* where the focus is on a strategic apex represented by an executive board of directors. This structure is prevalent in a small firm.

  − *Machine Bureaucracy* where the size of the firm is larger and the focus is switched to those activities and functions which plan and control such as planning of strategy and production planning.

  − *Professional Bureaucracy* arises where professionals within the firm provide the focus as with lawyers, doctors or teachers.

  − *Divisional Bureaucracy* is characterised by the functionally based firm with strong heads of functions being the "middle line".

  − An *Adhocracy* is represented by a firm where the support activities become key focus perhaps through research and development or public relations.

Box 4.1 Technology-driven fragmentation

With the advent of coal cutters and mechanical conveyors, the degree of technical complexity of coal getting was raised to a higher level. Mechanisation made possible a single long face in place of series of short faces, but the technological change had a number of social and psychological consequences for the work organisation and the worker's place in it, to which little thought was given before the change was introduced. The pattern of organisation in a short face working was based on a small artisan group of a skilled man and his mate, assisted by one or more labourers. The basic pattern around which the work relationships in the long face method were organised is the coal face group of forty or fifty men, their shot-firer and "deputies" (i.e. supervisors). The basic unit in mining took on the characteristics in size and structure of a small factory department, and in so doing disrupted the traditional high degree of work autonomy and close working relationships with a number of deleterious effects.

The mass production character of the long face method necessitates a large-scale mobile layout advancing along a seam, basic task specialis-ation according to shift, very specific job roles and different methods of payment within each shift. In these circumstances there are considerable problems of maintaining effective communications and good working relations between forty men spatially spread over 200 yards in a tunnel, and temporally spread over 24 hours in three successive shifts. From the production engineering point of view it is possible to write an equation that 200 tons equals 40 men over 200 yards over 24 hours, but the psychological and social problems raised are of a new order when work organisation transcends the limits of a traditional, small face-to-face group undertaking the complete task itself. As the social integration of the previously small groups has been disrupted by the new technology, and little attempt made to achieve any new integration, many symptoms of social stress occur. Informal cliques which develop to help each other out can only occur over small parts of the face, inevitably leaving some isolated; individuals react defensively using petty deceptions with regard to time keeping and reporting of work; they compete for allocation to the best workplaces; there is mutual scapegoating across shifts, each blaming the other for inadequacies (since in the new system with its decreased autonomy, no one individual can normally be pinpointed with blame, scapegoating of the absent shift becomes self-perpetuating and solves nothing). Absenteeism becomes the way miners compensate themselves for the difficulties of the job.

The work of Eric Trist and the Tavistock Institute reported in Hugh and Hickson (1989) reproduced by permission of Penguin Books.

The lessons from organisation academics relating the structure of organis-ations, the way managers behave and the way work has been organised has at times illustrated the dilemmas which arise in the context of business process re-engineering. How are we able to understand the process, organise the task and the people to gain the most? A case in point is described in Box 4.1 where the division of work brought with it loss of communication and reduced perfor-mance. It is interesting that technology in this form forced the loss of integration while technology associated with business process re-engineering as information technology may bring together disparate groups into a more cohesive whole. Mumford (1987, 1995), a lifelong proponent of socio-technical systems theory and design, has reflected on its strong similarities with BPR although she identifies aspects of emphasis and values which separate the two. She sees BPR having a macho ethos with an emphasis on efficiency – something of which managers who use BPR methodologies should perhaps be aware.

CHARACTERISTICS OF PROCESSES

Business process re-engineering aims to force managements to consider aspects of organisational structure and the way in which work is organised within the social and political framework of the organisation. As they do this they make an explicit recognition of the uncertainties which surround business processes but often without the means to resolve them. They would welcome a frame-work in which to make sense of the reality. Systems methodology, particularly that of exploring "soft systems" (Checkland, 1981) or in systems dynamics (Forrester, 1961; Senge, 1990), have strong principles which may help to bring meaning to the way in which processes are linked as part of a larger system. However, many managers and teams who are part of a process may not have the knowledge and skills to apply these methodologies. They do form part of the tools which are available for teams to which we will return in Chapter 17. At this stage we want to examine a more exploratory approach to processes and to identify those characteristics which are accessible to a wide range of process members.

The Nature of Processes

If we are using BPR to improve the way in which business processes perform we perhaps need to identify some of the ways in which processes are discussed. It seems to us that two approaches are useful, namely:

- The strategic "fit" of processes
- The characteristics of processes

Strategic fit of processes

One of the abiding concepts of strategy is the idea of strategic fit. We see this in the 7S model with components of superordinate goals, systems, structure, style, strategy, skills, and staff (Waterman, Peters and Phillips, 1980). A later framework is the *strategy compass* used to map a customer's view of the offering of an organisation and the producer's capability (Bowman and Faulkner, 1994). The concept of fit is reflected in the development of essentially functionally based strategies illustrated by the development of manufacturing strategy (Skinner, 1969) and the concept of a product/process matrix of Hayes and Wheelwright (1979). None of these propositions is negated by BPR, rather BPR approaches perhaps force organisations to think more clearly about fit because of the risks involved in major change.

Another theme which impinges on our understanding of strategy and processes is the concept of *competencies* and *capabilities* which have received wide coverage (Prahalad and Hamel, 1990; Stalk, Evans and Schulman, 1992) and in a direct link the idea of a competence building process (Ghosal and Bartlett, 1995). The essential message is that the organisation should build competencies which are *core* or *critical* to its success and develop these while at the same time being prepared to outsource non-critical activities or processes.

The characteristics of processes

Processes have a number of characteristics which help us both to describe them and explain their relationship to one another. We discuss in some detail in Chapter 11 on operations management the key features of processes. These can be summarised into three areas under the headings of *structural, operational* and *limiting output.*

Structural characteristics are associated with the basic concept of a process being one of transformation of inputs of resources into outputs. One process's inputs are the outputs of another process. So processes form networks and subsequent transformations are intended to "add value" to their inputs. Within any transformation process there is a series of activities which contribute to the overall process. Hence it is possible to identify and map the series of activities in one process and each process can be subdivided into a series of sub-processes as a hierarchy of other processes. The higher the level of the process, the greater the potential for sub-division. For example, a large business process such as product development may have several thousand smaller processes within it. We suggest three main levels for processes, process elements, process element activities and activity tasks. A customer service business process was considered to have three process elements, sales, customer order and transportation. Each of the elemental processes could then be broken down into activities and the tasks which allow them to operate.

Operational characteristics are concerned with the purpose of the process at whatever level and the identification of the "process task", i.e. what the process must do well if it is to play its part in the wider scheme of things. We are also concerned here with the ownership of the processes and the commitment and control of resources to achieve the task, along with measurement of performance (see Box 4.2).

Characteristics which limit consistent output are those which cause variability in a process or understanding constraints in the resources or capabilities. There are also aspects of uncertainty about any process. This uncertainty can be seen as the intangibility of processes which often arises in processes which are delivered

---

Box 4.2 The supermarket paradox

A supermarket will try to design its store to make it easy for customers to gain access and move around in comfortable conditions. It will establish supply networks and systems to support the replenishment of the 20 000 items it might hold. It will train its staff to greet customers and know about products. From day to day the store management will also manage their quality systems and schedule staff to be present according to the numbers of customers they expect each day. They known that their ability to judge the need for staff affects customer service and unit costs. However, at times the store will become busy to the extent that no more staff can be used to serve or to run the checkouts. The store is then "coping" and customer satisfaction will probably fall. The store managers need to consider how they can ameliorate the misery for customers in these circumstances by making sure the checkout process is not held up for any reason and by controlling the flow to fast checkouts (customers cheat at these times!). They could, of course, entertain the customers or give sweets or drinks to children. Inevitably in all services other things go wrong for all sorts of reasons and the staff need to 'recover' the situation for the customer. This may be by replacing goods which are damaged or taking shopping round to the home of a regular customer who inadvertently forgot some items.

Managers in all the major supermarkets are presented with essentially the same set of processes and similar resources. However, we all know from personal experience that one supermarket chain has differences from another and that different stores in one chain feel different. We may find it difficult to describe in detail what these differences are but we are affected by them.

---

mainly through people. It can be described in terms of "the way we do things". It is often difficult to identify these intangible aspects of processes and this leads to the concept of visibility of processes both to an organisation and to competitors who may be seeking to copy a process. Reed and DeFillipini (1990) speak of strategic "causal ambiguity" in this context. Often people in a process are not precisely sure why it works as it does.

CONCLUSIONS

There is much from our past learning about processes which we should not ignore in taking a new view of organisations. The lessons from the past remind us to pay close attention to the redefinition of how people work together and the influence of technology in the redefinition. We will see this reflected in Chapter 6. Finally, in the spirit of this book we need to look at all the management discipline areas if we are to gain a full understanding of how we might manage processes better.

Chapter 5

Managing by Business Processes

Colin Armistead and Philip Rowland

WHAT WILL YOU FIND IN THIS CHAPTER?

This chapter is about the structural changes in organisations which accompany BPR as part of the strategically driven change and the choices which are explicitly or implicitly made. We look at the approaches to "managing by process" and reflect the importance of measurement in the management process. Reading the chapter you will cover:

- A strategic drive by many organisations to become "lean" – what this means and the reasons behind the concept
- A comparison of a functionally based and a process-based organisation and the trade-offs which are experienced in making a move from one state to another
- A consideration of four structural taxonomies for organisations which address the function versus process balance, with examples of the way in which a number of organisations are changing
- The approaches companies are taking to measurement which attempt to link together processes to prevent the creation of process silos.

INTRODUCTION

Our contention is that strategy leads to the development of processes which serve the needs of individual markets. This movement has its recent roots in the strategy models of academics like Michael Porter (1980, 1985) and exposition in companies such as Motorola and Levi Strauss who have driven forward change under aspects of Quality and Customer Service. We have already made it clear earlier that we see the knowledge and methodologies of TQM as being complementary to BPR through the concept of the business process. The question which is raised in relation to radical improvement in performance is "how can organisations manage the new paradigm of processes while keeping the inherent strengths of functions?" This section addresses the issues arising from a strategic intent for management by process through the identification of processes and their exploration. We put forward principles of process management to the implementation of the new order in managing by process. Most of those who have completed BPR programmes reflect retrospectively that the mapping of processes and the conceptual model building of a process-based organisation is the easy part of the exercise, even if it didn't seem so at the time. The implementation of the exercise is what counts. The lessons from previous initiatives lead us to support this view if only from a comparison of other performance-improvement initiatives such as TQM, JIT and Simultaneous Engineering discussed in Chapter 11. We recognise that we are here dealing with managing change. All models for change include the possibility of returning to something like the original state rather than the intended changes becoming embedded. This danger is illustrated by the Mitel experience (Chapter 2). We present a positive view of managing by process as a way of preventing this reversal.

STRATEGY-DRIVEN PROCESS MANAGEMENT

We can see the movement over the last ten years towards management by process in the operational activities of a supply chain. Companies in markets which had strong Japanese competitors, including cars, electronics and electrical products, realised that they must achieve increases in performance on many dimensions quickly rather than over a period of time. It was no good just playing catch-up. Chapter 12 on Logistics tells the story well.

We can understand the strategic changes by using the simple model of the strategic compass (Figures 5.1 and 5.2) (Bowman and Faulkner, 1994). The model compares the customer's view of an organisation and what a producer must do, either to match the customer's perception or to change the perception of the customer through experience of the organisation's products or services.

The customer model compares price with the customer's perception of added value. Like many strategy models this is one for mapping the relative position of firms as a whole or product groups in different markets. The four segments

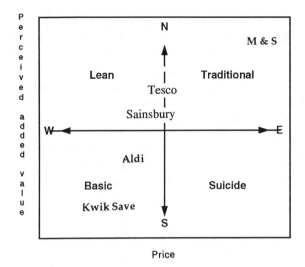

Figure 5.1 Strategic compass

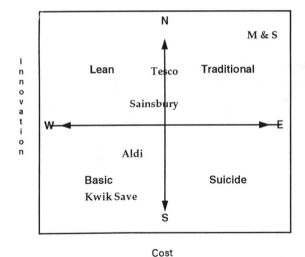

Figure 5.2 Strategic compass

of the framework correspond to:

- The Traditional quadrant where the prices are relatively high but the customers accept these as the products and services are regarded as being superior to other offerings
- The Basic quadrant where prices are low but less is given to customers often in terms of completeness of a service or reduced performance of a product

- The Suicide quadrant where the product or service are perceived to be overpriced. Being in this quadrant leads to the demise of the product or the firm. Exceptions arise with monopolistic or quasi-monopolistic firms, as with some privatised utilities in the UK
- The Lean quadrant is where customers perceive good value for money with an equitable balance between the make-up of the product and services and the prices which are charged.

We show how food retailers, in the UK can be positioned on the quadrant with companies like Marks & Spencer showing in the traditional quadrant and long-standing low-price providers like Kwik Save being joined by newcomers Aldi, Netto and Shopping Giant. Other key players in the market Tesco, Sainsbury, Safeways and Asda, are jockeying for a position more towards the Lean quadrant. As such they illustrate the effect for many organisations in very competitive markets. They seek to move the customer's perceptions towards the west or northwest on the strategic compass. Such moves have consequences for the producer's capability. This is reflected in the second framework (Figure 5.2).

Now the customers' concern with added value and price as experienced in anticipated consumption is replaced by the producer's capability to build added value through creativity and innovation and to control costs in line with the intended positioning. Hence the ability to survive in the Basic quadrant comes from developing processes which control costs very effectively while providing an acceptable level of product or service. This can be a delicate balance as demonstrated by the experience of Ratner's. Ratner's became one of the most successful jewellery retail chains in the 1980s under the chairmanship of Gerald Ratner. Unfortunately on more than one occasion he denigrated his customers by describing his merchandise as "rubbish" and suggesting customers were foolish to buy it. His first statements went unnoticed but finally they were picked up by the tabloid press. Gerald Ratner was forced to resign and the company image was so badly damaged that it changed its name to Signet, but even this move was not sufficient to change its fortunes.

The Lean quadrant is, of course, the most interesting as the ability to maintain costs while building perceived added value presents a competitive threat to organisations in both the traditional and basic quadrants. Having a strategic intent to "Get Lean" is the spirit of BPR notwithstanding getting "happy" as discussed in Chapter 15.

The manifestation of leanness is in the automotive industry with Japanese companies consistently showing comparatively higher quality (measured in terms of defects), faster development of new models and higher productivity. If Leanness is a metaphor for organisational success we have to see how implementation takes organisations away from a functional base towards processes and ultimately new organisational structures and ways of working.

As with any organism, we know often from bitter experience that leanness is not just about losing body weight, which we could equate to simple downsizing. Who would wish to see an "anorexic" organisation? Leanness involves also being "fit'. Here there are useful analogies with the quality concept of "fitness for purpose", the linking of products and services with market needs. So leanness in organisations is likely to come from concentrating the "body" on activities which make it fit for a purpose, i.e. the strategic goals. In the metaphor we can see processes as being the muscle systems which develop the capability and high performance coming from coordinated action on the part of a number of muscle systems, i.e. processes. Where are the organisational functions in the metaphor? Perhaps represented, at best, the senses and, at worst, by pockets of fat.

Box 5.1   The National & Provincial Building Society

The National & Provincial Building Society is the UK's 12th largest. It is based largely in the north of England employing over 4000 people in 320 branches and over 200 community network branches. It supplies mortgages, savings, investments, credit cards, insurance and other personal financial services to households. The Society was transformed under the direction of Chief Executive David O'Brien by attempting to change the mindset of the organisation, starting the programme change in 1990. In the words of David O'Brien, "At National & Provincial we mean the beliefs and principles that govern how people in the organisation behave towards each other, their customers and their suppliers. This includes what the organisation values, and what it is like to do business with, what members feel about working here. Such beliefs and principles give stability and cohesion to organisations."

The approach to change has been to reduce the number of processes within the Society from 18 to 10. An object-oriented methodology was used to design the processes using the concept of three kinds of objects: process objects, systems objects and people objects.

The language to describe the processes reflects the changed mindset. Processes were described as direction management, with implementation consisting of customer requirements, customer engagement and customer satisfaction within an understanding process. The use of terms like *events* to describe meetings, players for staff, role for job, process for procedure, teams for departments and team leader for manager all helped to change the way the organisation thought about itself and its people. Key team roles are described as team leader, coach and manager, analogous to positions in sport. The team leader is effectively the captain, the coach develops skills and provides resources while the manager sets the direction. Each member of the direction team leads an implementation management team.

The Society keeps track of the issues which concern people and uses this to reflect the changing mindset of the organisation. It calls this its "issueometer". It took time in the years following the launch of the programme for people to accept the new mindset for the organisation and become team players focused on the process rather than questioning the change or reflecting on the role of teams.

A key measure for David O'Brien of the success of the change is the strength of the Society's relationship with its customers. This is a comparison of the profiles of the financial services which the Society considers an individual customer could benefit from and the customer's actual use.

N&P's pre-tax profits increased by 51% in 1993 but at the same time its cost/income ratio rose sharply at a time when other societies were seeing the ratio fall or remain constant. In September 1994 David O'Brien resigned. About the same time he offered the view that the transformation was about two-thirds complete. In the previous year a clash of cultures was given as the reason for the collapse of the proposed merger between N&P and the Leeds Building Society which had a more traditional approach. In 1995 the N&P was taken over by Abbey National, the first Building Society to become a private limited company.

References: *Financial Times*, 29 September 1994, National Provincial ousts Chief Executive; *Financial Times*, 26 July 1994, Building society conundrum; David O'Brien and Judith Wainwright, 1993, Winning as a team of teams – transforming the mindset of the organisation at National & Provincial Building Society, *The Journal of Corporate Transformation*, **1**, No. 3.

Hinterhuber (1995) reports that business process management in 1994 was the top priority of 34% of a sample of European companies whereas three years previously it was not mentioned as a priority as such (cost reduction was then the biggest issue for 32% of companies). Some organisations have decided to move rapidly away from a functional base for their organisation towards processes to break the mould of the old culture as much as for operational effectiveness. The National and Provincial Building Society is a case in point with the introduction of a new language for activities and positions (see Box 5.1). Our proposition is that in making changes of this magnitude organisations must be capable of managing implicit or explicit trade-offs between functional and process management and managing the changed role for people.

UNDERSTANDING THE FUNCTIONAL AND PROCESS TRADE-OFFS

A fundamental shift from a functionally based organisation to being business-process based will require an appreciation of the strengths and weaknesses of functions as opposed to processes which cross old functional boundaries. Unless this happens, good aspects of functions may be lost in any transform-ation. These are the skills and expertise associated with a function which may drive their own internal processes, and in the best instances may act as a catalyst for improvement more generally throughout an organisation. Perhaps we should realise that in making any move towards process management we are likely to be trading off some of the existing benefits of functions at least in the short term. Operations management discipline is no stranger to the issue of trade-offs and how the subject has been advanced by challenging the accep-tance of trade-offs. For instance, we would no longer accept a trade-off between the consistency of the quality of a manufactured product with the cost of achieving this goal (i.e. quality consistency is free as proclaimed by the quality gurus). So too we would recognise that to increase the capability of a product would require increases in costs, i.e. there is a trade-off between cost and quality expressed as performance or capability; a Lexus car is more "capable" than a Corolla. However, over a period of time we would expect the capability of each car to rise.

We are not suggesting that organisations who accompany BPR with structural change necessarily abandon all aspects of functions, and indeed may choose not to. Motorola with their concept of advisory and operational processes present one model of compromise. We believe, though, that in order for an organisation to manage its own change, people need to determine what the trade-offs mean for them, establish whether they are real or imaginary and decide how they will manage them. This may only be in the short term while new methods of working with process management are established and the organisation can be sure it is not simply working in horizontal rather than vertical silos as happened initially for Mitel.

In order to understand the trade-offs we might be making with functional versus process management we can postulate changes associated with process management compared to functional management. Often in tackling the question of trade-offs it is useful to establish what is involved in the states for which trade-offs are being considered. So let us consider two models for the organisation. The first model consists of clear functional domains with strong barriers between the functions, typified in the current language of functional silos. Here whole processes or parts of processes tend to be owned by the functions. The processes which transcend functional boundaries are poorly integrated even when the flow of information, people or materials passes from one function to another. The second model is of a flatter organisational structure with processes running in concept across the organisation and aligned with the flow of information, people, or materials. These performance improvements result from the type of exercise as illustrated in the St James's Hospital case study (Chapter 20).

How can we describe functions and processes? We need a model to discuss the polar differences between functional and process-based management. We will use a model of the organisation of people, processes, and technology in the context for organisational culture and enabled by aspects of communication. In these elements we can identify other commonly held constructs associated with functions and processes. We put these forward as extremes as summarised in Table 5.1.

What are we likely to experience on a tour of a "pure" functionally managed organisation, perhaps represented by many traditional retail banks or an engineering manufacturing company? The organisational structure is very hierarchical often with 20 or so different identifiable grades between the most junior position and the chairman of the board if the company is large. We are

Table 5.1 Features associated with functional and process management

Dimension	Functional orientation	Process orientation
Organisational structure	• Hierarchical • Functional focus	• Devolved • Process focus
Operational processes	• Owned by functions • Functional boundaries • Disconnected flows • Sub-optimised operations	• Process-owned • Customer-focused end to end • Simplified flows • Optimised for customer service, costs and efficiency
People	• Functional allegiance • Limited "sight" of customer • Separation of specialist skills • Individual focus	• Process allegiance • Customer-focused • Integration of skills • Team focus
Technology	• Discrete in functions • Measurement of functional objectives • Loose connection of planning and control	• Integrate in processes • Basis for process measurement • Planning and control for the process
Communication	• Vertical orientation	• Horizontal orientation
Culture	• Front-office/back-room divide • Functional baronies • Language of disciplines	• Customer focus through the process • Process ownership • Language of service delivery

introduced to the functional heads who talk more about their own functional barony than the organisation as a whole and this view is reinforced by their staff who see the function as their route for advancement. There is a sense of certainty about the way things are done in the functions. It may be that staff have a professional status attached to the function and see themselves as expert designers, engineers, accountants, or bankers, for instance. The talk is of the activities in the function, or new technology which will assist the functional goals. Unless the function has a front-office role there is no direct contact with customers and no feeling that this should be the case. The functional domain provides a warm feeling of security and stability, a position which is reinforced by the internal communication system which filters out the news from outside whether it is good or bad. The language of the function is encouraged to isolate the new ideas coming from outside even if they are from another function within the organisation. "Job's worth" attitudes prevail to ensure non-cooperation.

We now embark on a visit to a "pure" process-managed organisation. We meet the executive team who explain the process architecture of the organisation. As we tour with various processes we are conscious of teams of people and process owners who recognise and tell us about the role of the process in meeting the strategic goals of the organisation. People we meet seem to understand who the end customer is as well as having a strong sense of being part of an internal customer chain. They relate anecdotes about the unconditional guarantees they give to the next teams in their process and interrelating processes. The tales are of gifts and nights out as recompense for shortfalls in performance. There is an air of uncertainty if not instability but this seems to engender excitement rather than fear. Some individuals who have expert and professional status reflect on the differences they found when they started to work for this organisation coming from a more traditional functionally based firm. They speak of being circumspect about their role as experts, how they thought they would miss the close relationship with other professionals of their calling, how they found a new way to use their creative talents to improve the processes they found themselves attached to and how they were able to share their expertise to improve the competencies of other members of the process teams. Technology in this process environment was used to enable performance improvement and when systems were introduced the integrative aspects were explored to build internal and external capabilities into suppliers' and customers' processes. In this process environment in the course of our tour we were able to understand simply how things worked and the way in which customers' requests were dealt with.

On reflection after our tours we are drawn to the functions for their sense of structure and security and their potential for reducing risk, while recognising their defensive attitude to change. We feel the sense of excitement about the unstable process structure with its possibility for rapid reconfiguring. Perhaps neither really exists to the extreme we have painted. Maybe the pure process view represents a Utopia which can be useful in making decisions about balance (Grint, 1995). However, most organisations will be left with dealing with trade-offs in moving from management through function to management by process and most reach a compromise position.

What are the trade-offs between functions and processes? Many organisations are moving in the direction of adopting some degree of management by process while retaining some functional elements in their organisation. If the differences between managing through functions and by process are at all real we might expect an organisation to encounter a number of possible trade-offs as they move from function to process. These trade-offs might only be short term but may also extend over a longer period of time. In either case trade-offs need to be recognised and managed. All organisations will experience different trade-offs to different degrees. The following are trade-offs which managers should look for:

1. *Customer focus versus utilisation of skills* Dispersing skilled resources from a function among a number of processes might mean that it is not possible to use those resources fully. This could apply to specialists in a number of disciplines, for example engineers or financial advisers. On the other hand, by being in the customer-facing process, specialists may become more innovative through gaining knowledge of customers' needs.
2. *Process versus functional silos* In changing from a functional to a process-based organisation the structure may only in effect be turned on its side when people are redistributed into processes which have as great a tendency to form barriers between the business processes as existed with the functional structure. Most organisations seek a balance between the two.
3. *Empowerment versus imposed control* Process management suggests devolvement and empowerment for the process teams which might be seen to threaten the control of performance. Individuals may also feel unable or disinclined to accept the greater responsibility which comes with empowerment. We return to the subject of empowerment in Chapter 6.
4. *Fuzzy matrix versus clarity of structure* Functional structures for all their complexity in organisations tend to be understood by people and may be exploited in power games. The structure of a process arrangement may not be as clear. Rather it may seem to be more of a fuzzy matrix especially if individuals play a role in more than one process. Gaining understanding of roles and structure could cause problems in staff motivation and performance.
5. *Process knowledge versus discipline expertise* While redistribution of people into business processes may lead to a greater understanding of the process and the needs of customers, the change may not allow for continued development of specialist knowledge from a critical mass of experts.

6. *Loyalty and motivation versus cost reduction* If the adoption of "management by process" is perceived only as a way to reduce the number of staff employed, staff who remain may be less loyal and have low motivation.

These trade-offs might also be seen in the context of problems we could associate with radical change. First, organisations may not be able to make the change quickly enough to realise any benefits, i.e. they are stuck with the worst aspects of the trade-offs. Second, the defence barriers of functions may be too great and the same individuals may regroup within processes creating equally impermeable horizontal rather than vertical structures. Third, while the concept of horizontal processes might make conceptual sense, the reality experienced by those in the new process structure may be confusing. Fourth, while the process concept obviously relates easily to operational processes, or those which are project based as in new product development, it may be more difficult for its implementation in support or enabling processes.

APPROACHES TO MANAGING BY PROCESSES

Managing by process is the concept of a horizontal organisation replacing the vertical functionally based organisation (Ostroff and Smith, 1992). The question facing organisation is what structure to adopt and how to make the change. Organisations seem to start their journey by defining the high level architecture of the organisation. This may seem very simple in concept (see Figure 5.3 for Royal Mail Business Processes Overview). A traditionally functionally based organisation is shown in Figure 5.4 and a "pure" process based organisation in Figure 5.7. Two other intermediate structures are seen in a number of organisations. First, Figure 5.5 shows the matrix-based organisation where functions still exist along with cross-functional processes. Here individuals have allegiance to both a function and to one or more processes. Second are processes which are close and supported by centres of excellence which support the cross-organisational processes (Figure 5.6). While these may be equated to functions their effectiveness in the new domain rests with the mindset of support rather than control which we might associate with functionality.

How do organisations decide how far to go in becoming horizontal? There seems to be no definite answer to this question. Perhaps there is an element of size of organisation. The National & Provincial Building Society moved as far as most in this direction. Some of the problems and the dangers for the CEO are highlighted in Box 5.2. Some essential components of a process-managed organisation are clear. One of the most important is the concept of the team-based organisation with a strong and clear ownership of processes at any level

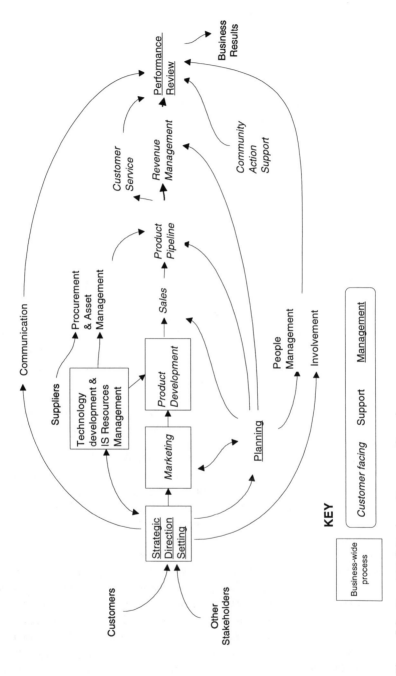

Figure 5.3 Royal Mail Business Processes Overview

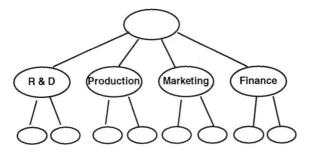

Figure 5.4 Managing by functions

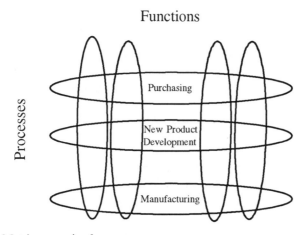

Figure 5.5 Matrix managing by process

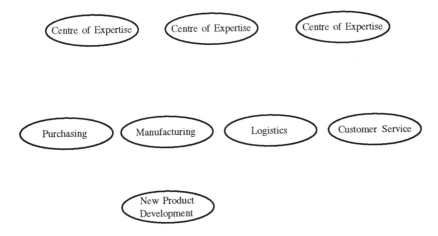

Figure 5.6 Partially managing by process

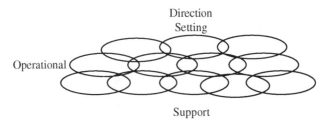

Direction
Setting

Operational

Support

Figure 5.7   Fully managing by process

Box 5.2   Holding BPR together

In the experience of Baxi, a Preston manufacturer of domestic boilers and heaters, only through painting an "Armageddon scenario" did the newly appointed chief executive convince his senior managers of the need for re-engineering. Even then, two directors resigned as the seven-month programme gathered pace. But re-engineering can be as costly for the more intrepid senior managers as it can be for their more obstructive colleagues, as Baxi's David Dry discovered. Despite the company making £14 million profit on a turnover of £73 million in 1993, Dry was shown the door. The board that had viewed him as its salvation felt it had a "tiger by the tail" as Dry said. With the prospect of more pleasant pastures, the board felt that Armageddon could keep its tigers.

Source: Marion Devine, Riding the re-engineering tiger, *Sunday Times*, 16 June 1994.

---

in the hierarchy along with a focus on customers and suppliers across the process.

The appeal of managing by process is one which is occupying the minds of large organisations. The question for them is often one of what is the best top-level "architecture" for us? A large and complex organisation will often first adopt a matrix type of organisation (Figure 5.2) but in a multiple form with each matrix being one company. Within one company, however, a different approach might be adopted. If the company has strong and well-defined operational supply chain processes there is a tendency to move towards integration of the supply chain with other disciplines acting as centres of expertise. Examples of the latter are found in companies like Kodak and Ericsson.

The other concept is that of managing the white space across boundaries (Rummler and Brache, 1990) so as to eliminate or minimise the effect of disconnects in flows of information, materials or people. The dangers of process silos replacing functional silos is a very real one as the Mitel case demonstrates. One company we know is dealing with this potential danger by having senior managers from high-level business processes which overlap making joint decisions.

There are, of course, dangers in moving to the horizontal. Not least is the resistance of managers to make the change. After all, we are asking managers to adopt new behaviour and possibly relinquish power. This kind of resistance is not confined to changes associated with BPR but needs to be confronted (Argyris, 1990).

MEASUREMENT FOR PROCESSES

The message of quality improvement has always been linked to the need to have good measurements on which decisions can be taken on the viability of processes. This has especially been the case in manufacturing. Many of the winners of the quality awards, for instance Florida Power and Light and Motorola, have based their success on measurement. Indeed the whole of the Motorola quality programme progressed under the banner of 6-Sigma as a target for process capability. While this approach to process capability is appropriate for manufacturing processes it becomes less so for service processes when customers become part of the processes. However, the need for good measures of performance remains the goal for process management. The question is often what to measure, where, and when and with what frequency as well as how to link together measures at different levels of process disaggregation and between processes at the same level.

The old tenet holds of "what gets measured gets done". Measurement has a place in the control of processes and setting targets for improvement linked to reward. It is perhaps obvious in the context of this book that no single measure is sufficient and we are seeking a range of measurements which will measure the performance of the organisation of the whole and drive improvement in performance. Measures which have an effect should be talked about and relate to the core capabilities. This requires a mix of hard and increasingly soft measures. The CEO of Pepsi talks about the changes in orientation for his team in the following way (Garvin, 1995):

"Our focus is completely different. Let me give you an example. Every Monday morning is a senior staff meeting, and much of the time is devoted to discussions of our core capability-building processes. Whether it is new product development, single voice communication or coaching and support for sales, we're constantly asking 'How do we leverage these processes for maximum advantage?' It's not as though we'd asked these questions before, they never came up. We were much too tactical and reactive ... There is a difference in the questions I ask. My first question on field visits used to be 'Are you going to deliver your volume and profit target'? You can imagine the message that gave. Now the questions are different. Are we giving great customer service? How is our relationship with Wal-Mart? The questions are much more attuned to the doing."

How can we devise a measuring system? Organisations take a number of approaches to measurement which have some common features:

1. Demonstrate where capability is being developed.
2. Link measures at different levels of the processes.
3. Include a mix of soft and hard measures of performance.
4. Have measures which capture the internal and the external environment.
5. Devise measures which support the management of interfaces within processes and between processes for the achievement of the overall process targets.

The first point is fairly obvious but can be disastrous if ill-conceived. For example, when the Royal Mail began their quality programme with the arrival of Ian Raisbeck, their quality director, there was a dispute about their performance. A critical measure is referred to as "quality of service" which is a measure of their success in delivering mail against target. The users were claiming the Royal Mail had a success rate of about 70% whereas the Royal Mail's own measures seemed to show the figure was over 90%. Ian Raisbeck questioned this discrepancy. It turned out to hinge on the way the measurement was made. Not unreasonably, the users measured from the point of posting to delivery at an address. The Royal Mail's internal measure was between sorting office and delivery office!

Examples of an approach using a range of measures of performance can be seen for those organisations who have adopted one of the major quality frameworks as a means of assessing performance. It is becoming increasingly common for large organisations in Europe to adopt the EFQM model. This influences measurement in a number of ways illustrated by the experience of the Royal Mail. They have embraced both the EFQM framework for driving improvement and the concept of the process-based organisation. Key business processes have been identified and characterised at least at the first level of disaggregation. The processes are recorded in a process atlas and form the platform for the establishment of a hierarchy of measures linking processes at different levels to the corporate core capabilities. Figure 5.8 shows this hierarchy for the main operational process for collecting and sorting mail in the Royal Mail. The process is referred to as the Product Pipeline. The approach to measurement illustrates some important aspects of managing large business processes. First, we still have to address the management of interfaces between different parts of the large process. These may arise simply because of

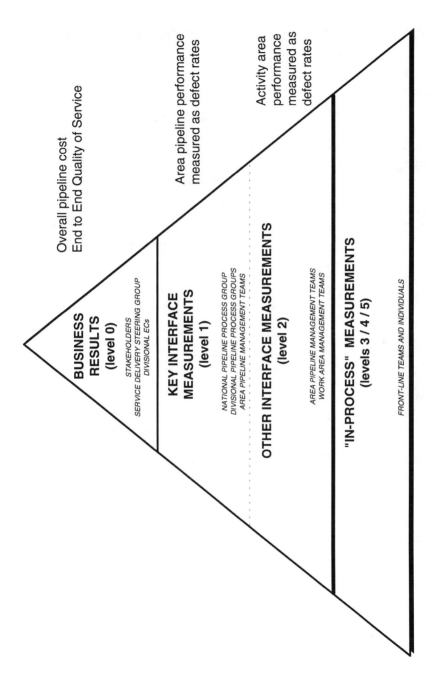

Figure 5.8 Product Pipeline framework for measurement. (Reproduced by permission of the Royal Mail)

Organisational self-analysis model

Leadership	Management act as individuals in taking and communicating decisions. They promote the need to develop and improve the organisation and to set targets.	Management act as a team, ensure two-way open communication, become involved in improvement groups. They agree plans and set priorities.	Managers develop and support improvement teams and make time available for them to work. They check progress and recognise involvement; they say 'thank you'.

Score 1 ▬▬▬ 2 ▬▬▬ 3 ▬▬▬ 4 ▬▬▬ 5 ▬▬▬

| **Policy and strategy** | Partial Business Plans exist—only concentrating on financial targets. Plans are not widely communicated or visibly championed by the top team. | Business plans encompass competition data eg. customer satisfaction measures. Key points are communicated; individuals understand and accept responsibility . | Strategic direction—Vision, Mission Objectives etc are communicated to all stakeholders. A new culture is being developed. Resource made available for continuous improvement. |

Score 1 ▬▬▬ 2 ▬▬▬ 3 ▬▬▬ 4 ▬▬▬ 5 ▬▬▬

| **People management** | Training is seen as a cost and people are employed to do a job. | The management team recognises that success comes from employees. Skills training is encouraged and training plans are agreed and aligned to company goals. | Delegation of responsibility to people at appropriate levels takes place. Appraisal schemes match the aspirations of the people and the organisation. |

Score 1 ▬▬▬ 2 ▬▬▬ 3 ▬▬▬ 4 ▬▬▬ 5 ▬▬▬

| **Resources** | Resource management tends to be directed solely at financial areas Decisions on stock and materials are taken using hunches and 'gut' feelings. Information is 'kept in people's heads'. | Information available—often talked about or over-analysed but rarely used to improve. Cash and working capital are seen by all to be important. Stock controls in place. | Decisions are made on the basis of information. Stock is related to customer requirements. Process improvement and evaluation of new technology takes place. Planning systems are in use. |

Score 1 ▬▬▬ 2 ▬▬▬ 3 ▬▬▬ 4 ▬▬▬ 5 ▬▬▬

| **Processes** | Few procedures exist apart from financial controls. Everyone does their best and firefighting is the norm. Changes are made to fix problems as and when appropriate. | Procedures have been written and imposed. A bureaucratic system exists with little chance for improvement. Non conformances are seen as 'bad'. Systems purpose not clear to operators. | Critical processes are owned and there is support to monitor and improve them. Ownership is assigned to management who review corrective action etc. |

Score 1 ▬▬▬ 2 ▬▬▬ 3 ▬▬▬ 4 ▬▬▬ 5 ▬▬▬

| **Customer satisfaction** | Customer satisfaction only considered in terms of external complaints. Complaints are dealt with when they arise with little attempt to find or correct the cause. | Customer satisfaction measures are available from surveys. This data is used to set performance standards and staff have been trained in customer service. | The need to meet agreed customer needs is reflected within the core strategic plans. A customer care policy exists and is widely published. |

Score 1 ▬▬▬ 2 ▬▬▬ 3 ▬▬▬ 4 ▬▬▬ 5 ▬▬▬

| **People satisfaction** | Disputes and grievances are resolved as and when they arise. Absenteeism and/or staff turnover are high. Morale at times is poor and management tend to concentrate on themselves. | People's views are sought through surveys. Staff are consulted on improvement but grievances are dealt with by 'personnel'. Health and Safety are treated seriously. | Two way internal discussions take place and some form of appraisal process is used for joint improvement targets. Communication and feedback on a broad range of issues happens—morale is good. |

Score 1 ▬▬▬ 2 ▬▬▬ 3 ▬▬▬ 4 ▬▬▬ 5 ▬▬▬

| **Impact on society** | Environmental and Social obligations seen as costly and a threat to competitiveness. Damage limitation exercises are used to counter 'problems'. Community work limited to individuals. | Environmental and Social requirements are dealt with to conform fully with legal requirements. Policy documents and internal standards have been written. | Strategic Quality Planning incorporates Environmental and Social obligations. Responsibility is allocated to senior managers. Environmental audits take place. Keen practitioners are encouraged. |

Score 1 ▬▬▬ 2 ▬▬▬ 3 ▬▬▬ 4 ▬▬▬ 5 ▬▬▬

| **Business results** | The financial results are available and some non-financial indicators published. They are seen as management data by the majority of staff. | Systems exist to monitor and display financial and non-financial indicators. They are communicated to staff and improvement targets indicated. | Indicators are used to measure process & output and available for improvement teams. Trends are monitored and used to set targets. Supplier quality is measured and shared. |

Score 1 ▬▬▬ 2 ▬▬▬ 3 ▬▬▬ 4 ▬▬▬ 5 ▬▬▬

Figure 5.9 Organisational self-analysis model based on the European Foundation of Quality Management Framework

Starting with Leadership, read all the statements across the page and choose and circle the number you feel best reflects the situation within your organisation. Multiply the number you have chosen by the factor shown and enter your score in the box on the right. Repeat the exercise for the other eight criteria and total your scores to produce a Grand Total. Overleaf, we interpret the result.

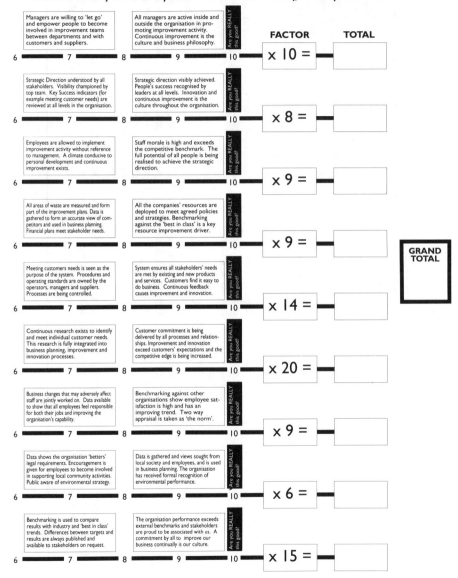

Figure 5.9 *Continued*

Table 5.2 Process capability assessment. (Reproduced by permission of ICL)

	Exists in name only	Designed and developed support systems set up	Partially deployed	Fully deployed	Reached world-class standards
Ownership	No-one owns this process	An owner has been appointed	Owner has fully accepted responsibilities, understands process tools and techniques	The success of this process impacts the owner's personal rewards, skilled with process tools and techniques, effective leader	Recognised role model process owner. Owner has been rewarded for improving the process
Definition	It exists, and may deliver an output	The transformation, inputs and outputs have been agreed and documented, accurately flow charted	Measurement mechanisms included in process definition	Audits show process and documents match	The process is stable, proven and fully understood
People operating and managing this process	It is not clear who does this process	People have been appointed to operate and manage this process	All know their own responsibilities and are competent	All highly competent and committed, work as team, know outline of others responsibilities, rewarded for success of this process	Recognised role models, working with process customers and suppliers to improve the process
Effectiveness	Outputs of this process not identified	Deliverables to all process customers assumed	Deliverables confirmed with all process customers, sometimes being achieved	Deliverables to each process customer being achieved most times	Outputs to all process customers being consistently achieved every time

geographic separation as with networks of sorting and delivery offices or banks and processes centres or factories and distribution centres. Interfaces can be addressed by the use of the "service level agreements" set up between the sides of the interface. Second, we still employ the process control measures and use these to drive forward increases in process capability.

The EFQM framework has also been used as a vehicle for self-assessment within the organisation. The EFQM assesses enablers for performance and results in the areas of customer satisfaction, employee satisfaction, business results and impact on society. The assessment process examines the extent to which there is evidence of high achievement in the enablers and of deployment of the practice across the organisation rather than in isolated pockets. Results are judged against appropriateness of the degree of excellence of the results and their scope. The categories of assessment require both soft and hard measures and require some degree of agreement among assessors as to what demonstrates good and bad practice.

Using this form of assessment has involved the Royal Mail in training senior managers who have carried out assessment in teams according to the EFQM practice first at Division level. The Royal Mail has also participated in the EFQM award by preparing a full submission of 75 pages and being assessed by external assessors. This has given valuable information about areas which require improvement. The EFQM categories for assessment have also been adopted by the British Quality Foundation as a means of judging organisations for their quality awards. A simplified assessment framework for use in small firms is shown in Figure 5.8, which shows the holistic nature of the approach.

The use of these types of frameworks for assessing performance are useful because they capture qualitative and quantitative data from a range of individuals. It may be used to focus on one aspect of capability. An example for assessing the development of capability for managing processes developed by ICL is shown in Table 5.2. The role of this type of measure is that it gives both a snapshot of how far a process has developed and acts as a route map for developing the process capabilities.

CONCLUSIONS

Understanding how to manage by process seems to us to be essential for managers who are seeking to improve performance by adopting a combination of BPR and continuous improvement. A mindset change is required the more the institution moves towards complete management by process and away from old-style functionality. We have tried to address some of the issues which arise in getting the right balance by using the concept of trade-offs. Clearly the ability to manage by process is dependent on the people and we look at the people issues more closely in the next chapter.

Chapter 6

The Role of People in Processes

Colin Armistead and Philip Rowland

WHAT WILL YOU FIND IN THIS CHAPTER?

It is a truism that people are an organisation's main asset. In the context of this book we will look more closely at Human Resource Management issues in a subsequent chapter. Here we want to cover a number of issues which we regard as being important for managing by process and BPR and on-going continuous process improvement activities. They are:

- The view from the top managers. How do they see the new organisation and communicate the message?
- The role of the team in the process-based organisation. The majority of process-based organisations have adopted the concept and practices of managing by teams.
- The question of empowerment. What do we mean by empowerment? Do we always want individuals to be empowered? How do we try to arrive at the best balance of empowerment and control?
- People in flatter process-based organisations find their changed circumstances confusing. Traditional career progression is no longer available. What are the issues and how are organisations addressing these?
- Development of specialist skills and abilities, once the preserve of the

functions, may be weakened as the organisation moves more towards a process-based organisation. How can this problem be overcome?

- A tool for managing culture. While this subject is dealt with extensively in many books we include some thoughts to help to link the management of change to managing the BPR project which we cover in the Appendix.

THE VIEW FROM THE TOP

The experience of BPR programmes has identified the need for strong commitment from senior managers. Success or failure depends on their actions. It is easy to see why things go wrong. Senior managers in commercial firms are often preoccupied with short-term demands on their time for profit improvement. They may also already be engaged in a wide range of initiatives: to expand or contract, to invest in systems, or to improve customer service. This inevitably raises the question of why they should engage in a process view of the world and be willing to commit to the pain and effort of trying to make it work. The BPR literature makes the role of leadership clear for success. Also the quality frameworks of the EFQM and the Baldrige Awards make an explicit assumption that leadership is an essential component in the scheme of things.

The experience of large organisations such as Rank Xerox, SmithKline Beecham and Pepsi-Cola (Garvin, 1995) has been a change in the nature of the top team. Now managers must be technically competent. They must have the soft skills needed for communication, and the ability to work as a team. Craig Weatherup, the president and CEO of Pepsi-Cola in North America, expresses the leadership needed in the following way:

> "When I was considering someone for promotion a few years ago, I looked at only two criteria. One was *idea leadership*. The person had to have the ability to find, create, borrow, steal or reshape ideas, especially big ideas, because that was the essence of our culture. The other thing I looked for was *people leadership*. Pepsi's managers had to be able to mobilise the troops and energise the organisation, get it moving fast and aggressively. Today we've added a third category, *capability leadership*, by which I mean a manager's ability to build and institutionalise the capabilities of people, the organisation and systems. To do that well requires a focus on core processes."

Changes in the style and competencies of top management are clearly essential to the success of the improvement programme. As the new order is going to emerge only over a period of time it is not possible at this time to make the same didactic statements about the "role of leadership in the process-based organisation" that we might be confident about doing for the improvement approaches for processes themselves (see the Appendix).

THE TEAM-BASED ORGANISATION

The idea of teams as the vehicle for improvement is not new. It fashioned much of the thinking and practice of the quality and customer service initiatives of the 1980s. The initiators of change were those companies in Japan and the United States which were identified as role models of seemingly successful companies who had adopted the team model either for the front-line service team or as quality improvement teams or quality circles. This set the tone for talking about teams to the extent that is has become something of a heresy to suggest alternatives. Has anything changed in the process-based organisation formed by BPR? Are teams now more important? The answer to these questions would seem to be yes. The principles of BPR suggest integration of activities which can lead to the formation of teams, for instance for customer order processes, installation of equipment and customer service. The adoption of a process-based organisation in a large process like order fulfilment still requires working across geographical boundaries. These boundaries could easily become barriers in the same way as functional silos were in the function-based organisation. Teams which transcend the boundaries are seen to be the way in which this regression is prevented.

The role of teams is clearly identified in our previous listing of the principles of the process management. The new teams require a shift of mindset which some organisations, such as the National & Provincial Building Society, have tried to deliver by changing the language of the organisation to align with a sporting analogy of teams (Box 5.1). Such moves require the training and development of new skills to support the new structure and ways of working. The use of a skills matrix for the process allows members of the team to attain the range of skills necessary for the process team to work effectively and improve their performance. The Mitel case gives an account of the actions which might be taken. It may be that BPR leads to a complete redefinition of the job. The case of National Vulcan's move from insurance process clerks to insurance professionals is a case in point. Such examples are perhaps in line with Peter Drucker's predictions of the rise of *knowledge* workers (Drucker, 1993).

The management of teams is driven by the structure of the organisation. As most large organisations seem to be adopting the matrix of the process/centre of excellence model the role of the process leader becomes paramount. Many organisations are using the approach of making members of their executive team individually responsible for broad key processes. This approach is designed to overcome the traditional situation where there may be owners of processes, for example in manufacturing or logistics, but board-level executives could still override their decisions. In the new structures there are sometimes attempts made to differentiate roles between persons who have broad responsibilities for a key business process, called *process sponsors* or *champions*, who are able to break any cross-functional barriers which remain and *process owners* concerned with the day-to-day running of the process.

Where there is a matrix structure organisation we may still find barriers. The teams which transcend old functional boundaries can still be frustrated by the allegiance of managers and staff to old functions often because of personal focus or "rewards" for such loyalty.

A QUESTION OF EMPOWERMENT

Much of the literature on team and process-based organisations mentions the need to empower staff. The problem is that the term itself is rarely clearly defined so its use is ambiguous. We could draw parallels to the way in which the term quality was employed in the past, particularly with regard to service quality. Managers often hid behind the "intangibility" of quality and refused to look closely at more detailed descriptors. It might be argued that this failure of definition contributed to the existence of gaps in understanding and capability characterised in the servqual model (Parasuraman, Zeithaml and Berry, 1986).

There seems to be a similar danger in the term empowerment. It is clear that senior managers, in using the term, wish it to represent an unlocking of the capabilities of individuals and teams to contribute more to the running of existing processes and the redesign or re-engineering processes. However, from the individual's perspective changing in this direction may seem threatening rather than liberating.

We find it useful to use the framework for the position of empowerment as shown in Figure 6.1 (Armistead et al. 1994). The framework represents the organisational perspective as expressed by senior managers and the perception of individuals through the organisation. Management's view may be of an organisation which has tightly imposed controls or one which expects individuals and teams to take decisions about their own actions. This view is set against the perception or wish on the part of the individual for discretion over what is done and when. The model has four domains, two of which are congruent and two dysfunctional:

1. The *Compliant* domain represents the situation of high imposed control with little autonomy for the staff who for the most part are content to work in this environment which feels supportive of them.
2. The *Adaptive* domain is characterised by a high level of empowerment with low imposed controls and a great deal of autonomy for individuals and teams and again support for this state of affairs. This domain has traditionally been associated with professional groups.

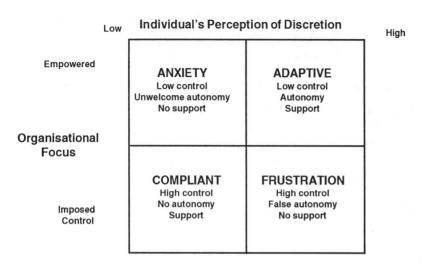

Figure 6.1 Empowerment

3. The *Anxiety* domain arises when organisations speak of empowerment in ill-defined ways and expect individuals to respond without giving any real support for them to cope with the change. The autonomy given feels unwelcome and threatening. Reasons for anxiety include lack of confidence to work in the new way, a lack of understanding of what is being asked of them, and a fear that they are being set up to fail and consequently may lose their jobs.

4. The *Frustration* domain results when individuals are led to believe that they are being empowered and are given training to enable them to work more autonomously, only to find that the reality is different. High control exists and they feel unsupported and consequently frustrated by what is happening.

The question for managers and staff in any organisation is one of where they want the organisation as a whole to be positioned and where individual groups of staff should be positioned. If the desired state is different from the existing one the question is then one of how best to manage the change. Our assertion would be that many of the defensive actions of individuals to change result from being moved into either the anxiety or frustration states.

We might wish people within the changed organisation to be more empowered to enable them to respond quickly when things go wrong and to be able to put them right for customers especially. This might be in circumstances of service recovery. Empowerment may also result in a more innovative process team who push for improvements to be enacted. It might be argued that the concept of a "learning organisation" which is innovative is only possible by adopting some degree of empowerment. Organisations which have moved to control staff more have often found frustration takes over, as many professionals in the public sector organisation have experienced during recent years.

Actions which help to make changes easier are:

- Clarity on why and when empowerment rather than control is needed. What are the risks entailed in making major shifts? Remember the Baring's Syndrome.
- Clear communication on the need for change and what empowerment means in their organisation for individuals, teams and process owners.
- Demonstration of support for individuals in making shifts through training, appraisal and rewards.

REWARDS

The question of rewards in the new type of organisation is perhaps one of the most contentious issues. There is general agreement that the old rewards systems, which were based essentially on the functional model of the organisation with its hierarchy and implied advancement over time up through a grading system, are no longer viable.

As organisations become flatter and if they adopt the paradigm of management by process the old order of rewards is no longer appropriate. In addition, staff are increasingly employed on shorter-term contracts and often different contracts. This can result in people in one team being employed on different terms and conditions.

There is no doubt that reward systems need to be considered early in any re-engineering programme. Cigna Insurance Company, which is included as one of our case studies (Chapter 24), reflects on the difficulties which were caused by not taking action sooner. The question for many organisations is what to put in place. Perhaps one of the most radical and imaginative is that used by Rank Xerox (Gavin, 1995). Rewards are linked to two key measures. One concerns performance against corporate objectives for the whole of the company (including financial and customer satisfaction measures). The second relates to the performance of specific processes. A bonus is paid against a metric computed by multiplying the two measures.

It is clear that a reward system can only succeed in motivating staff when the measurement used by the organisation makes sense to all concerned. Measures which drive one factor at the expense of another are self-defeating (see Box 6.1). Halifax's reward system threatened the very concept of the organisation of security, integrity and trust which a building society would traditionally wish to project.

Box 6.1   Halifax drops bonus for cut-price houses.

The Halifax estate agency last night said it had withdrawn a controversial bonus scheme which rewarded staff who persuaded sellers to drop their prices. The about-face came because of "hostile" public reaction to the scheme under which sales staff received a £200 bonus if they persuaded vendors to drop their prices by a third.

A spokesman said that all bonuses owed to staff, due to be paid at the end of a trial period in December, would not now be honoured. The policy disclosed in a leaked memo had been condemned by Labour as an "opportunity to cheat the public" with consumer affairs spokesman Nigel Griffiths urging the Director of Fair Trading to investigate. "This is driving prices down rather than getting the best prices for sellers, at a time when 1.5 million people are trapped in negative equity," Mr Griffith said. Halifax Property Services argued it was merely trying to encourage staff to break the log-jam in the property market.

David Harrison, *Observer*, 24 September 1995.

CAREER PROGRESSION

In the same way that rewards systems are affected by the shift to a process-based management system so are the career paths available to individuals in the company. Traditionally progression meant climbing what was often a very long ladder and each rung allowed the climber to collect more symbols of their status and position; grade 4 gets a car, grade 5 petrol as well, grade 6 a special car parking space, grade 7 a nicer car and an office and so on. Many re-engineering projects result in much shorter ladders with considerably fewer rungs. To make matters worse for the already-concerned managers the symbols which went with it are also often changed – gone is the management canteen and the reserved parking space; instead a more equitable regime is to be installed. All this change results in serious issues in retaining and motivating staff as well as providing some means for them to feel they are making progress, albeit of a different kind.

One solution which is emerging within organisations is that "promotion" occurs when someone moves from one task to another which has significantly more complexity attached to it. There may be no movement up in the sense of the traditional ladder-based hierarchy and yet there is a discernible increase in the responsibilities of that person. Movement between processes may provide for such opportunities as well as giving the person wider experience which should also be seen as important development steps. More traditional examples may also fit as in the case where a move for a finance director from a business unit whose revenue was $10 million to another with a revenue of $50 million clearly provides "promotion" even if the levels in the hierarchy remain the same.

Many organisations are combining the above ideas as well as introducing a more entrepreneurial culture. In a sense they are seeking to minimise the problems of removing the ladder by emphasising the upside of staff having considerably greater responsibility and authority in their work, leading to greater fulfilment.

SPECIALIST SKILLS

Another area of disruption in organisations moving to a process orientation is in the development of specialist skills and abilities. In the traditional organisation the functions acted as "schools" for each respective discipline. People served "apprenticeships" in marketing or finance and as they developed within the function their skills and abilities in these areas increased. While this is true to an extent we also believe that much of the upward progression in the function served to develop other, less valuable, skills more oriented towards the political nature of the functional organisation and the need for managers to act as communication channels, or scramblers, depending on your perspective.

Real marketing and finance skills can still be developed without a large hierarchy developing, or without the need to have a large central resource group. Value-added is once again the name of the game. Developing a detailed budget breakdown which soaks up management energy yet provides an analysis which is well beyond the needs of the business is not what is required. Instead those with specialist skills must use these to give most leverage to those needing help. Amoco's re-engineering started through just such a move in its own budgeting process (Hammer and Stanton, 1995).

Many of the organisations which have been re-engineering have maintained their functions, albeit that the numbers of people may have been reduced and those that remain may work in process-based teams. In these organisations there is still then a kernel around which the "schooling" process can take place. These functions can also continue to act as collectors of new approaches and ideas in their respective fields from outside sources such as academia, professional societies and institutes and conferences.

In other organisations, however, the functions may have virtually disappeared, and some may have been outsourced. In these cases the organisation will need to develop alternative mechanisms for fostering professional expertise and collecting ideas. Small centres of expertise may be maintained to ensure that processes or business units receive the necessary help in a particular field that they require to augment their own skills. Such centres may also provide the mechanism whereby staff development can over a number of different assignments develop individual skills in any given area.

MANAGING CULTURE

The whole field of managing by process which results from BPR is a change management process in itself. The greater the scale of the re-engineering, the more important the way the change is managed is to the overall success. There is an extensive literature on managing change and our intention here is to summarise what we see as being some important points, particularly relating to culture and its importance to BPR and managing by processes.

Changing organisations is ultimately about changing the way in which individuals do things. The more challenging the change, the greater will be the need for fundamental changes to take place. The change programmes associated with BPR have many of the characteristics of changes in previous times. Perhaps what is different is the spirit of the unknown associated with the process-based organisation. This gives management difficulties and opportunities. It creates difficulties because it makes it more difficult to describe what the future state will look like. The resulting ambiguity allows organisational defences against change to swing into action. It creates opportunities because it may free the organisation in ways which make opposition more difficult.

There are many models for describing organisation culture but we have found the cultural web notion (Johnson, 1992) useful in thinking about change. The framework (Figure 6.2) describes the organisational culture in terms of six components and a central paradigm which describes the values of the organisation:

- The *organisational structures*: the formal layout of the organisation, as can be described on an organisation chart or in a process atlas. The balance between process and functions would be described here.
- The *power structures*: there is in most organisations an informal structure working beyond the dictates of any form of organisation chart. Who are the prime movers in the organisation? Does real authority lie with the executive or elsewhere? Who has the power to block change?
- *Control systems*: how are things planned and controlled? How tight are the control systems? Do the measurement systems address both soft and hard measures?
- *Routines and rituals*: how do things actually get done as opposed to the way the procedures say? How are decisions made on such things as promotion and appraisal?

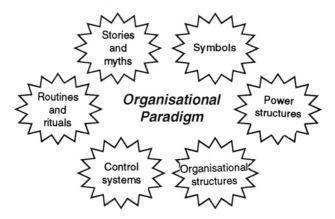

Figure 6.2 A cultural web

- *Symbols*: what are the status symbols which represent power or position?
- *Stories and myths*: what stories of past glories or failures abound? Do they tell of support for individuals or the consequences of stepping out of line?

The concept of the web is that the six factors must support the paradigm. An organisation which declares itself to be responsive to customers' needs by empowering its staff would probably fail if the control systems prevented autonomy and the stories told were of lack of support for people who committed resources on their own initiative to helping customers.

A snapshot of the cultural web as perceived by different groups in an organisation gives a pointer to where the barriers to change may originate. Changes in organisations of the type which we are addressing often bring a change in the central paradigm because the external environment has changed, for instance customers are different or have changed expectations. We have tried to present the issues to be addressed by thinking through the options for structural changes to managing by process, the measurement systems and the approach for HRM. However, it is always important to look for forces which create barriers and to devise action which will minimise the effects, the force field analysis. The following are common, and quite natural, reactions to change:

- Ignorance of what is happening – what on earth is going on?
- Fear of the unknown – will I lose my job?
- Tradition – we have always done things this way, why should we change now?
- Comfort – it sounds like a good idea but it's too much trouble and for what?
- Politics – what will I and my group gain or lose from the change?

- Mindset – probably the most important for we may not see the potential of the change because we are stuck in the mindset of the past. This is very relevant in the function versus process debate.

CONCLUSIONS

Changing people's behaviour is difficult enough, but changing underlying values takes even more time or may not be possible at all. Managers forget this at their peril. The cultural web helps to identify different aspects of an organisation's culture which will shape both values and behaviour. It helps managers to identify necessary actions in different dimensions so that improvement programmes can be tailored to cover all the areas where change is needed. Pay, rewards, career development, recruitment and training are all areas which are likely to be affected by a BPR project and require on-going consideration as the organisation shifts to managing by process.

Part Three

Perspectives from the "Operating" Disciplines

Principles of Managing by Processes – Summary

Colin Armistead and Philip Rowland

Having discussed aspects of processes and process management we try here to suggest a number of principles for managing by process. In doing this we are not so much taking a didactic approach but rather wanting to reflect a number of approaches which we have observed in organisations who have made the changes discussed in this part of the book. Hammer suggested principles for Business Process Re-engineering. The quality gurus, including Deming, Crosby, Juran and Feigenbaum, also have their own prescriptions for quality improvement programmes. We see our principles as going beyond all of these to address the new order of the process- and team-based organisation.

REDUCING UNCERTAINTY

So what might organisations do to reduce the unknown of managing by process? There is much more advice written on how to carry out improvement programmes than on how to manage by process. In the absence of any detailed researched approach to managing by process in Box 7.1 we present ten steps based on our observation of companies and reports in case studies of organisations in articles, at conferences and from our own research (Armistead, 1995).

Box 7.1   Principles of Managing by Processes

1. Designate a process champion
2. Know the process
3. Understand the linkages
4. Work on the trade-offs
5. Train within the process
6. Teach others about the process
7. Measure the process
8. Manage careers
9. Build specialist expertise
10. Improve the process

There is the need for clear leadership and commitment to any move in the direction of process management as well as for considerable training to enable individuals to understand their new roles and develop the skills needed. The use of a skills matrix is one means of ensuring that all the skills and expertise are available in the process. It must be clear where and with whom the skills and expertise lie or can be obtained. Perhaps more than anything else it is a question of managers recognising the trade-offs in their own organisations and working creatively to minimise their effects.

In this context the ten principles are:

1. *Designate a champion* who will manage and improve the process. There are strong messages from supply chain management that personal responsibility for an end-to-end customer-facing process leads to improvement in performance.
2. *Know the process* and monitor its evolution through high-level process mapping to understand the activities and flows. Place the customer relative to the process, and determine the service operations task for the process. Establish the performance of the process according to what is important for customer service and efficiency. Find out where value is created or costs are incurred unnecessarily. Finally, probe to untangle the intangible – those aspects of the process which are inseparable from the people involved.
3. *Understand the linkages* with other processes within your organisation and with your customers. Are you adding value to those processes which are concerned with your organisation, your customers or your suppliers?
4. *Work on the trade-offs* if the process is being created from a cross-functional background. Understanding functional versus process trade-offs will allow each organisation to make clearer decisions about what is the best balance for them.

5. *Train within the process.* Cross-functional customer-facing processes require new roles, tasks, skills and expertise, often organised around teams. A skills/expertise matrix may be displayed showing where they lie and with whom and how they are being developed. Rewards and recognition should be clear and set in accordance with the targets and goals in the service operations task for the process. The use of imposed controls or empowerment needs to be recognised in the training process.
6. *Teach others about the process* who may need to supply or receive outputs. Moving to management by process is a learning opportunity for organisations. Process owners and teams should be expected to have a responsibility for spreading their learning.
7. *Measure the process* for control, improvement, and benchmarking, using a range of financial and non-financial measures.
8. *Manage careers* in the new process-oriented, possibly flatter organisation. Align expectations and aspirations with a different kind of progression emphasising cross-skill training and the importance of gaining wider business experience both within the process and in other processes.
9. *Build specialist expertise* in the context of the new organisation taking account of any weakening in this role where the traditional functions in the organisation are made weaker. The process teams will probably need a mix of specialist skills as well as more general skills. In addition, these teams will need to draw on groups of staff with advanced skills.
10. *Improve the process* continuously. The world won't stand still and neither should you.

CONCLUSIONS

We can observe organisations such as Kodak, Motorola, Royal Mail, and Rank Xerox struggling with the consequences of managing by process and addressing issues around the principles. Managing by process is proving to be problematic but then what could we expect after so many decades of working in functionally based structures? It seems clear that the payoff for those who succeed will be large but that success is not guaranteed and experimentation will be required to fit general principles to the specific needs of each organisation.

Chapter 8

Operating Disciplines

Colin Armistead and Philip Rowland

This part deals with the disciplines which we call "operating" in contrast to "enabling" disciplines which we will cover in Part 4. The operating disciplines are:

- Strategy
- Marketing
- Operations
- Logistics

Here we aim to give an overview of how these disciplines have changed over the years, to postulate on their place in the new world order of process management and the issues which relate to them in any BPR initiatives. The following four chapters in this part cover each discipline in more detail and will give you an insight from the viewpoint of a discipline expert.

WORKING IN UNISON OR OPPOSITION?

A fundamental issue in re-engineering and managing by process is the paradigm shift. In moving from a traditional functionally based structure an organisation does not want to lose the inherent expertise from functions. But it also wants to integrate activities which were previously the sole property of a single function. Such changes require the relinquishing of power and authority in the functions to a new order in processes. We have already seen that this can itself be threatening for individuals who may engage in counterproductive behaviour.

While not wishing to oversimplify the way all organisations have worked in the past we can see reflected in the detailed chapters a number of features. The four discipline areas work almost in isolation being very inward-looking.

Strategy is concerned with planning, often carried out remotely from the rest of the functions, fed to the board and imposed throughout the functions where it is subverted or ignored. Marketing is more concerned with sales or with operating the techniques of marketing research or advertising depending on the nature of the organisation. Where marketing is more prominent the function views itself as determining strategy. The marketing paradigm is driven by the concept of the 4-Ps of product (or service), price charged and terms of the sale, promotion and communications programme, and place through the distribution channels. This model for marketing was essentially a transaction-based model; one company supplies something for a price and the customer essentially takes it or leaves it.

Operations in manufacturing is concerned with managing the plant. The view is one of excluding the customer and being driven by output volume, plant utilisation and labour productivity. Demands from marketing and sales are seen as disruptive, imposing unnecessary if not impossible demands on production. Everything is output driven, making the planned volume or more is everything. Quality often takes second place. Excess demand in many markets means that customers, while not happy with poor quality and delivery, still buy. Major errors in design are sorted out once a product has been launched. From manufacturing after-sales service is seen as a "necessary evil', although the revenue from spares is always appreciated. In service organisations things are little better. The producer mentality prevailed in commercial and public sector services. The attitude could be summarised as "you the customer are lucky to have our service – complain at your peril!"

Logistics does not exist. The term is probably not well appreciated and recognised by many managers except in a military context. Distribution is the focus, moving the product from a factory through a network of warehouses. Control of materials is often haphazard and shortages commonplace.

This bleak picture would suggest that firms are not successful. Obviously that is not the case while demand outstrips supply and the competition is limited by regulation. However, once the world starts to change and new competitors enter domestic markets in the West either from the USA in the case of service companies or from Japan for manufacturing companies, everything changes. Toyota, Sony and Canon from Japan and Amex, McDonald's and Federal Express from the USA have an impact which stretches beyond the boundaries of their industry sectors.

THE NEW WORLD ORDER

The effect of the changed environment can now be traced back to the 1970s, with a greater need for change occurring during the 1980s, and continuing into the 1990s. Many commercial organisations in the manufacturing and service sectors focused on quality improvement to change the culture of the organisation. The effect of this move was often to get manufacturing operations under control in so far that the consistency of quality of products in sectors such as electronics moved from defect rates measured in percentage terms to parts per million. The price of non-conformance was recognised as were team-based improvement programmes of the quality circle type. The Japanese concept of Kaizen, continuous improvement, was often adopted. In the UK great store was often placed on the installation of quality systems such as BS 5750, now part of the international standard ISO 9000.

Companies were often forced to look at reducing their cost base and improving customer service. In manufacturing companies this led to the adoption of practices which reduced the level of inventories through just-in-time techniques. At the same time, companies found that these practices also led to a reduction in cycle times which potentially enabled them to be more responsive. The adoption of just-in-time as a method of managing supplies between a producing and consuming company along a supply chain laid the basis for the development of supply chain management and logistics.

What has caused organisations to go further over last few years and look for radical changes, in some cases to believe in process-based management? We see a number of factors at work not all of which would obviously be recognised in all organisations which are developed in the chapters in this part of the book.

Strategy

- The adoption of the *resources-based concept of the firm* encouraged companies to identify core competencies and capabilities. Once this step was taken it quickly became apparent that the way in which the competence and capability was operationalised involved more than one function The idea of broad business processes gained favour. These were for developing products, procuring supplies, fulfilling orders and providing customer service and support. The consequences of this approach are explained in Chapter 9.
- If processes are to be re-engineered it becomes important to understand to what end. The strategy process is defined. No longer can it be left to a top-down approach. It becomes necessary to take a communal view of the direction. In some instances companies found that they were able to bring together and define what had until then been an emerging strategy. In Chapter 9 Susan Segal-Horn and Cliff Bowman discuss the new paradigm

for the strategy process, i.e. how strategy is formulated as much as what is in the strategy. For instance, Rank Xerox as part of their Xerox 2000 review asked experts and managers about the future and complied a list of 60 assumptions which, once refined by probability of happening, were used to help formulate the strategy.

Marketing

- Marketing started to change. The rather obvious concept of *customer retention* took hold. The premise was if customers are loyal and remain with one company the latter is in a position to reduce the costs of gaining customers and will also benefit from an audience to whom it can sell more products/services. Moreover, if it provided good service customers will act to promote that company to other potential customers: a virtuous circle. In the same vein the concept of relationship marketing gained favour. No longer is the relationship between supplier and customer viewed as being transaction based. Rather companies look to build partnerships. But what relationships are concerned? Quickly the concept expanded from existing and potential customers to include employees, suppliers and those who might influence a sale through recommendation or referral. In Chapter 10 Jim Lynch explains how the role of marketing changes to be more strategic and to prevent the organisation being inward-looking.
- Products and services are no longer easily separated. Most companies are offering an intricate mix of products and services which require a more intimate understanding of what customers value. Once defined the offering can be delivered only through an understanding of the requirements.

Operations Management and Logistics

- The Baldrige award for quality in the USA followed by the EFQM award placed processes firmly at the centre of the assessment model. This in itself would probably not have brought about change as the processes might have been interpreted in the context of the functional paradigm. What changed the paradigm was that organisations who were winners or high performers in the assessment were already starting to think about processes which ran across the old functions. They acted as a role model or benchmark companies for others and changed the mindsets of many senior managers. This group saw the potential for process orientation allowing them to reduce their cost base and improve customer service. We look at the lessons which have been learned within the quality movement in Chapter 11.
- Operations in those companies which have developed their capabilities to incorporate Japanese manufacturing practices are described in Chapter 11. These companies were in effect re-engineering the manufacturing processes

in the 1980s and building partnerships with suppliers. The barriers between purchasing and supply and manufacturing and distribution began to be dismantled. Chapter 11 also makes this point.

Logistics

- Logistics and supply chain management became both necessary and possible as ways of managing the production of goods from parts manufactured anywhere in the world, followed by the distribution of goods on a global scale. The growth of the Benetton Group is an excellent example. In Chapter 12 Jim Cooper explains the interlinking of the manufacturing activity and supply and distribution.
- Information systems have the potential for integrating activities which make possible configurations previously excluded to managers. Examples are seen in direct banking and insurance, telesales, customer service and support with remote monitoring of equipment, teleworking and the development of EDI systems for linking customers and suppliers.
- Mass customisation as a practical proposition only becomes possible with well-developed operations and logistics systems coupled with effective information systems. The idea of time-based competition (Stalk et al., 1990) captures the goal of being more responsive to customers with the potential of increasing the value of what the customer is buying, while not increasing the price significantly.

Our assertion is that all these influences have now come together and the basis for radical improvement comes from taking a process management approach to an organisation. For this to be effective requires an integration of the processes for strategy, marketing, operations and logistics.

QUESTIONS TO BEAR IN MIND WHEN READING THIS PART

1. To what extent is the role of the operating disciplines undergoing fundamental change as the result of process engineering?
2. What have been some of the main influences on driving organisations to look for radical improvement in performance?
3. How important is the participation of all operating functions in a process re-engineering initiative?

Chapter 9

Strategic Management and BPR

Susan Segal-Horn and Cliff Bowman

WHAT WILL YOU FIND IN THIS CHAPTER?

This chapter focuses on the relationships between BPR and business-level strategy. The following issues will be discussed:

1. BPR initiatives will always have a strategic dimension and it is important to understand the strategic relevance of BPR to the business.
2. BPR initiatives can have unintended strategic consequences which may be positive or negative.
3. Only if the organisation provides a learning context can BPR inform the strategy of the business.
4. A BPR "mindset" is a necessary but not a sufficient condition for effecting quantum (rather than incremental) change in the organisation.
5. BPR initiatives can alter their strategic significance over time.

We develop the arguments to support these assertions through a simple four-cell matrix. Then we employ a case history of the role of BPR initiatives in an international hotel chain to illustrate the main points of our argument. Finally, the chapter closes with some conclusions.

THE DEVELOPMENT OF STRATEGIC MANAGEMENT THINKING

Before applying the ideas and mindset of strategic management to BPR, it may be useful for some of the background and history of strategic management thinking to be reviewed. One of the most readable texts to attempt this in recent years is Whittington (1993). He discussed the historical development of the field which has become known as strategic management from its emergence in the 1960s. At that time it was more likely to be called "business policy" and had its roots in the ideas of Alfred Chandler, a business historian; Igor Ansoff, a management theorist; and Alfred Sloan, a businessman and renowned industrialist who was the founder of the giant American car firm General Motors.

Ansoff was a professor at the Carnegie Institute of Technology in the USA. His job title is instructive. He was professor of "Industrial Administration". His best-known and most influential book published in 1965 was called *Corporate Strategy* and subtitled *An analytic approach to business policy for growth and expansion*. This gives a clear feel for the approach to management he espoused and was one of the first coherent statements of this relatively new field of strategy. Together with Chandler (1962, 1977) and Sloan (1963), they established a perspective which Whittington (1993) calls the "classical" school of strategic thinking. The focus for them was strategy as deliberate and rational, directed towards profit maximisation, and very much the restricted domain of top management. It drew heavily on notions of military leadership and viewed corporations as hierarchies to be directed from the top. For a more modern example of this genre see Ohmae (1987) and Porter (1980, 1985). The definition Chandler gave of strategy was "the determination of the basic long-term goals and objectives of an enterprise, and the adoption of courses of action and the allocation of resources necessary for those goals" (1962, p. 13).

This represented a view of strategy as planning. The focus of Chandler's work then, not surprisingly, was the organisational structures that would enable these managerial hierarchies to work efficiently by allowing top managers to allocate resources as they saw fit to achieve their strategic objectives. Companies and organisations were seen as efficient and rational resource-allocating mechanisms. Strategy is seen as a rational process of analysis which is designed to achieve (in the phrase popularised by Porter, 1985) "competitive advantage" over the long term.

Since then, strategy has progressed through at least three further phases. To use Whittington's (1993) terminology, he calls these the Evolutionary, Processual and Systemic perspectives on strategy. The Evolutionary approach to strategy (Henderson, 1989) sees rational planning as frequently irrelevant, due to permanent environmental turbulence. Markets are seen as dynamic and businesses (and their strategies) must evolve or die. In this school of thought, it is markets, not managers, which force choices. Successful strategies emerge in response to turbulence and the role of managers is to fit their strategies as well as possible to the environmental turbulence.

The Processual approach to strategy, whose best-known exponent is Henry Mintzberg (1987), also perceives "long-range planning" (also the title of one of the best-known practitioner journals in the strategy field) as of less relevance than the process by which strategy emerges within the organisation. Thus from this perspective, strategy is emergent, rather than deliberate, and also, very importantly, is neither top-down nor rational. Strategy reflects not only the views of top management but also a set of pragmatic compromises between various stakeholders in the organisation (Pettigrew, 1985). The implication of this processual view of strategy is that those strategies which are imposed top-down, without incorporating other organisational constituencies, are unlikely, in practice, to be realised strategies.

Systems thinkers (Granovetter, 1985; Shrivastava, 1986) see strategy as the child of context: social context, geographic context, political context, cultural context, etc. It follows that strategy must always be contingent on that context rather than absolute. Therefore Asian or Middle Eastern strategic thinking may vary considerably from West or East European strategic thinking. Viable strategies will therefore be context-specific.

Finally, in this brief summary of the developing field of strategic management, it may be helpful to indicate the current perspective on strategy which has its closest links with BPR. That is the approach currently called the resource-based view of strategy (Prahalad and Hamel, 1990; Grant, 1991; Peteraf, 1993). In terms of our summary of types of approaches to strategy, the resource-based view fits the classical view and is a recent version of it. That is because it takes the view that organisations are bundles of resources which managers have to develop and build towards achieving their strategic objectives. These resources form the inputs into different clusters of competences available to the organisation, the outputs of which are different levels and types of performance. Therefore in the same industry firms may pursue different strategies and achieve different performance levels as a result of their differing resources and the differing competences which result from them. The relationship between this and BPR should be clear. It is the role of management to use approaches like BPR to create relevant processes internal to the organisation, so that appropriate clusters of competences may be developed.

As we have just argued, a useful distinction can be made in the strategy literature between the **content** of strategy and the **process** of strategy. The content of strategy refers to what the strategy is addressing, and a distinction is usually made between different levels of strategy (i.e. corporate level, business unit level, functional or operational level strategy). We would expect a corporate-level strategy to address issues like the logic or rationale for the corporation (i.e. why have we collected these different businesses together?).

Strategy content at the business level would set out the markets the business is attempting to compete in, and the way in which it seeks to gain and sustain advantage. At the operational level we would find functional or divisional strategies (e.g. finance strategy, marketing strategy) which, in an ideal world, would explain the role that function would play in delivering the business level strategy. Thus strategy content refers to what the strategy is addressing.

In contrast, strategy process refers to how the strategy came about. Did it result from a deliberate attempt to plan the future direction of the organisation? Or perhaps it just emerged from a series of *ad hoc* decisions made over time. The strategy could be the vision of one person, which may not be communicated in its entirety to other people in the organisation. Or there may be no explicit strategy, but the culture of the organisation may provide a strong and stable influence over the actions of the members of the organisation.

STRATEGY CONTENT AND PROCESS

In selecting a theme for this chapter we have concentrated on the role of BPR in the strategy *process*. Although there are clearly vital issues of strategy content that need to be addressed, many of these will be raised in other chapters of the book. In order to explore the process issues in the relationship between BPR and strategy we shall use the four-cell matrix in Figure 9.1.

The vertical dimension of Figure 9.1 refers to Strategic Intent. We are simplifying a great deal of complexity here by assuming that there are only two possible states that a business can be in: that there either is or is not a clear view of where the organisation is trying to go. The horizontal axis refers to the presence or absence of BPR initiatives within the business. These two dimensions generate four possible states that a business could be in, which we have labelled as follows:

- Cell 1: Drifting
- Cell 2: Disconnected
- Cell 3: Deckchairs
- Cell 4: Driven

We shall now explain the status of a business in each of these four cells. We loosely use a sailing analogy to capture the essence of each of the four states.

Cell 1: Drifting

Here there is no clear strategic view of where the business is heading, and at the operational level there are no BPR-like initiatives. The business is drifting, with no-one effectively shaping its evolution or direction. The clear danger here is that the firm may be drifting towards disaster. Aimless and rudderless,

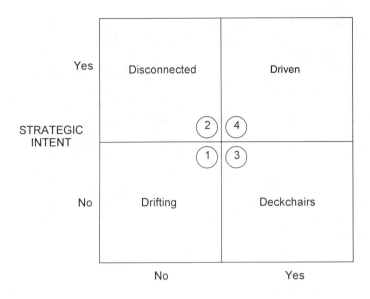

Figure 9.1 Strategic intent and BPR

drifting places the firm at the mercy of its environment, unable to negotiate hazards, or to steer towards calmer seas or favourable winds.

Cell 2: Disconnected

In Cell 2 there is a vision, or statement of intent for the business. This may be in the form of a five-year strategic plan for the business, or a mission statement. However, there are no actions at operational level that are supportive of the vision. To use our analogy, it is as if the captain on the bridge is sending messages to the engine room, but the messages are not getting through: the strategic intent is disconnected from the day-to-day actions at the operational levels of the business. This is a worryingly common state of affairs in many organisations, and has led some to be rather sceptical of formal planning systems.

Cell 3: Deckchairs

There is a popular if rather morbid analogy used in discussing strategy that refers to the Titanic disaster. The story goes that many efforts to change things in the organisation are akin to rearranging the deckchairs on the Titanic (see Hammer, 1990). So we are rather provocatively asserting here that where BPR initiatives are adopted that are not informed by a clear vision of where the organisation is headed, they run the risk of being as effective as deckchair rearrangement would have been in averting the sinking of the Titanic.

BPR can operate as a substitute for strategy. Where a management team is unclear about the direction the firm should take, the need to do something (to be seen to act) can make initiatives like BPR seem attractive. We could cite previous popular initiatives as playing similar roles as substitutes for having a genuine strategy: TQM, MBO, Quality Circles, Corporate Planning. Downsizing, delayering and outsourcing could also be regarded as fulfilling the requirement that BPR meets in this cell. The advantage to top management of initiatives like TQM and Quality Circles, as examples, is that they are unlikely to do any harm to the business, and they may be beneficial. However, the same could not be said of delayering and BPR, an issue which we will explore later in the chapter.

Cell 4: Driven

This is the cell the business should strive to be in: here there is a clear vision for the organisation, which is being implemented by supportive BPR initiatives. The business is being driven at both the strategic and the operational levels. Obviously this assumes that the content of the strategic vision is appropriate, which may or may not be the case. But determining what is appropriate strategy content is outside the scope of this contribution (some suggestions for exploring this issue can be found at the end of the chapter).

Using this four cell matrix, we shall develop our arguments to support the assertions we made at the start of the chapter.

1. BPR initiatives will always have a strategic dimension and it is important to understand the strategic relevance of BPR to the business. Where the firm is firmly into Cell 4 (it is "Driven" at both the strategic and operational levels) then BPR has a clear strategic dimension: it is a primary means of implementing the strategic changes required to realise the vision. However, BPR initiatives may be uninformed by a strategic intent (hence the firm would be classified into Cell 3, "Deckchairs"), but they may nevertheless have strategic ramifications. If BPR is employed as an "action" substitute for real strategic behaviour, there is a danger that unintended negative consequences may unfold. We take this issue further under point 2 below. Our point here is that BPR will always have strategic ramifications, that these may be positive or negative, and it is crucial that whatever is undertaken by way of BPR, is addressed from a strategic perspective.

2. BPR initiatives can have unintended strategic consequences which may be positive or negative. Depending on the scope of the BPR initiative, there will be predictable strategic ramifications flowing from it. Clearly, a minor process-orientated restructuring of a small part of the organisation is not likely to have

the same strategic impact as an initiative which spans the whole organisation. We would expect positive strategic outcomes where BPR enables the firm to deliver higher levels of perceived use value to customers, at lower costs. These changes are most likely to be incremental improvements to the organisation's ways of doing things, and may well not alter the existing product market scope of the business. These strategic consequences are likely to be those that would be anticipated by the top management team that sanctioned or promoted the BPR initiative. Unintended positive outcomes may result in the form of a challenging and questioning of issues outside the planned scope of the initiative. We pursue this further in points 4 and 5 below. But major problems can emerge with Cell 3 (Deckchair) BPR actions that may not surface until months or years later. In order to explore this argument, we need to refer to a growing stream of literature in the strategy field, usually referred to as Resource Based Theory (Grant, 1991; Peteraf, 1993). This approach highlights the role that inimitable, valuable resources play in sustaining competitive advantage. A key feature of the resource-based perspective is the argument that know-how (which confers advantage) may be so embedded in the culture of the firm that no one individual is able to identify or explain quite how the firm manages to perform so effectively. This know-how has been referred to as tacit or implicit knowledge which also has the quality of being "causally ambiguous" (which means that it is difficult for outsiders to understand the way things are done in the firm).

The potential problem with "crude" BPR is that it might not recognise the role that tacit, embedded knowledge plays in delivering value to customers. And an uninformed attempt to redesign or reengineer processes may destroy this source of advantage. Therefore, we would argue that there is every likelihood that as any BPR initiative may have important strategic consequences, all such initiatives should be approached from a strategic perspective.

3. Only if the organisation provides a learning context can BPR inform the strategy of the business. The beneficial outcome of BPR leading to a shift in the way the business is managed strategically (i.e. Cell 3 to Cell 4) can only occur in an organisation that fosters learning. Otherwise the business remains firmly in Cell 3, and runs the risk, among other things, of unintended outcomes destroying the firm's sources of advantage. But this is true of other potentially valuable operational initiatives (for example, quality circles) which, in order to deliver their full potential, require top management to empower lower levels of the organisation. By empowerment we mean attitudes at the top which encourage lower-level employees to exercise initiatives; allow them to experiment (and provide the space and resources for this to happen); encourage them to challenge the status quo; permit (and expect) them to fail sometimes, but to see that as a learning opportunity.

In this type of culture BPR can lead to the refinement and development of strategy. Here the broad ground rules (or strategic intent) would be agreed by the top team, allowing scope to the rest of the organisation to flesh out the emerging shape of the organisation. The ground rules would focus on, for example, the core competences of the business (and how they should be developed and augmented), broad definitions of product market scope and measurable high-level performance targets. Within these broad guidelines the detail of strategy can emerge, drawing upon the continual learning and challenging that a BPR approach can foster.

4. A BPR "mindset" is a necessary but not a sufficient condition for effecting quantum (rather than incremental) change in the organisation. By BPR "mindset" we mean the type of thinking that is consistent with a BPR philosophy. We understand this to include a challenging of existing ways of organising the business (in particular, a challenge to functional specialisation); a focus on outputs rather than inputs; and an orientation towards the delivery of customer value, not products. For many firms this thinking would be a preliminary condition for a major strategic transformation, as it probably challenges the prevailing mindset (or paradigm), which may well exhibit contrary beliefs and assumptions (i.e. the need for functional structures; emphasis on delivering products; measurement and control of inputs via costing and budgeting systems).

But the BPR mindset, though a necessary precursor to transformational change in the business, is not a sufficient condition for it to occur. Such thinking needs to be combined with three other elements before change is likely to occur. These are a feeling of dissatisfaction with the existing state of the organisation, shared by enough influential members of the top management team to motivate them to seek to radically change things; a vision of where the organisation should be headed (i.e. a strategy); and a set of understandable first steps that will move the organisation in the desired direction. So a BPR mindset can be helpful in implanting a new way of thinking inside the firm that eventually leads the firm from Cell 3 to Cell 4 in our matrix. This leads us into our last point.

5. BPR initiatives can alter their strategic significance over time. It is important to recognise that any change initiatives will have different strategic significance depending upon the context of the organisation. For example, in a public sector organisation used to years of working in a stable, regulated environment a change initiative of quite limited organisational scope (e.g. restricted to one department) could have substantial impact on the culture of the whole organisation. In contrast, an organisation that has a history of continual change and adaptation can more easily absorb additional changes.

Hence the same BPR initiative will clearly have different strategic ramifications depending on the particular organisational context. We can take this argument further by suggesting that the context of an organisation will change over time, as its environment, strategies and structures evolve. Therefore we need to recognise that a set of BPR-inspired change initiatives may change their strategic role over time. In order to explore the significance of this temporal dimension we shall use the case of Novotel hotels.

INTEGRATING STRATEGY AND BPR: A CASE STUDY OF A MULTINATIONAL HOTEL CHAIN

The case history which follows of the French hotel chain Novotel, and the events and the actions it describes, will be used to illustrate the strategic management mindset within which successful implementation of BPR is most likely to occur. The first Novotel hotel was opened by two entrepreneurs near Lille airport in France in 1967. The first Novotel outside France was opened in 1973. By 1995 the chain had grown to 280 hotels in 46 countries around the world. The hotels provide 43 000 rooms and employ 33 000 people. Novotel is just one of the hotel chains belonging to the Accor Group of France, which operates more than 2000 hotels worldwide offering more than 2 million rooms at different ratings and service levels. Other chains in the Group include Sofitel, Mercure, Ibis and Formule 1. These range from 4-star (Sofitel) to 1-star (Formule 1).

The Novotel Concept

The fundamental characteristic of the Novotel hotel concept is of international standardisation of the offering. What is therefore required is consistency of the offering in every location in which it is available. This is one of the elements of globalisation of a service that is especially problematic. Standardisation of the offering means putting in place a service delivery system that is robust enough to survive transferability across borders and generate consistent service standards to satisfy customer expectations, irrespective of local conditions or infrastructure. Some of the elements of standardisation were more easily realisable. The design, style and layouts of the hotels were reproduced to precise specifications. For example bedroom size is standard throughout Europe at 24 metre square.

The Novotel chain is positioned as a 3-star chain worldwide which means that certain facilities such as quality of bedroom furniture, fixtures and fittings or outside amenities such as swimming pools and amounts of free car parking space are always available at all Novotel units. Figure 2 captures some of the key elements in the Novotel business chain. However, the more interesting elements of the Novotel offering for the purpose of this discussion are the management processes which enable the standardised service levels to be delivered at all locations worldwide and the changes (re-engineering) of these processes which were carried out as the business strategy was developed and modified.

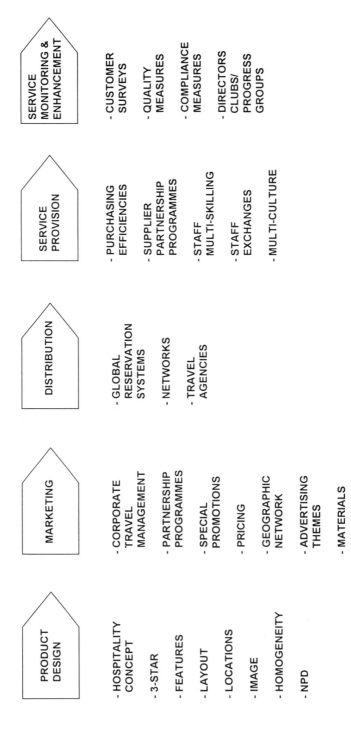

Figure 9.2 Novotel's strategy and process elements. (Source: Segal-Horn, 1995)

Processes for Direction and Control

Since hotel design and guest bedrooms are standardised, basic housekeeping and maintenance functions can in turn be standardised. This means that training of staff in all basic functions may be simplified and the procedures for training can be themselves standardised. Indeed, one of the features of the Accor Group is the "Academie Accor" set up in 1985, as the centre for all staff training within the Group. Its "campus" is located on the site of Group corporate headquarters just outside Paris. From there, all training is designed and delivered. This standardised approach to the core service concept places special requirements on the staff as the key medium for delivery of consistent service standards wherever the customer is staying. Standardised procedures and centrally designed training programmes are one of the core mechanisms for securing such consistency.

Taking the concept of consistency one step further, the Novotel senior management developed a new approach to staffing in the hotel sector which is described as "multi-skilling'. The idea behind multi-skilling is to develop staff as a team able to perform all tasks and work as needed in a flexible manner. Obviously, this would have many advantages for hotel management, not least in smoothing the need for certain types of staff at peak bottleneck periods of the day or evening. Pressures on checking-in or checking-out at reception cluster at early morning and evening or getting rooms cleaned while guests are at breakfast, and these are common bottlenecks dramatically affecting patterns of staffing. With the Novotel approach to flexible skilling and team working, a new pattern emerged. Flexible working patterns broke down the staff demarcation normal within the rest of the hotel industry. Reception and front-of-house activities (e.g. showing guests to rooms) were carried out by the same staff who served in the restaurant at peak mealtimes or performed housekeeping or room-cleaning tasks at other times of the day. The benefits of this to the firm were enormous leading to a reduction of core staff levels and a more resource-ful workforce. However, maintaining universal quality standards as the chain grew rapidly over a 25-five year period became more and more problematic, especially when many new staff were recruited from other hotel groups with different working practices.

A system to monitor standard procedures was introduced in 1987 which became known as the "95 Bolts'. These 95 points or regulated systems applied to the thirteen main points of staff/customer interaction. These "moments of truth" included reservation, arrival/access, parking, check-in, hall, bedroom, bathroom/WC, evening meal, breakfast, shops, bar, outdoor games/swimming-pool and check-out. Each of these key interaction points were divided into a series of compulsory directives for staff, e.g. how to set out a bedroom, lay a place setting in the restaurant or welcome a guest. A booklet containing the 95 Bolts was issued to all staff and was a mainstay in induction for new staff.

Monitoring of standards was carried out by an internal team of inspectors who visited each hotel approximately twice each year. They functioned in the same way as "mystery shoppers" in that they made reservations, arrived, stayed and departed incognito. On completion of their stay they would make themselves known to the General Manager (GM) for review and discussion. Percentage grades were awarded and recommendations made. This system, while helpful to control and consolidate after a period of rapid growth, gradually became over-rigid and procedural in orientation and was replaced by a more adaptive system in 1992.

Processes for Sharing the Learning

At a meeting in 1992 for Novotel managers, using the "Open Space" format (i.e. where participants may propose topics for discussion, move from group to group according to preference, or indeed, leave), the relationship of the hotel GM and his staff team was redefined from hierarchical to enabling. A new corporate slogan "Back to the Future" ("Retour vers le Futur") was adopted to reflect the outlawing of the bureaucratic style of standardisation and a return to Novotel's entrepreneurial roots. In addition, mixed-level (i.e. beyond just the top team) working parties were established in three key issue areas: communication (marketing and image), management and commercial. Inter-functional groups were set up across hotels and countries and GM groups of clusters and interest types across countries were established to share ideas, innovations or best practice. These GM interest groups were constructed around common hotel types within the Novotel chain e.g. all GMs of motorway, airport or city-centre locations, etc. The 95 Bolts were abolished for being too rigid and were replaced by three simplified general measures of performance – clients, management and people. One and a half layers of management were eliminated leaving only one direct reporting layer between GMs and the two co-Presidents of Novotel. The role of the GM was rethought and redefined as capturing the spirit of "Maitre de Maison", much closer to the social role of a ship's captain. This led to a need for reassessment and redevelopment of all GMs, all of whom were required to go through an assessment activity incorporating role-play in such situations as conflict resolution with subordinates or guests.

While great effort was made to position these assessments and changes as constructive inputs for identifying positive training needs rather than negative grounds for dismissal, this emphasis on new styles of working for both management and all staff created much anxiety and uncertainty which the top team had to transform into a positive atmosphere of empowerment and opportunity. As an illustration of the imaginative ways in which this extremely delicate problem was tackled, one example is the two Benedictine priests who were guests at one of Novotel's large management conventions in 1993. The Benedictine fathers were invited to speak to the gathering about the principles of Benedictine hospitality and welcome which have graced their order since its founding centuries ago. Benedictine principles, duties and procedures were described and explained. It is also worth noting the continuous active involvement in the redevelopment process of the two original founders of Novotel (now co-Presidents of the Accor Group), as well as the visible public involvement of the co-Presidents of Novotel.

Implications

In summarising the outcomes of the process changes described above, both the structure and operations of Novotel's corporate headquarters, as well as operations and routines in every hotel in the chain, were transformed, although in differing degrees and over different time scales. The transformations reflect the new roles and tasks of management to give priorities to innovation and service which represent defensible sources of advantage for Novotel. Some of the obvious points to mention include:

- Delayering led to reduction in headcount of management staff and staff per hotel. Labour costs in the hotel business are significant. However, the benefit was measurable in value-added to both staff and customers as well as in management of costs.
- Information flows throughout the company have changed. Flattening the hierarchy has enabled more relevant information to be conveyed faster to relevant people.
- The role of Headquarters has changed. It now acts as an information coordinator, collator and channel, rather than the instigator of time-consuming demands for central performance statistics. This releases GMs' time for performance driving. For example, the centre filters useful information to all hotels which they store as the "Pilot Case" file for shared reference.
- Collaboration across and between levels has increased. GMs organise self-help clusters; training sessions are shared across the group; "reflective clubs" (Clubs de Reflection) have been created in some hotels as mixed informal groupings of staff, meeting to discuss innovations. Significantly, they contain staff from across all service areas in the hotels and discussion covers the hotels as a whole, not the specific responsibility of any individual staff (club) member.
- The role of the GM has changed to that of coach, optimising the service and amenities available to guests by developing the competences of his or her team.
- Ways of working for all staff have changed. In addition to more respon-sibility, the horizons of staff have been broadened, giving greater awareness of the business as a whole, encouraging cross-functional links and increased autonomy which adds value for staff and guests alike.

APPLYING THE MATRIX TO NOVOTEL'S EXPERIENCE

Having briefly told Novotel's history, and summarised some of the changes it has made during that history, we can relate it back to the four cells in Figure 9.1. This will allow us to map Novotel's progression through each of the phases of the cells during its own historical development. Each cell of course represents a better or worse "fit" between BPR and strategy. In our view, the line of ascent is from Cell 1 "Drifting" as the poorest strategic position, rising to Cell 4 as the strongest strategic position. Cell 4 is in this sense superior to Cell 3 in that the "Deckchairs" strategy, a popular one, represents piecemeal tinkering at the operational level, which may work for a time, or be wholly inadequate to the competitive situation in which a company finds itself. A context in which BPR both contributes to, and is the primary tool to implement outcomes of, the strategy for the business is where the high ground lies (Figure 9.3).

Cell 2/Phase 1: 1967–77

In our view, the place to begin mapping the history of Novotel's strategic and process initiatives is with Cell 2, since the company began with a strong

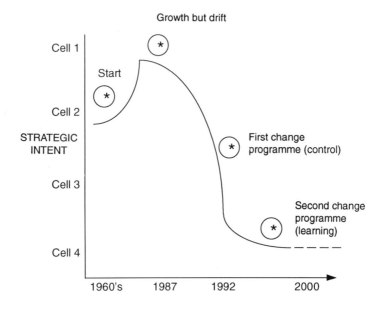

Figure 9.3   Novotel's strategy and process shifts

strategic vision and a clear business idea. In fact, the concept with which it was begun by the two entrepreneurs who founded it is one of the most innovative things about this company. They started with the strategic intent of building a 3-star chain. After a business start-up phase in Paris in 1967, and a rapid growth phase in France, Novotel International was incorporated in 1970. Expansion, both in France and internationally, was fuelled mainly by organic growth, i.e. building their own hotels but also with some acquisition of other hotels.

Cell 1/Phase 2: 1977–87

The company had become big very quickly. It retains clarity in its strategy of building an international 3-star chain, but its ability to implement has lost focus due to the spread of the business. In management control terms it is drifting. In spite of the setting up of the "Academie Accor" on the headquarters site just outside Paris to provide a centralised training facility for all staff worldwide, there was a sense that standards were slipping. In a replaying of a classic corporate growth scenario, the systems that were adequate for the early stages of managing the company were proving inadequate as it changed shape and enlarged its geographic and cultural scope. The piecemeal ways the central management had attempted to address these issues were themselves inadequate. A more thorough review was needed.

Cell 3/Phase 3: 1987–92

In a dramatic attempt to reassert control of the delivery of the strategy the "95 Bolts" programme was developed and implemented. It was based on top-down direction and control management systems. Every managerial and front-line staff activity was defined, structured and monitored. The dominant objective was to ensure that the standardisation required of all Novotel hotels was achieved. However, this was done in such a way that the innovation and entrepreneurial style and vision which had distinguished the business earlier was extinguished and replaced by procedures designed to ensure watertight reproduction of the concept without deviation at all locations. It was belatedly realised that the systems had lost touch with the strategy.

Cell 4/Phase 4: 1992 – current

In response to the over-rigidities of the "95 Bolts', and following the appoint-ment of the two new Co-Chairmen in 1992, the current phase was begun. The aim in 1992 was to get the strategy and the processes back in alignment and meet the needs of all customers internationally at the 3-star level. In order to get both the staff and the customer centre-stage again, the "Back to the Future" change programme began. The new processes were for the company to reinvent itself and recapture its entrepreneurial roots. But perhaps the most important element in Cell 4 is the refocusing on *outcomes* not on tasks, which is what had been so damaging about the "95 Bolts" initiative described in Cell 3. The new processes were once again clearly recognised as the inputs to enabling the managers and staff to achieve the outcomes of the strategic intent.

The Future?

It will be interesting to follow the impact of Novotel's internal processes into the future to see whether the learning context that they have aimed at creating is indeed able to deliver the intended strategy: a self-monitoring organisation, responsive to product, market and customer needs.

REVISITING THE FIVE KEY ISSUES

This chapter has argued that to be effective, BPR must be strategic. That means there must be ownership at the top of the organisation and a strategic direction in mind for the firm to which the re-engineering clearly contributes. If these conditions are not met, BPR risks building in just the types of rigidities it is supposed to alleviate. To reinforce this argument, the five key issues set out at the beginning of the chapter will be revisited. Their focus is the creation of a constructive rather than a destructive relationship between strategic management and BPR. In that light, the events described in the case study will be matched to the key issues as a means of testing out their relevance in practice.

1. Emphasis was placed on the importance of the interface between strategy and BPR at the business unit level by understanding the strategic relevance of BPR to the business. In the case of Novotel the company had a clear strategy, and at the time of its inception in the 1970s, a unique strategy in the 3-star hotel segment internationally. Its development and redevelopment of its managerial and operational procedures was driven by a precise outcome, what they needed to get right to implement the strategy effectively.

2. It was asserted that BPR initiatives could have unintended consequences over and above any intended consequences. Although such unintended consequences may, of course, be positive or negative, it is the negative outcomes that may destroy potential benefits of the re-engineering. A classic example of this appeared at Novotel when the 1984 change programme, aimed at tightening international standardisation, had the unintended (but perhaps predictable) consequence of excessive control, over-rigidity and stifling inflexibility. This in turn was threatening the company's strategic

positioning rather than enhancing it. It led in due course to a round of process change, yielding more appropriate outcomes.

3. BPR initiatives which are effective in the short term may be counterproductive in the longer term. Figure 9.3 illustrates precisely this shift in significance over time. Paradoxically, growing the business, which has such a positive feel to it, may actually embody strategic drift, as in Novotel in the 1970s. Also total process change, as in Novotel in the 1980s, may become inappropriate over time. This suggests that to be effective, BPR must be continuous.

4. Following on from the previous point raises issues of a BPR "mindset". Certainly the change in Novotel's approach between the first change programme and the second change programme was a shift in mindset from inputs (controls) to outputs (enhanced learning/customer satisfaction). However, that BPR mindset was a necessary but not a sufficient condition for effective change in the company. The factor driving the move from phase one of international standardisation worldwide, as control and routinisation, to phase two of flexible team processes within a learning context was the clarity of the strategy. The international 3-star concept was what gave drive and strategic intent to the business. It was also what drove the company to reinvent itself again and from first principles, because the strategy was not being realised. It was the existence of a clear strategy which made it possible to evaluate the BPR needs.

5. Our final key issue concerns the necessity of a learning context in order that BPR fulfils its potential to successfully contribute to a living, evolving, strategy. In many ways, the processes that Novotel evolved for continuous improvement, continuous monitoring, continuous motivation and continuous enrichment by best practice are the most positive illustration of the need for BPR to feed continuously back into strategy to fulfil its own potential.

CONCLUSIONS

In this chapter we have explored some of the strategic process issues that arise when an organisation embarks on BPR initiatives. The arguments advanced here constitute a call for BPR to both implement and inform the strategic direction of the firm. There can be only a very poor second place for a BPR which addresses operational processes in isolation from strategic intent. If BPR practitioners can harness the relationship between BPR and strategic intent, the two forces can indeed create what Quinn (1992) has called the "intelligent" enterprise.

Chapter 10

Business Process Re-engineering: A Marketing Perspective

James E. Lynch

WHAT WILL YOU FIND IN THIS CHAPTER?

Marketing has not been involved in the BPR movement to the extent to which we might have expected. This chapter reflects on some of the reasons why this has happened and why some organisations are reappraising the role of marketing. In the chapter you will find:

- A discussion of the dual role of marketing as both a strategic activity for an organisation and as the custodian of functional activities like marketing research and the role ambiguity this can cause
- The potential for marketing in changing markets to prevent BPR projects becoming inwardly focused
- Examples of the different approaches taken by organisations to retailer/manufacturer relationships. In the best cases benefits to both parties result from structural changes to marketing and buying functions

INTRODUCTION

This chapter reviews the BPR phenomenon from a marketing perspective and considers both the opportunities and the challenges which BPR poses for marketing practitioners and academics. At the superficial level the potential threat which BPR poses to conventional marketing functions in organisations is apparent. The essentially holistic approach to organisational design which characterises BPR clearly challenges the value and continuing relevance of traditional departmental or functionally based structures. This obvious threat means that it is easy to overlook the major benefits which BPR offers to the marketing discipline. More specifically, BPR offers the organisation in general and marketing in particular the opportunity to reassess customer relationships and interfaces in a fundamental manner which offers major developmental opportunities. This very positive potential contribution from BPR has tended to be overshadowed because BPR has risen to prominence at a time when marketing has been encountering considerable internal and external criticism for a perceived failure to respond adequately to a much-changed environmental context.

MARKETING AND ITS CRITICS

These are difficult times for the marketing profession. Increasing critical comment from both practitioners and academic sources, coupled with widespread evidence of organisational reassessment of marketing's contribution, suggest that both the concept and the profession are at a developmental watershed. These developments, which have been labelled "marketing's mid-life crisis" (Brady and Davis, 1993) are summarised below:

1. *Duality and ambiguity in marketing* Marketing theorists have always highlighted the essentially dual role that marketing occupies (or should occupy) in the organisation (Lynch, 1994a). First and foremost, at the strategic level, marketing is conceived as an external orientation or philosophy which should permeate the decision processes and operations of the whole organisation. Additionally, but at a secondary level, marketing is also conceptualised as a series of specific functional activities (such as advertising, market research and new product development) which are traditionally the province of a specialist marketing department. The potential tensions and ambiguities inherent in this duality are self-evident and have often been cited as a major cause of organisational underperformance (Ames, 1970; King, 1985). In particular, it is argued, too much emphasis on marketing's functional dimension dilutes or impedes its core philosophic purpose. Conversely, proper appreciation of marketing's dual role has been suggested as a key factor in organisational success (Hooley and Lynch, 1985).

   It could be argued that the potential role ambiguity inherent in marketing's dual nature did not prove to be an issue of the highest significance in the lengthy period after the Second World War, when most environmental conditions favoured growth and the development of mass markets. This was an era of rising economic prosperity, population growth and increasingly easy access to the marketplace via rapidly evolving mass media and generally weak distributors (Lynch, 1991). The last 20 years, however, have seen major changes in most of these environmental conditions and it is these changes, which are discussed below, that have led many commentators to question the continuing relevance of marketing as conventionally practised.

2. *Marketing and the new environmental paradigm* The contributing environmental factors which were associated with marketing's post-Second World War growth phase have all undergone significant change. Several key dimensions of change are shown in Figure 10.1. The customer base and media channels have tended to fragment in a highly competitive and saturated marketplace in which retailers and distributors are increasingly powerful. The new environment can be characterised as chaotic, fragmented and unpredictable (Gleick, 1988; Brown, 1993). In this new, complex and turbulent environment, the new organisational imperative is to deliver sharp improvements in corporate flexibility, sensitivity and responsiveness (Lynch, 1994b). Increasingly, organisations must have the capability to anticipate changing market needs and to respond to them rapidly via increased innovation and a continuing commitment to change.

The current wave of critical comment directed at marketing essentially suggests that marketing has traditionally demonstrated a tendency to functional self-absorption which renders it increasingly irrelevant or peripheral to the new environment. In particular, it is suggested that this excessively narrow functional focus generates an aversion to risk and a general lack of responsiveness and market agility (Mitchell, 1993; Brady and Davis, 1993; Clark and Fujimoto, 1990; Webster, 1992). The validity or significance of this questioning of marketing's organisational role is supported by marketplace evidence that many organisations with a traditionally strong commitment to marketing have begun to reshape or even dismantle their existing marketing structures (Murray, 1994; Mitchell, 1994; Heller, 1994; De Jonquières, 1993).

The current increase in critical questioning and self-doubt relating to marketing's organisational role has coincided with the emergence of a radical new managerial approach – Business Process Re-engineering. BPR is expressly designed to deliver the new environmental imperatives of corporate flexibility, sensitivity and responsiveness. BPR and its fundamentally antifunctionalist perspective have significant implications for the current marketing debate.

Old environment	New environment
Continuity	Discontinuity
High growth	Low/no growth
Mass markets	Fragmenting markets
Loyal customers	Volatile customers
Mass media	Fragmenting media
Weak retailers	Strong retailers
Innovation important	Innovation vital
Technology important	Technology critical

Figure 10.1 Environmental paradigm shift

BUSINESS PROCESS RE-ENGINEERING

The central theme of BPR is that a new environmental paradigm demands that organisations adopt radical or even revolutionary new perspectives on the operation (Hammer, 1990). In particular, advocates of BPR emphasise the centrality of defining and responding to the core processes which underpin customer satisfaction and competitiveness (Hammer and Champy, 1993; Johansson et al., 1993). Focus on core processes, it is argued, will allow the organisation to slough off the bureaucratic systems and structures which are inevitably generated by specialist functional departments, which tend to build empires and pursue their own often narrowly sectional interests. As a result of emerging from these "functional silos" the organisation, it is suggested, will be able to take a holistic, flexible and innovation-orientated view of those core activities and processes which are at the heart of the creation and profitable retention of customers. The attack on specialist functions (such as the specialist marketing department) is central to BPR thinking, which is driven by a cross-functional, multidisciplinary perspective. BPR stresses the need for fluid, cross-functional teams which constantly evolve and reshape to handle environmental uncertainty and increasing competitive challenge.

The central thrust of BPR, therefore, has significant implications for the role and structuring of marketing in the organisation. What has not yet been fully debated, however, is the extent to which BPR represents a threat or an opportunity for marketing. Self-evidently, BPR challenges the notion of the marketing function as conventionally conceived. But, as has been argued earlier, the purely functional dimension of marketing is a secondary element in genuine marketing orientation. Indeed, as many observers have suggested, it is the tendency of organisations to overemphasise marketing's functional aspect at the expense of its core philosophic perspective which has proved a major barrier to effective marketing implementation. McDonald (1994), for example, has argued powerfully that the root cause of the failure of British business is to be found in its view of marketing as a practical, tactical function rather than as a core philosophy.

If we adopt the perspective that says that marketing is first and foremost a philosophy of doing business which puts customer satisfaction at the core of the decision-making process, then the impact of BPR on marketing can be perceived in a very positive light. If the "core philosophy" view of marketing is adopted, then its essential compatibility with the aims and objectives of BPR becomes apparent. Table 10.1 compares key statements on BPR from one of its leading exponents with the perceptive and classic description of marketing's true meaning by Peter Drucker. Although the statements are 20 years apart in time, it is clear that they reflect an essentially similar sense of organisational priorities. What BPR does in a very powerful and effective way is to make marketing face up to its duality as both philosophy and function and to force a

Table 10.1

- "A capability is a set of business processes strategically understood ... business processes that deliver value to the customer."
- "Competitive success depends on transforming a company's key processes into strategic capabilities that consistently provide superior value to the customer" (Stalk, Evans and Schulman 1992)

- "There is only one valid definition of business purpose: to create a customer."
- "Marketing is so basic that it cannot be considered a separate function ... It is the whole business seen from the point of view of its final customer" (Drucker 1974)

---

decision as to where primacy should lie. There should, of course, be no contest. Marketing is first and foremost a holistic, organisation-wide perspective. The aims of BPR and marketing are not antithetical but complementary and this is why BPR presents marketing with a major opportunity. BPR offers a vehicle whereby the crucial philosophic dimension of marketing can assert its rightful organisational dominance. It is instructive to recall that the key drivers behind the emergence of the BPR idea are market-related – the need to deliver more significant customer benefits through heightened market responsiveness and more rapid and relevant product innovation. BPR, if effectively implemented, works with the grain of the marketing idea not against it.

Traditionally, marketers sought to achieve organisation-wide acceptance of and commitment to the marketing idea by exhortation and education. This sub-optimal solution to the dilemma proved broadly viable in a generally forgiving and helpful external environment. Now that organisations face a new and harsher environmental paradigm, this exhortatory approach is no longer adequate (if it ever was). BPR offers marketing the chance to become genuinely institutionalised in the organisation's core processes. This suggestion can be illustrated at the anecdotal level by the phenomenal success of "new start" operations such as Direct Line and First Direct. In these organisations, customer satisfaction, retention and profitability have come about because they have had the courage to revolutionise traditional operating methods and systems and, in effect, to re-engineer conventional industry practices and processes from a customer perspective. The outcome of this radical approach is the development of formidably market orientated and competitive organisations which have found completely fresh ways of operationalising the marketing concept.

THE SIGNIFICANCE OF NEW TECHNOLOGY AND REVISED ORGANISATIONAL DESIGN

Although it is apparent that marketing and BPR have broad conceptual congru-ence, the effective implementation of BPR-driven marketing improvement depends upon the resolution of important strategic and structural questions within the organisation. The adoption of a BPR approach raises fundamental questions concerning the future shape of marketing's contribution to organisational success. At the strategic level, perhaps the most significant issue raised by BPR concerns the potential opportunities which it creates to strengthen an organisation's long-run relationships with its customers. As Hunt (1994) has noted, the decade of the 1980s saw a sharp shift in organisational priorities towards the need for deeper and more long-lasting relationships with the customer base. BPR, with its core commitment to new and imaginative uses of information technology to reshape key processes, holds out the potential to far-sighted organisations to redefine their relationship marketing policies and systems in radical and innovative ways. Examples of this can be seen in the exciting developments which are now taking place in EDI (Electronic Data Interchange) and database marketing (Houlder, 1995; *Economist*, 1995). Progressive organisations have recognised that information technology, if coupled with the incisive strategic redefinition of process which BPR offers, can open up a wide range of new relationship possibilities. BPR-driven information technology not only creates new ways of relating to existing customers but also helps shape the organisational context in which new forms of relationship can evolve and develop.

It is already apparent, however, that the improved relationship marketing potential inherent in the BPR idea can only be realised if there is appropriate structural change within the organisation. Unless the marketing specialists understand and appreciate the significance and potential of the new technology and are able to work with it, new relationship opportunities are unlikely to be realised. For this reason it seems probable that conventional marketing departments staffed by traditional marketing specialists are unlikely to be the most appropriate future organisational expression of the marketing idea. Many observers have already noted a move towards a more interdisciplinary and cross-functional organisational model (George, Freeling and Court, 1995; De Jonquières, 1993; Mitchell, 1993).

While the move towards cross-functional teams seems strategically sound in the current environmental context, it does, however, raise the question of the precise relevance and role of the functional specialist in an increasingly holistic organisation. While the cross-functional imperative is an obvious outcome of a BPR perspective, it is equally obvious that there is a danger of the loss of valuable specialist expertise in the rush towards team working. Some aspects of the marketing tasks (e.g. market research; advertising development) clearly require a level of specialist expertise which cannot be delegated to a cross-functional team. This process of redefining the appropriate role for the functional specialist in the cross-functional team is currently only in its infancy. One imaginative solution which has been reported involves the retention of specialist pockets of marketing expertise in small centres of functional excellence even though overall strategy is customer process-driven from a team perspective (Mazur, 1995). This whole topic is one where further discussion, experimentation and research are urgently required since the most appropriate solution may vary for different industrial and structural contexts.

BPR MYOPIA

Despite the complex organisational and structural issues which are raised by a BPR-driven approach to marketing, it seems clear that BPR can deliver a wide range of positive benefits to the promulgation of the marketing idea. Conversely, however, it is important to note that the marketing perspective itself must form a vital input to the BPR thinking process. Without a strong marketing vision, BPR risks becoming myopic and overly inward-looking. It is instructive to note that when BPR has failed to achieve its objectives or encountered major criticisms (an increasingly observable trend), it is because it has been implemented in a narrow or incremental fashion which understates market imperatives (*Economist*, 1994; Lorenz, 1994; Lynch, 1994b). There are real dangers as well as real opportunities in any increased emphasis on process and process redesign. Too narrow a process focus can generate an inwardness, an internal orientation which turns the organisation in upon itself – the reverse of the marketing idea. Overall, therefore, it is possible to hypothesise that marketing and BPR are mutually supportive and mutually necessary. Marketing without a holistic perspective becomes functionally narrow and self-serving. Equally, BPR without a marketing perspective tends to be a trivial tinkering with systems.

THE PILOT STUDY

In order to explore the working hypothesis that marketing and BPR are not antithetical but complementary, a small-scale pilot study is now in progress with a range of cooperating organisations. The business area chosen for the pilot study concerns the rapidly changing and highly complex interface between major UK retailers of packaged goods and their suppliers. The retailer/manufacturer relationship was chosen because it is a prime example of the new environmental paradigm. Traditionally, the channels of distribution were dominated by large and relatively sophisticated manufacturing companies who were able to impose their will on generally weak and unsophisticated retailers. The current position, however, represents a significant change in roles. Increasing retail concentration levels, coupled with a sharp mix in retailer strategic and marketing sophistication and ambition, have produced a major shift in the distribution of power in the channel. Figure 10.2 outlines in

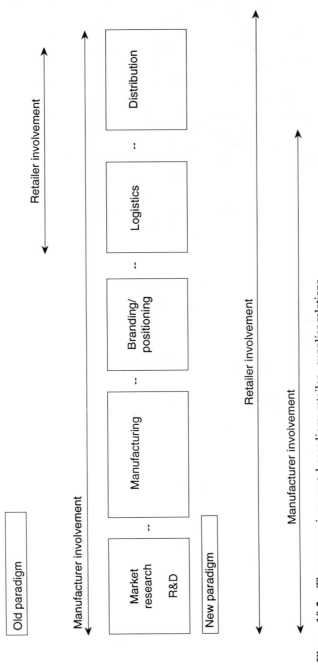

Figure 10.2 The new environmental paradigm: retailer–supplier relations

diagrammatic form several of the key elements in the retailer–manufacturer relationship. As the figure demonstrates, successful and powerful retailers have gradually become more and more involved in the major elements in the supply chain. No longer are retailers passive elements in the channel which suppliers manipulate as part of their "marketing mix". Indeed, the retail sector is now highly proactive in a whole range of areas which were once the sole province of powerful suppliers, including branding, positioning, market research and manufacturing (own label).

Methodologically, the choice of packaged goods retailer–manufacturer relationships for the pilot study offers both benefits and disadvantages. On the positive side, the high degree of concentration in the sector means that a relatively small sample of respondents (in this pilot study instance, six retailers and six suppliers) can offer coverage of organisations which represent an important proportion of the relevant total market. However, the highly sensitive and volatile nature of retailer–supplier relationships also creates obvious difficulties in terms of research design. Because of the sensitive, complex and evolving nature of the area under research review, a conventional cross-sectional, quantitative study would be an inappropriate form of data capture. The chosen approach, therefore, is both qualitative and longitudinal (repeated in-depth interviews and, where permitted, observation). Paradoxically, this kind of qualitative, longitudinal approach, while generally agreed to deliver richness and depth of insights, has nonetheless tended to be the exception rather than the rule in the marketing field (Hunt, 1994; Brownlie et al., 1994).

Because of the small-scale pilot nature of the study and its longitudinal nature, any early results can only be regarded as indicative and exploratory. Nonetheless, it is encouraging to note that it would appear from the preliminary phase of the research that important developments can be identified which are consistent with the basic hypothesis being explored.

A crude skeleton typology of respondent organisations is sketched in Table 10.2. It would appear that some organisations have begun to reflect quite radically upon the significance of the new environmental paradigm for their traditional operating methods and systems. These organisations, tentatively labelled "The Visionaries", demonstrate not only the capacity for fundamental reappraisal but also the ability to develop a new mindset which challenges prior assumptions and a willingness to engage in organisational redesign. Thus, for example, one major multinational manufacturer, with an established reputation for marketing sophistication, observed: "We now have to accept that the customers [i.e. the retailers] know far more about our consumers, [i.e. the final purchasers] than we do." In similarly radical vein, one top retailer commented: "We no longer rent shelf space to manufacturers; we control it on behalf of our customers." Significantly, the major manufacturer cited had already radically restructured its marketing effort based on a process redefinition – with the abolition of the once-sacrosanct marketing department, and the reallocation of

Table 10.2 A skeleton typology (preliminary pilot study results)

Visionaries	Reactors	Tweakers	Inerts
• Fundamental reappraisal	• Limited reappraisal	• Relabelling of functions	• Low awareness of key issues
• Mind-set redefinition	• Minimal mindset redefinition	• Window dressing	• Inertia
• Significant structural change	• Limited structural change	• Minimal structural change	• Minimal change
• Partnership/ relationship focus	• Increased collaborative emphasis	• Transaction orientation	

its activities to new organisational teams labelled "brand development" and "customer development". The customer development activity reflects a basic new distinction being drawn between consumers (the final users) and customers (the retail distribution chain). The customer development team focuses on retailer relationships and aims to bring the retail voice into the organisation's decision processes. The perspective adopted by this group is not brand based but total category based – to reflect the retailer mindset. The brand development group, by contrast, now concentrates solely upon market research, innovation, market communication and long-run brand building. This willingness to use process redefinition to redefine organisational structure was also apparent in the top retail organisation already cited which had abolished its traditional (and once equally sacrosanct) buying function and moved to a more fluid management structure which subsumes both buying and brand/product development activities.

As Table 10.2 illustrates, the respondents in the other categories showed less radical tendencies, with varying degrees of urgency and responsiveness to environmental change. These ranged from partial response or "window dressing" to virtual inertia or ignorance. Interestingly the four-way responsiveness classification shown in Table 10.2 has some resemblances to the typology which emerged from a recent study of BPR by Andersen Consulting (Mackenzie, 1994). The Andersen Study found three categories of organisational response – "First Movers", "Quick Reactors" and "Also Rans". The current pilot study would support the Anderson view that diffusion of the BPR concept is moving at very different rates in different organisations.

While the small sample size and the preliminary nature of the research suggest caution in reading too much into the early findings, it is perhaps noteworthy that those organisations which have undertaken BPR in a significant way appear to have begun to see a range of organisational benefits. The initial evidence suggests that these benefits may prove to derive from several sources. For example, the radical rethink of customer-related processes which BPR demands would appear to facilitate fresh perspectives on innovation, particularly in relation to speeding up the new product development process. Additionally, the "back to first principles" reviews of retailer–supplier linkages (which BPR can trigger) appear to offer the potential for developing an improved working relationship across the supply chain. Perhaps the most crucial benefit which BPR appears to generate for marketers is the opportunity to ensure that a genuinely market-orientated philosophy operates throughout the organisations. The research suggests that this objective can be best achieved not by exhortation but by embedding the marketing perspective into the organisation's fundamental definition of core processes. Overall, it is possible to suggest that far from reducing marketing''s role and significance in the organisation, the effective implementation of BPR may actually increase it.

CONCLUSIONS

This chapter has suggested that far from seeing the end of marketing (as the more apocalyptic critics have suggested) the new environmental paradigm and BPR represent a major opportunity for the marketing philosophy to become more effectively institutionalised in organisational core processes. It has been argued that marketing now has the chance to avoid the dangers of excessive functionalism and to drive for wider recognition and implementation of the customer-focused philosophy which is marketing's true *raison d'être*. If the marketing profession embraces the potential of the new BPR-driven approaches now emerging, the preliminary research is already suggesting that the organisational pay-offs could be considerable. Conversely, if marketers retreat into the functional palisade, they run the risk of irrelevance and being shunted into the organisational periphery. It is also becoming apparent that unless BPR is implemented in a way that recognises the centrality and complementarity of the marketing concept, it can become overly narrow and inward-looking, thus running the risk of decline into yet another passing management fashion or fad.

Chapter 11

Business Processes: Lessons from Operations Management

Colin Armistead, Alan Harrison and Philip Rowland

WHAT WILL YOU FIND IN THIS CHAPTER?

This chapter is about operations management. Operational processes have been the focus of many BPR-type programmes first in the manufacturing domain. The transfer of these approaches into non-manufacturing environments has been a feature of BPR. In this chapter you will:

- Define operational processes
- Explore the characteristics of business processes
- Link the principles of BPR with other improvement approaches including total quality management (TQM), just-in-time (JIT), lean supply, and simultaneous engineering (SE)
- Identify lessons for implementing improvement programmes which are relevant to BPR
- Learn where operations management cannot add to the knowledge base for BPR

INTRODUCTION

The adoption of the process paradigm for organisations has resonance within the operations management discipline. BPR is concerned with activities to improve performance which have many similarities with existing concepts and techniques in the domain of operations management. We believe there is rich learning to be gained from the areas quality management, just-in-time and simultaneous engineering which may be disregarded or hidden from those engaged in BPR programmes. In this chapter we aim to highlight the relevant learning.

The development of the concept and practice of Business Process Re-engineering from "The Management in the 1990's" research programme at MIT (Scott Morton, 1991), Hammer's well-known initial article on re-engineering in *The Harvard Business Review* (Hammer, 1990) and Davenport's book on process innovation (Davenport, 1993b) was at first sight highly biased towards the exploitation of information technology. However, it was clear that many of the examples given of BPR had a very strong operations management and services management content.

Some authors on BPR do, of course, already acknowledge antecedents in manufacturing, logistics and supply chain concepts (Johanson et al., 1993). We do not claim BPR as an operations management approach but to examine the concepts and techniques of the field which might have application for BPR. Hence the learning which has been gained from other improvement philosophies may be valuably transferred to BPR programmes. We can see this demonstrated in the St James's Hospital case study in Chapter 20.

Implicit in the various definitions of BPR is the consideration of organisational structure. If an organisation is viewed as a collection of processes, how do the processes impact on a functional view of the organisation? The debate about the relative importance of processes over functions where processes cross traditional functional boundaries is likely to be a feature of implementation of BPR (Womack and Jones, 1994).

As a prescription or framework for how to undertake BPR we have combined the *principles of re-engineering* proposed by Hammer and the *characteristics of a re-engineered process*, suggested by Hammer and Champy (1993) into a list of eight "rules" for the improvement of business processes:

1. Organise around outcomes not tasks.
2. Have those who use the output of the process perform the process.
3. Treat geographically dispersed resources as though they were centralised, creating hybrid centralised/decentralised organisations.
4. Link activities in a natural order and perform them in parallel.
5. Perform work where it makes most sense, particularly decision making, information processing, checks and controls, making them part of the process.

6. Capture information once and at the source, minimising reconciliation.
7. Combine several jobs into one, possibly creating a case manager or case team as a single point of contact.
8. Create multiple versions of processes when appropriate.

We will use this list to examine and consider which techniques and concepts originating in the operations management domain provide insights into the implementation of the rules for BPR.

WHAT RINGS TRUE FROM OPERATIONS MANAGEMENT?

Operations management is concerned with the management of processes, people, technology and other resources in the production of goods and services. Any textbook on operations management includes chapters dealing with the main areas of the design of products and operations and planning and control of capacity, materials, quality and resource productivity. The content of these main areas may be essentially descriptive and qualitative or may include a quantitative approach to solving operational problems.

There exists in the operations management domain two main areas which have resonance with the concept and prescription of BPR: first, the use of the process paradigm and second, the concepts and techniques for designing, managing and improving operational processes.

Defining a Process

Operations management is a useful place to start in the quest for a definitive statement on what is a process. This is not simply because the authors belong to that discipline, but because the whole subject is based on the concept of managing the transformation process. "Process" refers to the conversion of inputs (resources) into outputs (goods and services) (Slack et al., 1995; Armistead 1990) (see Figure 11.1).

Inputs to the transformation process

Inputs to the transformation process can be classified as either:

- *Transformed resources*: the resources which are converted in some way. Usually, these are some combination of materials, information and customers themselves. For example, a bank primarily processes information, although materials (money, statements) and customers (advice, cash transactions) may also be transformed.

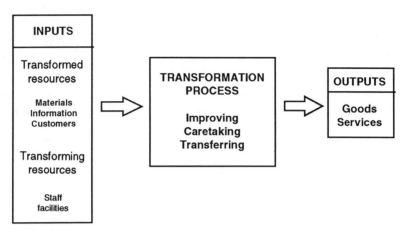

Figure 11.1 Transformation process model

- *Transforming resources*: resources which act upon the transformed resources. The two key inputs here are facilities (hardware such as buildings and equipment) and staff who operate, maintain, plan and manage the operation.

Both types of input are needed in any transformation process.

The transformation process

The transformation process uses transforming resources to convert the transformed resources. Conversion may follow a number of different routes characterised as *improving*, *caretaking* and *transferring*:

- Materials may be *improved* and converted *physically*, such as steel strip into car bodies. Or their *location* may be transferred, as in the case of postal delivery. Or a *storage* process may be involved in *caretaking*, as in warehousing.
- Information may be *improved* and *reconfigured*, such as in financial services. Or its *location* may be *transferred*, as in telecommunications. Or *caretaking* involving *storage* process may be involved, as in meteorology records or the creation of data "warehouses".
- Customers may be *improved*, such as hairdressing. They may also be *improved physiologically* (as in health care), or *psychologically* (as in entertainment). Or their *location* may be altered, as in airline or rail travel. *Caretaking* takes place as with accommodation in overnight hotels or places of entertainment.

A relatively small number of types of transformation process (improving, caretaking and transferring) emerge. In practice, transformations are often combinations of two or more of these basic types. In the same way that operations management must be capable of explaining transformations in a wide variety of environments, so should BPR principles be applicable to any business process.

Outputs

Outputs of the transformation process can be characterised by two extremes:

- *Goods*: which are tangible, storable and transportable. Quality from the customer viewpoint is basically product-related.
- *Services*: which are intangible and cannot be stored or transported. They are typically produced simultaneously with their consumption. Quality depends not only on the outcome of the service but also on the customer's perception of the delivery system.

Again, outputs from most transformation processes are combinations of the two.

BUSINESS PROCESSES

Operations should be viewed as one example of a business process. The key point is that transformed resources originate from outside the boundaries of the organisation, and that outputs in the form of goods and services leave the boundaries of the organisation. It is this "end-to-end" property which should be used to distinguish business processes. They start with inputs to the business boundary and finish with outputs from the business boundary. This view is consistent with the BPR message of "reinventing the corporation", and not simply streamlining parts of processes as in Davenport and Short's (1990) ideas.

There are not many examples so far of organisations which have "started with a clean sheet of paper" in carrying out BPR. Work at Alcoa in the UK has been in this category (Thomas, 1993), and yet re-engineering produced only four "business processes". These are illustrated in Figure 11.2:

- *Strategic flow*: to develop strategy to ensure long-term profitability and to optimise tactical business performance.
- *Customer service*: to respond effectively to customer needs as a total business system.
- *Operations flow*: to ensure support and development of all processes.
- *Administration flow*: To ensure support and development of all processes, development is carried out elsewhere in the company, so it would be necessary to add this business process in many organisations. However, it is

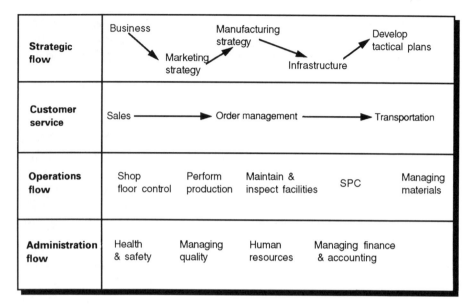

Figure 11.2 Redefining business processes: outcomes of a BPR exercise. (Reproduced by courtesy of Alcoa)

surprising how simple the new organisation is after re-engineering, as indicated by Figure 11.2.

Breaking Down Business Processes

Managing business processes needs to take into account their aggregate nature. A hierarchical structure is needed in the same way as project management needs a work breakdown structure to allocate tasks (work packages) to project teams. The analogy with project management is further reinforced by the changes envisaged by BPR – from functional departments to process teams. This approach gives rise to a proposed "business process breakdown structure".

Using the Alcoa work as illustration in Figure 11.3, the names given to the levels in the hierarchy can be explained as follows:

- *Process elements*: these are the major elements into which a business process can best be organised. For example, the Customer Service business process was allotted three process elements. These were Sales, Order Management and Transportation.
- *Process element activities*: process elements can in turn be broken down for ease of management into recognisable activities. In the case of the Sales

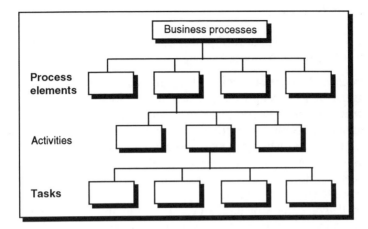

Figure 11.3   Business process breakdown structure

process element, just two activities were defined. These were Management Customer Accounts and Claims Processing.

● *Activity tasks*: finally, activities can be broken down into tasks which are written up as standard operating procedures for individual "process owners" to carry out.

Characteristics of the four levels in the hierarchy are that they share the process characteristics that were identified earlier. They are all transformations, but differ only in scale and in that most level 2 to 4 processes are internally rather than externally supplier/customer focused. It is only necessary to carry out the breakdown in order to achieve a concise, manageable and defined series of tasks so that overall business process objectives may be met. Therefore, the number of levels should be kept as small as possible, and the number of processes at each level should also be kept as small as possible. For example, Alcoa needed only seventeen process elements to cover the whole business (see Figure 11.2). Progress in re-engineering over time should reflect process reduction in terms of the number of processes, elements and activities.

Properties of Processes

Having postulated that business processes can be broken down into a hierarchy of smaller processes which share the same characteristics, this section reviews what we have learned in operations management about the properties of processes. These properties are grouped under three main headings: *structural*, *design and operational*, and those which *limit consistent output*.

Structural characteristics

There are a number of features of processes which we can categorise as being structural. These relate to processes being:

- *Hierarchies*: all processes can be disaggregated into hierarchies of smaller processes with increasingly detailed activities as we have seen.
- *Networks*: all processes form part of a larger network at the same level of disaggregation. Networks offer the potential to share resources to meet demand where and when required. Telecommunication networks are able to do this easily. Networks which require physical movement of people or materials may not be able to manage the flows in times which are sufficiently responsive to customer demands.
- *Process mapping*: the structural aspects of hierarchies and networks makes it possible to map the relationship between processes at any level of disaggregation of place in a network. However, it is not easy to map all aspects of the process where there is a high level of human participation in the process (see limitations below).
- *Value chains*: all processes comprise elements or activities which add value and those which do not. So treating a patient clearly adds value in accident and emergency treatment whereas the patient waiting to be seen does not.
- *Customer participation*: customers participate or influence the nature of processes. Even where processes are remote from customer participation they should still be directly influenced by the needs of customers.

Design and operational characteristics

The following are characteristics of processes which we relate to the design and operational management of processes. These correspond to:

- *Ownership*: all processes benefit from a clear identification of a process owner which assists integration of activities within the process. Within the materials supply chains in manufacturing, it has been shown that integration is correlated with improvements in timings, and quality and costs (Armistead and Mapes, 1993).
- *The operations task*: the purpose of all processes can be defined by an operations task or service operations task consisting of four parts (Figure 11.4): first, descriptions of critical *customer service* and quality dimensions the process should achieve; second, the *productivity* and cost targets to be attained; third, the *demand* for products and services with which the process must deal. Demand is considered in terms of volume and variety of output and variations in volume and variety over time. Variety may also be expressed according to certainty associated with commitment of resources

and timing of demand. The terms runners, repeaters and strangers (Parnaby, 1988) are used in this context. Demand is described in terms of the certainty of demand for a particular period and the amount of resource needed to satisfy that demand.

– *Runners* are activities which are part of a regular routine. The timing of demand and the amount of resource needed to satisfy that demand are well known.

– *Repeaters* are intermittent activities. While there is information about the amount of resources which will be needed to satisfy demand there is uncertainty about when those resources will be needed.

– *Strangers* are activities whose occurrence is much less predictable. The resource allocation needed to meet demand is also unknown.

- *Any constraints* which hinder the achievement of customer service or resource productivity targets. So, for instance, the operations task for the process of providing maintenance and repair for domestic products such as washing machines or dishwashers would have its task defined in terms of the time to respond to a problem and the time to repair the equipment as key customer service dimensions. Productivity targets would be expressed in terms of the utilisation of engineers in repair and maintenance work rather than travelling or doing other things and also in costs of spares. Demand would be expressed as the number of service visits expected in a time period which might vary according to the model and also time of the year. In this type of operation one would expect a high level of runners in the mix of tasks which the engineers were expected to undertake, thereby containing costs.

- *Focus*: processes are more likely to achieve the objectives of the service operations task if they are focused on the production and delivery of one service or similar activities (Skinner, 1974). A computer manufacturer might choose to focus one of its help centres on one small product group

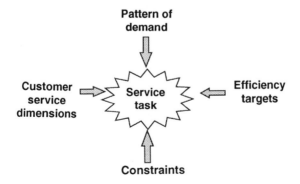

Figure 11.4 The service operations task

directing all calls through this one centre rather than all help desks dealing with all products.

- *Resource capacity*: all processes have resources which enable the process to achieve the operations task. However, making the link between the amount of the resource available and the actual output from a process in a given time period is not always simple. For example, the number of customers served at the check-out in a store depends on a number of factors, including the number of customers in the store and the amount of groceries they each buy.

- *Cycle time*: All processes have a time element associated with them, often called the cycle time. Cycle time can be measured in several different ways. However, here we see cycle time as being the time it takes for inputs into any process to be transformed into the outputs of the process. Often in BPR cycle time reduction is an important goal.

- *Measurement*: all processes are inherently capable of being measured by a mixture of quantitative and qualitative dimensions. Measurement can be for control, for improvement, for benchmarking. Critical questions about processes relate to "where is the value and where is the cost?" Measurement allows these questions to be addressed with information rather than uninformed argument.

- *Operational elements of control*: all processes require control through a series of planning and control strategies. First, these are concerned with managing capacity to achieve a balance between the load imposed, the demand and the availability of resources. Second are planning and control strategies for managing quality and resource productivity. Third are strategies to cope when the process is either under or overloaded and quality of service and or productivity will suffer. Finally there are the strategies to recover when things go wrong (Armistead and Clark, 1994).

Characteristics which limit consistent output

Finally there are some aspects of processes which limit consistent output.

- *Variability*: all processes are variable so that output is not constant. Variability is due to inherent factors within the process and to external effects which impinge on the process. The skill of a surgeon and the condition of the patient are inherent factors within the process of surgery. Availability of operating theatres or support staff would be external factors. The aim for process managers is to keep processes within defined limits of variability in order to ensure consistency of outputs.

- *Uncertainty*: The greater the extent of human involvement within a process, the higher the uncertainty as to why the process works as it does. The reason for not being able to capture all the process knowledge by process mapping techniques is that it is held in the expertise of the staff and customers and in the way they work together, i.e. the intangible aspects of processes.

- *Constraints*: all processes are subject to some constraint on their output, often described as the rate-determining step. Other constraints may be availability of resources to processes. Understanding constraints is important in managing load and capacity.

DEVELOPMENTS IN OPERATIONS MANAGEMENT

There have been three important developments in the operations management field which have a bearing on BPR. First has been the concept of *operations strategy* (Skinner, 1969; Hill, 1985; Heskett, 1986; Armistead, 1990), for providing a link between the competitive strategy of an enterprise and its operational capability. The overriding concept in operations strategy is one of fit between the competitive intent and operational capability on the premise that no one operational configuration of resources can do everything, i.e. produce the highest quality product or service in a customised form in the shortest time, on time every time and at the lowest cost.

The second development has been the widening of the operations management field from its manufacturing origins to include services and the effect of a customer as part of the operations (Sasser, Olsen and Wycoff, 1978; Heskett, 1986).

The third influence has been the development of specific operations concepts as a result of the actions of practitioners in enterprises rather than the work of academics. The biggest change has come in the last 15–20 years from the work in Japanese companies manufacturing cars, electrical and electronic products and their followers in the USA and Europe (Shingo, 1989; Schonberger, 1987). These developments have brought to the fore concepts and practices of total quality management (Juran, 1975; Crosby, 1979; Deming, 1986; Oakland, 1989), just-in-time (Harrison, 1992), supply chain management and lean production (Lamming, 1993; Womack and Jones, 1994), and simultaneous engineering (Voss, Russell and Twigg, 1991; Clark and Fujimoto, 1991).

THE APPLICATION OF OPERATIONS MANAGEMENT EXPERIENCE TO BPR

Without necessarily developing in detail all aspects of each area of operations management we have tried to abstract the key features which seem to us to have a bearing on the development of a BPR programme under the eight "rules" of BPR developed earlier. The results are:

1. *Organise around outcomes, not tasks* The message from operations strategy in either a manufacturing or a service domain is the importance of establishing the *operations task*. The operations task defines what the operational processes need to do well to meet customer requirements efficiently. Here the concept of order winning, order qualifying and order losing criteria for features of a product service offering is key to establishing the nature of the delivery process.

2. *Have those who use the output of the process perform the process* The concept of internal as well as external customers has been central for TQM. This concept brings with it the idea of partnership between different entities along a chain of activities in any process or along a supply chain. In practice the dangers of focusing only on the next step in the chain rather than the customer at the end of the chain have been realised. A BPR approach offers a resolution to the problem by challenging the idea that any departmental, and thus internal customer, boundaries are legitimate. BPR makes end-to-end processes supreme.

3. *Treat geographically dispersed resources as though they were centralised, creating hybrid centralised/decentralised organisations* The operational linking of geographically dispersed operations is key within service operations which are facilitated by the use of telecoms, for example telephone response centres situated geographically to give 24-hour global service. Similarly Just-in-Time supply may make physical inventories visible across a network with the capability to transfer material from one or a small number of locations without the need to hold stock locally.

4. *Link parallel activities in a natural order instead of integrating their results* Simultaneous engineering and design for assembly has enabled organisations to speed up new product development and improve quality by linking the development of new products to the development of the processes by which they will be manufactured.

5. *Perform work where it makes most sense, particularly, decision making, information processing, checks and controls, making them part of the process* Quality assurance within the context of TQM has tended to drive a move from final inspection of products to inspection at source by operators. Such quality control has in some cases been driven hard by the application of statistical process control (SPC) to reduce the variability within the operational processes. Such moves can require considerable training in the understanding and application of SPC techniques. Motorola's successful 6-Sigma programme is one of the best examples of this approach. The Just-In-Time principle of *Jidoka* places further emphasis on control, with the people actually doing the work allowing them to halt production to fix a problem as it arises.

6. *Capture information once and at the source, minimising reconciliation*
   Developments in integrating supply chains, utilising electronic interchange,
   have allowed organisations to track the movement of materials through each
   stage in the chain without the need to re-key data at each point. This
   minimises the need for reconciliation by ensuring each party is working on
   the same information.
7. *Combine several jobs into one, possibly creating a case manager or case
   team as a single point of contact*   The move to create manufacturing cells
   responsible for a significant part of the production process requiring multi-
   skilling of the cell operators is now being widely mirrored in service
   operations through BPR. Cells reduce lead time, movement of materials and
   worker movement and build commitment among members of the cell.
8. *Create multiple versions of processes when appropriate*   The concept of
   focus referred to earlier and the application of the categorisation of demand
   into *runners, repeaters* and *strangers* is widely taught in operations
   management as a way of understanding the process requirements of
   products and services. Matching the appropriate process approach to product
   complexity and volume has long been a mainstream task in operating
   systems design.

A further operations management technique from the TQM/JIT philosophies
which is increasingly applied to BPR programmes is that of micro-response
analysis. This technique takes a ratio approach to understand the performance
of process in three main ways: lead time to work content (or throughput
efficiency), process speed to use rate and pieces to work station, operator or

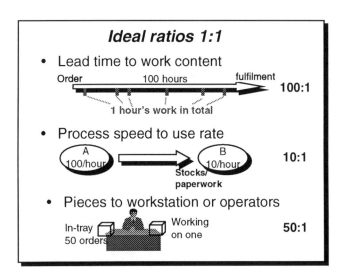

Figure 11.5   Micro-response analysis diagram

office worker. This concept is shown in Figure 11.5 (Peppard and Rowland, 1995).

The ideal ratio for all ratios is 1 : 1 yet in many cases ratios are significantly greater than this. The last of the three ratios is particularly challenging when applied in office environments as the notion of only one piece of paper being worked on with none sitting in the in-tray challenges the fundamental assumptions of how an office should work. Yet this challenge is necessary if poor throughput efficiency is to be understood and improved.

LESSONS FOR BPR FROM OPERATIONS MANAGEMENT

The examination of the aspects of operations management within the framework of the BPR rules focuses attention on key areas of TQM, JIT and simultaneous engineering. It is here that there has been research to investigate reasons for success and failure (Schaffer, 1993; Katz, 1993; Easton, 1993; Billesbach, 1991; Siegel, 1991). Such lessons would seem to be relevant to BPR.

1. *The role of the CEO* is important in setting the direction for TQM and in establishing the reasons and extent of JIT. Commitment from the top is all-important and responsibility cannot be delegated. CEOs should treat improvement programmes as any other strategic priority.
2. *The application of TQM and JIT must be in the context of the business environment* of each organisation. The use of benchmarking, however, to establish best practice for specific processes can be useful in breaking paradigms and providing clues for a better way of working.
3. *Training at the right time and for the right level.* Training should take place once support is established and should not be conducted as a mass exercise ahead of any action but rather rolled-out to support implementation. Don't miss out middle management in training and implementation. These people may feel most threatened and need the training most in order to adjust to new roles.
4. *Listen to customers*, suppliers and employees seeking facts to build understanding. Actions must be focused on those aspects which are a priority for customers. Facts should be sought throughout the research to support assertions and communicate the actual situation without a blame mentality being adopted.
5. *Don't focus on technical tools* too early or too much; people, leadership skills and creativity are more important. Sophisticated process mapping tools can shift attention from redesign to understanding existing processes and can deter non-technical staff from participation, stifling innovation and commitment.

6. *Involve suppliers in the programme* where they influence the outcome. Organisations are only as good as their supply chains and a partnership approach to supplier and customer relations within the supply chain can yield significant benefits for all parties.
7. *Don't try to do too much at once.* Celebrate successes to bolster confidence and momentum, recognising that it may take years to gain enough experience before the new orientation starts to work well. As with anything, there is a learning curve to improvement methodologies.
8. *TQM and JIT contain challenging messages which must be disseminated.* This communication process can be facilitated by the use of games and simulations to explain and demonstrate the message (Graham et al., 1991; Wiesbord, 1989). Indeed there are already indications of the same approach being adopted for BPR.
9. *Use the right measures to demonstrate success.* An over-reliance on short-term financial measures without understanding key operational indicators may paint a false picture of the operation's performance and the improvements made (Kaplan, 1992; Neely, 1993).

As the case histories of BPR grow it is clear that theses messages seem to be relevant to BPR programmes. Percentage failure rates may correspond to a 20:80 success to failure which have been suggested over the years for the essentially operations based programmes we have been discussing and for similar reasons (Hall, Rosenthal and Wade, 1993; CSC Index, 1994; Hammer and Stanton, 1995, are typical).

CAN OPERATIONS MANAGEMENT HELP WITH ALL ASPECTS OF BPR?

We have tried to indicate where aspects of operations management knowledge can help BPR programmes. However, we can also see some aspects of BPR where it does not provide answers. There seem to us three areas which are vital to the success of BPR.

First, if BPR is adopted it will lead organisations to adopt a process paradigm. While this is useful from a systems point of view it does nothing to indicate to managers how they should manage an organisation in this form. It raises the question of what it means to manage processes at different levels or managing operational, strategic and enabling processes and the interaction between the different types.

Second, if the process paradigm is used, how can measurement and control systems be re-aligned to support this mode of operation? It is our assertion, based on what companies tell us, that the debate about how to construct an appropriate performance measurement system has never been satisfactorily resolved. Indeed this question goes beyond the operations management domain to include finance and accounting, human resources and strategy (Kaplan, 1992; Neely, 1993).

Third, there would seem to be an emerging conflict in method between information systems developers and operations staff. The explosion of computer tools to support BPR demonstrates the demand which exists for sophisticated process mapping tools. Yet these types of tools are difficult for non-technical specialists to use. As detailed in our lessons from previous philosophies, emphasis on the use of these tools may prove damaging to BPR initiatives. This dilemma, again, cannot be resolved in the domains of IS or operations in isolation. As with MRP, only by working on all aspects of process, people and technology can success be achieved.

WHAT HAVE WE LEARNED?

The operations management discipline can provide a number of valuable insights into how pitfalls likely to befall BPR programmes might be avoided. JIT, in our opinion, offers some prescription on how to construct processes while TQM and simultaneous engineering offer more on how to go about the change. Like these other philosophies, BPR can only succeed with the commitment of top management and a cross-disciplinary approach. Because many of BPR's principles seem to be a transfer of manufacturing principles to the office and service environment, it would be worth more organisations considering the inclusion of skilled manufacturing people in their BPR teams.

Defining a "process" is no simplistic task. Like defining "quality", there are many interpretations and there has been much confusion. We need to tighten up on our understanding of the term "process", if only because it is at the centre of Business Process Management.

- A process may simplistically be defined as a transformation of inputs (resources) into outputs (goods and services).
- A business process is an end-to-end version of this definition, that is, its inputs are from outside the boundaries of the organisation, and its outputs are delivered to customers outside the boundaries of the organisation. Business processes in a re-engineered organisation are typically few in number.
- Other processes can and indeed should be ordered hierarchically under business processes. There should be few levels (four are proposed), and the fewer, the better.
- Processes at any level in the hierarchy share similar properties: a mix of value-added and non-value-added, inherent variability, capability of measurement, logically linked with each other (networked), benefit from ownership, and should be automated after being re-engineered. However,

there are intangible aspects of a process when people are involved which make exact characterisation difficult to achieve.

The field of BPR is in the developmental stage and there is a recognition that effective BPR exercises require an input from all management disciplines. Success is more likely to be achieved if the concepts of each discipline as they apply to BPR are well understood so that lessons gained in the course of implementation of other improvement initiatives are not lost. The contribution from operations management would seem to be potentially very valuable. In this chapter we have attempted to provide the link between operations management and BPR to this end.

Chapter 12

Going with the Flow: Re-engineering Logistics

James Cooper

WHAT WILL YOU FIND IN THIS CHAPTER?

This chapter considers the interrelationship between logistics and BPR. There is a strong link between logistics and operations management in the management of the supply chain and you will find interlinking themes. The development of the logistics field has been one of integration of previously disparate processes, a theme which is echoed in BPR. We also think that the concepts which underly the movement of materials also have application for the movement of information. In this chapter you will find:

- A description of the role of logistics in improving corporate performance
- The changing requirement from logistics resulting from the intensification of competition leading to the concept of flexible fulfilment driven by time-based management and mass customisation
- The contribution BPR can make to effective logistics management

THE LOGISTICS CONTRIBUTION TO IMPROVING CORPORATE PERFORMANCE

There is growing acceptance in most businesses that effective logistics management makes a significant contribution to corporate success. This is perhaps most evident in the manufacturing industry, where the flow of materials, work-in-progress and finished products is core to the business. But it is also true of many other business sectors, including retailing and even financial services, where the flow of documents has many parallels with the production line.

At the heart of the logistics contribution to corporate success is customer service. The availability of products to intending purchasers; the frequency and reliability of delivery; and delivery lead times – these are key dimensions of customer service in most businesses.

To a certain extent, customer service and logistics represent an updated response to that old business truism: a company with excellent products that cannot get them to market will fail. Clearly, superior customer service will contribute to corporate prosperity and the aim of logistics management is to promote service by configuring the physical flow of products to meet both actual and potential needs of customers.

Much of this configuring takes place within the organisation but, increasingly, the scope is extending to embrace external relationships. This is entirely a logical development when most supply chains start with suppliers and end with customers. Aiming to improve the effectiveness of the whole chain must be the best approach for all concerned.

The way in which the configuring is done will naturally vary according to the individual circumstances of organisations participating in a supply chain and also with the prevailing business climate. When, for example, inflation is high and real interest rates are negative, companies will not be concerned so much about reducing levels of inventory. On the contrary, they can profit through holding generous levels of inventory.

However, in recent years, with price stability and positive levels of real interest rates, most companies' logistics strategies have been oriented towards minimising levels of inventory, so long as customer service needs are not compromised. The need to achieve improved corporate financial performance has been a growing driver behind this development. As investors make discriminating choices between companies, a key consideration will be how well they are doing according to a variety of financial performance indicators, one of which is *return on net assets* (RONA). Since inventory is an important asset held by many companies, adjusting levels of inventory to improve RONA performance and so enhancing the attractiveness of a company to investors is a vital consideration.

In a similar vein, improvements to cash flow put a company on a stronger financial footing, and logistics management can make a vital contribution in this respect. Some retailers, particularly the multiple chains, have accelerated the flow of products through their stores and distribution centres to such an extent that they receive payment from shoppers before they have to pay their suppliers.

There is also much that can be done within manufacturing businesses to improve their own cash flow. It has been estimated (Barker, 1993) that, during the production process, products can spend up to 95% of their time as static work-in-progress, without any value-adding activities being applied to them. If, by management action, this idle time can be reduced, then the elapsed time between receiving revenues from the sale of the products and paying suppliers can be compressed.

Time compression within the supply chain can bring many valuable benefits to companies. Importantly, the time horizon for making forecasts can be reduced and this can contribute substantially to forecast accuracy. Even better, companies can order materials or components against what they know will be sold, which helps eliminate waste in the process of manufacture and obsolescence of the finished products themselves. For these reasons, the mission of logistics management in some businesses is now stated in terms of achieving superior customer service at acceptable cost through the time-based management of resources.

Yet, all too often, working to a mission statement of this kind is easier said than done. Suppliers of materials or components will need to conform to much stricter terms and conditions, namely:

- Acceptance of orders in smaller lot quantities
- More frequent delivery
- Time-definite delivery
- Complete fulfilment of each order, with no items missing.

As a consequence, a new set of relationships may well have to be forged between the customer, the supplier, and even the freight company which is responsible for the delivery of orders. This will require:

- More intimate knowledge of each other's businesses
- More flexible allocation of available capacity
- Integration of management information systems throughout the supply chain.

This is difficult enough to achieve within a stable business environment. For many businesses, however, the competitive landscape is changing fast. In *Through the Looking Glass*, Alice spoke of having to run just to stay in the same place. As competition intensifies, many companies find themselves in the same predicament, which represents a major challenge for logistics managers charged with the responsibility of achieving ever-better performance.

What, then, needs to be done? In the following sections of this chapter we first examine current and future business trends to map out the changing face of competition. We then focus on evolving logistics system requirements as competition becomes more intense. Finally, we examine the potential contribution of business process re-engineering (BPR) as a means to more effective logistics management and improved corporate success.

WHERE DO WE GO FROM HERE?

Global competition is now a fact of life for many companies, especially in manufacturing. In a growing number of countries the customer no longer has to buy whatever is available from a dominant supplier. The cars we buy may have been assembled anywhere from Michigan to Malaysia. The components they contain may have been sourced from dozens of countries. Price, quality and service are now the key buying considerations in all kinds of business sector.

The result is a familiar one to most managers. Markets are fragmenting, product life cycles are shortening – along with total production runs. Enabled by new technology in manufacturing, lot size is on the decrease as we aim to meet the more exacting needs of our customers. In consumer electronics, companies like Sony are gearing up to *retailer*-specific products, as long as at least a pallet-load is ordered. But in other sectors, the drive is towards *consumer*-specific products – mass production in lots of one. We are already there in motor manufacturing, with buyers being able to specify their preferred options in an almost infinite number of combinations. Now this trend is spreading to other business sectors as well.

Take, for example, Motorola's production facility for Fusion, its range of pagers which are designed to be readily customised. Customers can specify their requirements in terms of colour, size and performance features, such as their own paging tune. Production starts only on receipt of order and then all the relevant parts have to be routed to the assembly line. This represents a complex and varied logistics task in which all components have to be tracked to ensure proper control.

All our logistics operations are time-critical when making to order, as a recent article in *Fortune* on Dell Computers illustrates very well (Losee, 1994). *Fortune* followed one machine from the moment a customer placed his order until it was delivered 46 hours and 42 minutes later. The following is the sequence of events:

Wednesday (Austin, Texas)
10.49 am	Dell receives call from Mr Cozzette who orders a PC with special features
12.50 pm	Credit check and order ID issued
1.00 pm	Assembly process starts on ordered PC
2.01 pm	Customized fax modem inserted

2.10 pm	Customized tape back-up unit inserted
2.26 pm	Computer's barcode scanned to identify components used and update inventory
2.28 pm	Circuit test
2.40 pm	Assembly completed
7.25 pm	Extended test completed
8.20 pm	Tested for safety certification
8.37 pm	Finished computer is packed for despatch
9.25 pm	Airborne Express collects by truck

Friday (White Plains, NY)
10.31 am   Computer delivered to Mr Cozzette in his office

Where else might we see similar *fast* mass customisation in the future? Already we have the prospect of everyday products, such as jeans, being customised. Levi's have recently completed a successful pilot in Cincinnati, Ohio, which marries the bespoke to the mass-produced (Laurence, 1994). The Levi's Personal Pair Jeans service works as follows:

• A store assistant measures the customer and feeds the measurements into a computer terminal.
• The customer verifies the measurements and selects colour and finish details.
• An EDI link transmits the order details to a robotic cutting machine at the company's Tennessee factory.
• After machining, the finished pair of jeans is despatched direct to the customer.

Importantly, the new service is directed at women, who are generally less tolerant of poor fit than men. The payoff for Levi's from the Cincinnati pilot was a sales boost in women's jeans of no less than 300%.

One key to the spread of tailor-made products is in automated manufacturing where machines produce perfect customised products both inexpensively and quickly. Furthermore, this need to be flexible in how we make a product will be mirrored in where we make the product. It is now rare for companies to feel tied to a particular location for production purposes. The dynamics of global competition mean that companies look for competitive advantage through location. As a result we now see countries taking part in beauty contests to attract foreign investment. Several Asian countries emphasise political stability and their proximity to developing markets. Germany prefers to attract companies with its promise of a highly skilled workforce giving high productivity. Northern Ireland offers generous relocation grants and new facilities ready and available. In March 1994 the UK government agreed to pay Jaguar (owned by Ford) £9.4 million to stop assembly of the next-generation XJS being moved to Portugal (Done, 1994). Now there is discussion of making Jaguars in the United States. Production everywhere is on the move.

As a consequence of mass customisation and locational change, the focus for many companies will be on making logistics systems as flexible as possible. In effect, we are at the threshold of a paradigm shift for the twenty-first century and about to break away from current ways of managing logistics (Figure 12.1).

Until the 1970s, the emphasis was on "production push", where the task of logistics management was to respond to the requirements of production schedules which were designed to maximise operational performance at the factory. Products were, in effect, pushed down through distribution channels to the customer.

But during the 1980s, the customer service revolution heralded a dramatic change in approach. Logistics systems became driven by customer needs and the demands of the marketplace. In other words, product was being called down from production in response to customer requirements, and this "demand pull" approach continues to dominate logistics thinking in the 1990s.

For the future, however, a new approach will be required. Following on from production push and demand pull, the emphasis will increasingly be on "flexible fulfilment". Under flexible fulfilment, logistics systems will be driven by the need to customise, to satisfy the exact requirements of the consumer in terms of both product configuration and service. The need to be flexible is underlined by the great variety of possibilities in each case. In some business sectors, each product may be unique in its specification and customers will want to exercise their preference on how it reaches them much more than they do now. The word "fulfilment" says it all; customers will only be fulfilled in their purchase of a product if they get it their way and that will be a competitive necessity in the years to come.

Importantly, the principle of flexible fulfilment needs to be applied throughout the supply chain, and not just in finished product distribution. For example, inbound logistics systems will need to be flexible to accommodate different permutations in sourcing, as both manufacturers and their suppliers

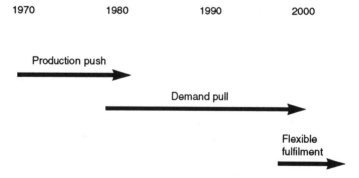

Figure 12.1   The changing logistics paradigm

relocate much more frequently than they have done in the past. These same systems will also need to exercise perfect control over a variable mix of components destined for customised assembly. Motor manufacturers and business equipment producers such as Dell have shown us the way in many important respects. Others will have to follow.

LOGISTICS SYSTEM REDESIGN TO MEET FUTURE NEEDS

Having the right kinds of system – from information to transport through to organisational structure – has always been one of the most important keys to effective logistics management. In designing logistics systems, managers should always have three principal aims in mind:

1. The system should deliver high performance and reliability.
2. The system should be designed in such a way that problems can be easily corrected.
3. Replacement or modified systems should be capable of being developed both inexpensively and quickly.

As we enter an age when flexible fulfilment in logistics becomes an overriding requirement, the need for systems redesign at frequent intervals is emerging as an issue of fundamental importance. It follows that the way we approach logistics systems redesign has to be given a great deal of thought. Shortening product life cycles, the frequent relocation of sourcing and production, the need to customise products and service – all these factors must be accommodated in our logistics systems of the future and the way we design and redesign them.

Here we can usefully draw on the lessons that have already been learned in the development of new products – there are many useful parallels here with systems development. The traditional way to develop a new aeroplane or car was to build a mock-up, to see whether the many thousands of parts would fit together properly. Physical mock-ups are all very well, but making them and testing the fit of parts is a time-consuming task. In many industries, mock-ups of products now take place in the computer rather than in the development workshops. An individual component is no longer modelled in wood or clay, but within a computer-aided design (CAD) program. A key advantage is that it allows necessary changes to be made quickly and accurately. Moreover, new-generation CAD software can deal with ripple effects – if one component is changed in some way then the program will automatically work out the consequences for other related components to keep the entire design consistent.

For the first time a Boeing aircraft has been designed using the CAD approach without a full-scale mock-up. The first 777 will be a flying version rather than an earthbound one whose sole purpose is to check the design configuration. The results so far seem to have been good, as *The Economist* (1994) reported: "When the wings of the first 777 were attached to its waist, the port wing tip was out of position by a thousandth of an inch; the starboard wing was positioned as accurately as the gauges could measure." This approach has not only meant that the 777 has been brought quicker to market, but also has dramatically changed the structure of life-cycle costs for the aeroplane. Now there is more "front-loading" of costs since more changes can be made at the conceptual stage when the design is still in the computer rather than at later stages in the product life cycle, as has traditionally been the case.

Flexible fulfilment in logistics requires a similar transformation of development practice. All too often logistics systems are designed on the back of the proverbial envelope. Many necessary changes are incorporated only when the system goes into operation. Increasingly, companies will find that this approach is inadequate as they have to respond to the needs of flexible fulfilment by redesigning their logistics systems more frequently and have them work on a "right-first-time" basis. The exacting requirements of the future marketplace will have far higher expectations of service performance in logistics. Figure 12.2 illustrates where most companies are at the moment in the development of logistics systems – Stage 1. It shows substantial "backloading" of life-cycle costs as system problems are tackled "on the fly" after the conceptual stages of development have been completed.

Some companies, however, are now taking a more advanced approach, at least in certain areas of logistics system design. Take, for example, distribution centre networks in Europe. Many companies now have the opportunity to integrate and rationalise their facilities which support the distribution of finished products across Europe. The question that invariably arises is "How many distribution centres do we need and where should they be located?" There is now sophisticated computer software which allows managers to answer these questions and find the cost and service implications of suggested solutions. Moreover, there is the important opportunity to ask "what if?" kind of questions. "What if we put our distribution centre in Madrid rather than Barcelona?" The software can give all the vital answers.

These companies are effectively at the beginning of Stage II in the way they are developing their logistics systems (see Figure 12.2). Just as for the 777 at Boeing, the design initially exists in the computer. Potential problems can be detected and corrected at this early stage of design development.

Even so, Stage II will still be insufficient for flexible fulfilment; the overall life cycle – from concept inception to system decommissioning – remains long. Flexible fulfilment will work on the basis of short system life cycles and rapid redesign when systems become obsolete. Stage III systems for flexible fulfilment will therefore require significant time compression in each of their life-cycle phases (see Figure 12.2). While only a few companies can yet claim

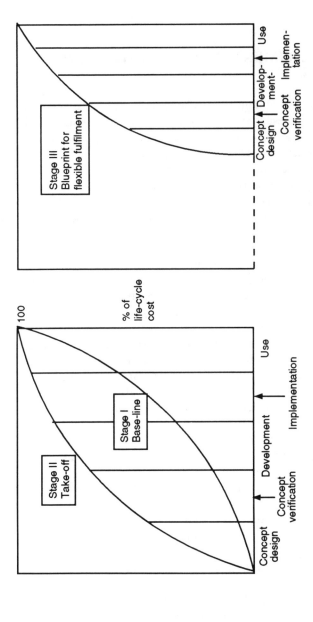

Figure 12.2 Life-cycle costs for logistics systems

to be on the path to Stage III, many more need to start preparing the way. When flexible fulfilment becomes a competitive necessity, a direct jump from Stage I to Stage III may be asking too much of both managerial and organisational capabilities.

CHANGING TIMES MAKE FOR CHANGING REALITIES

Having shown ways of doing things better in logistics management, it would be misleading to suggest that we are on the point of becoming "Masters of the Logistics Universe", to coin a phrase. For many companies, there is a significant gap between needs and competences, and it is one that will grow unless radical new approaches are adopted.

Integrated approaches to logistics management have brought to companies impressive gains in service, cost reduction and – increasingly – flexibility. Yet we have been fortunate in being able to exercise a great deal of control over the areas in which change has been sought, either because we have been given the responsibility and authority to make changes within our organisations or because we have been in a position to exert strong influence over working relationships with external organisations, such as suppliers. Difficulties seem likely to grow in the future as we need to resolve emerging problems that arise in areas where our control as logistics managers is weak.

The matrix in Figure 12.3 is based upon two dimensions already implicitly referred to in the foregoing discussions: *control* (which can be high or low) and *context* (which can be either internal or external to the organisation). Our focus in the 1980s and 1990s has been to the left of the matrix, in areas where we have inherited – or attained – a high degree of logistics management control. So in the top-left corner of the matrix (high control, internal context), we can identify initiatives in logistics which have brought good results. Included in what, for many companies, is a very long list are make to order; customised service levels; rationalisation of distribution centres; integrated information systems; postponement techniques.

As well as in the internal context, there have been many important logistics initiatives in the external context, where high levels of control have been evident. So in the bottom-left corner of the matrix we can list the following initiatives which have brought excellent results in many cases: co-makership with suppliers: just-in-time delivery of materials and components; logistics alliances with service providers; and EDI links with all kinds of external organisations.

But what of the right-hand side of the matrix? Could this represent the challenge from now on? In a recent Delphi study (Cranfield, 1994), correspondents foresaw a major increase in transport activity by the year 2001, but few

	High control	**Low control**
Internal context	Make to order Customised service levels Rationalisation of distribution centres Integrated information systems Postponement techniques	Speed and quality of decision making in the total organisation
External context	Co-makership with suppliers Just-in-time delivery of materials/components Logistics alliances with service providers EDI links	Transport restrictions/delays

⬆   ⬆

Current initiatives   **Future challenges**

Figure 12.3 Logistics management control: current initiatives and future challenges

governments in Europe have the kinds of plan in place to cope with the projected levels of demand. Also, on the question of introducing road pricing (which would control some of the otherwise inevitable congestion), our experts indicated both unease and uncertainty in their predictions. While half of them thought that most European cities would operate road-pricing schemes by the year 2015, the other half thought road pricing would never happen. It goes without saying that future plans for efficient and cost-effective delivery operations into cities critically depend on the eventual outcome.

There may well be other problems in this low control/external context position which affect our ability to achieve the highest levels of effectiveness in logistics management. The slow pace of agreement on international standards is a case in point. But we also have potential problems to solve in the top-right quadrant of the matrix in Figure 12.3, where, in our internal context, we commonly have a low level of logistics management control across the organisation as a whole. Arguably, one of the major problems afflicting organisations concerns the widening gap between managerial intent and capability. Increasingly we see companies developing sophisticated strategies and setting logistics goals which they are organisationally incapable of achieving. To appreciate the implications for the supply chain it is vital to understand both the evolution of logistics management and the barriers to effectiveness that exist within many, if not most, business organisations.

At one time, most companies used to have separate operational responsibilities for transport, warehousing and inventory. The result of this fragmentation was sub-optimal operation with low levels of service and high costs. Warehouses often had handling systems which were not the same as those used in transport. Again, information systems were often different, making the operational interfaces hard to manage. The list of problems was usually a long one.

The answer was to have a combined management structure – physical distribution management – in which transport, warehousing, and inventory operations were integrated. As a consequence of this approach, systems marched to the same tune, and the flow of finished products from the factory to the customer improved measurably.

The success of physical distribution management made it all the clearer that other aspects of moving and storing product were not as efficiently run as they could be. For example, the movement of components into factories for assembly and the flow management of work-in-progress were rarely integrated. Given the success of physical distribution management, there seemed to be significant opportunities for realising the available potential by integrating management responsibilities back up the supply chain.

However, in many instances, implementation has proved to be difficult. In particular, integration up the supply chain meant crossing more formidable organisational boundaries than those separating the components of physical distribution management. For example, production managers invariably hold a powerful position within manufacturing industry and many have showed an understandable reluctance to yield decision-making responsibilities to logistics managers in the interests of supply chain effectiveness. As a result, the nature of management responsibilities changed in the transformation from physical distribution management to logistics management.

Physical distribution management involved both planning and operational responsibilities for the movement and storage of finished products. Logistics management, however, has emerged as a strategic planning and coordinating approach to the movement and storage of product throughout the supply chain. To a large extent, this represents an example of what Beier (1973) describes as the "functionalism–coordination dilemma". Widening the boundaries has meant excluding the direct management of activities which are now seen as an integral part of the logistics process (Schary, 1994).

The coordination of supply chain activities within a company which is structured along functional lines is valuable, but it suffers from inherent weaknesses which undermine overall effectiveness. Coordination is necessary, not least to reconcile the often-conflicting positions of the different functional managers. Take, for example, the likelihood of different perspectives on the level of inventory held by the company. Most marketing managers would prefer high levels of inventory to minimise the possibilities of lost sales through products being unavailable. Production managers, too, will often advocate high levels of inventory, but for different reasons. Their concern is that unexpectedly high demand against slim inventory holdings will mean bringing forward production for the items in question. The consequence will be extensive rescheduling of the production master schedule – often a complex and time-consuming task.

An opposite position is likely to be taken by financial management within the company. They will be aware of the cost of holding excess inventory and will

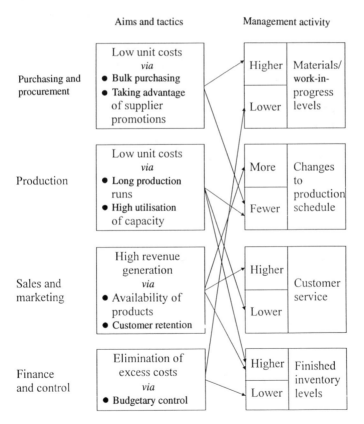

Figure 12.4 Implicit conflicts of interest in supply chain management

often prefer leaner holdings than either marketing or production, subject to the proviso that customers can still be satisfactorily served to ensure long-term profitability. The task of the logistics manager, therefore, must be to reconcile intrinsic differences between colleagues so that the best overall interests of the company are being met. Figure 12.4 gives a good indication of the potential complexity of the task and why coordination can take some time to achieve satisfactory results.

THE BPR PROMISE IN LOGISTICS

As argued above, the new logistics paradigm of flexible fulfilment means that companies will have to move more swiftly than ever if they are to remain successful and competitive. Yet logistics management through coordination is unlikely to bring about change sufficiently quickly in this demanding environment. That explains why some forward-thinking companies in logistics have been exploring new ways of serving customers more effectively. For a significant number of them, the answer has been found in business process re-engineering.

Figure 12.5 shows the model used by Hewlett-Packard for its process-led approach to management, which was formulated in the late 1980s. The model shows "order fulfilment" as one of the key processes identified by Hewlett-Packard. Order fulfilment is also represented as a process which spans the boundaries separating the different functions of the company, so its relationship to the coordination model of logistics management is clear.

However, in the Hewlett-Packard model, the management of order fulfilment does not imply coordination. Rather, the emphasis is on driving the *entire process* of order fulfilment – to make excellence in that and other

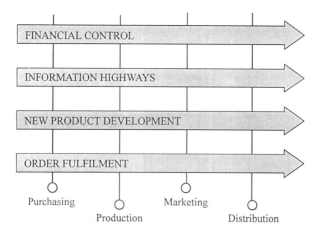

Figure 12.5   Realigning the organisation

processes the overriding management consideration, instead of trying to reconcile the entrenched interests of the individual functions.

Pioneers of BPR, such as Michael Hammer and James Champy (1993), cite examples of impressive savings from BPR, which can only be achieved through a process-led approach to management. The essence of BPR is to consider the process as a whole, rather than a sequence of tasks, and to establish the scope for new ways of working.

Since BPR represents a new approach, there is still a great deal of experimentation going on within companies and no consensus has yet emerged on which new ways of working will yield the greatest benefits. For some companies, small interdisciplinary teams, charged with the responsibility for devising new and better ways of managing processes, may be the preferred solution. Others might want to build on past experiences with matrix management structures, despite their uneven record of achievement, with internal conflicts being readily generated but proving difficult to quell.

Lack of buy-in and commitment represent two of the greatest dangers to the process-led approach. Consequently, management structures which are designed to minimise these dangers have the best potential for success. For this reason, the management structure represented in Figure 12.6 is a promising basis for BPR in logistics.

First, it secures the involvement of executive directors in the functional areas through the formation of a supply chain executive whose purpose is to oversee the order-fulfilment process. Second, it builds upon specialist knowledge from within the organisation by establishing a supply-chain support team drawn from the functions. This team then provides the basis for the third key component of the management structure, namely the logistics director, whose role it is to drive the order-fulfilment process. A further consideration is that the structure is designed to capture both top-down and bottom-up initiatives in the order-fulfilment process, which are then channelled through the logistics director.

At this point, it is important to provide an explanation of the terminology used in the management structure, particularly the distinction that is made between "logistics" and "supply chain', which is deliberate rather than accidental. When the responsibilities of the executive are decided, for example, it is vital to include external relationships with suppliers and customers. Hence the designation of supply chain executive. However, in developing strategies and plans to drive the order-fulfilment process more effectively all the knowledge, skills and techniques of logistics management must be leveraged. It follows that the individual charged with this responsibility must be a highly qualified logistics professional, so the title of logistics director is an appropriate one in the structure outlined in Figure 12.6.

Importantly, taking a process-led approach to logistics management will highlight a need for new relationships in the supply chain as a whole, especially

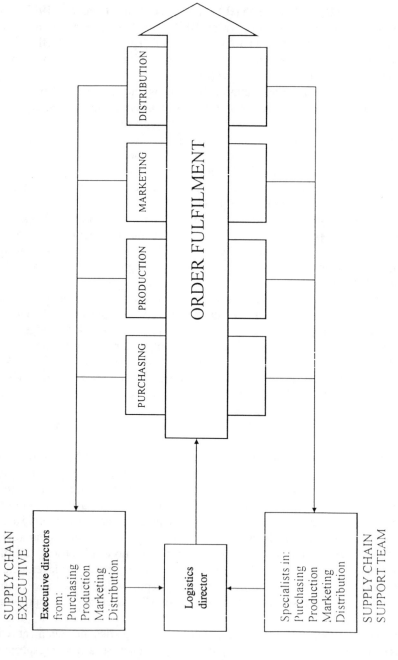

Figure 12.6 Organising for effective order fulfilment

relationships linking buyers with their suppliers. The traditional buyer–supplier relationship is summarised in Figure 12.7(a), where the sole point of contact is between the buyer and the sales manager of the supplier. This inhibits supply chain development as it creates an artificial and unnecessary division between key buyer–supplier activities. For example, the R&D department in the supplier organisation would be better informed of new product needs if it enjoyed a dialogue with the buyer's marketing department.

On a highly practical level, the distribution department is able to work more effectively if it has a more intimate understanding of its "departmental customer" within the buying organisation. This could be the production team in a manufacturing enterprise or another distribution department in the case of a retail customer which organises its own store-bound distribution from a network of retail distribution centres.

An improved way of working is illustrated in Figure 12.7(b), where there is an interface between the activities to improve the management of business processes, including those relating to the supply chain. Critically, the "buyer" and "sales manager" roles are reformulated as "supplier development manager" and "key account manager", respectively, to reflect the changed nature of the business relationship. The transaction of orders is no longer the main focus of attention, but rather a commitment to growing the business together. This is well illustrated in the motor manufacturing industry, especially among Japanese producers, and can result in innovation practices.

Nissan (UK) Ltd, for example, links many of its suppliers with its production master-schedule. This means that the supplier of exhaust systems, say, can determine how many of each type needs to be sent to the factory, and when. There is no need for Nissan to give explicit instructions on requirements and delivery any more. Similarly, payment is initiated when exhausts are fitted to cars on the assembly line, without the need for paperwork. The big advantage that these practices give to both companies – and they naturally work best in the context of using single suppliers – is in the area of overhead reduction. Supply-chain innovations have contributed significantly to the production cost advantage Nissan has enjoyed over its competitors, although the gap has closed somewhat since the early days as rivals have improved their own techniques.

Lastly, we turn to the nature of work itself, and how BPR seems likely to underpin some major transformations. For example, few would dispute the proposition that BPR will frequently result in the use of multi-skilled personnel rather than specialists in particular tasks. While this change often gives rise to understandable concerns, for all sorts of reasons, multi-skilling need not be as daunting a prospect as it might at first appear. This is because individuals can be given essential back-up by means of information systems. Some companies use what they call "knowledge highways" – giving instant information whenever and wherever it is needed – to support the work of process-oriented personnel. In this way, decision making can be informed by making all the

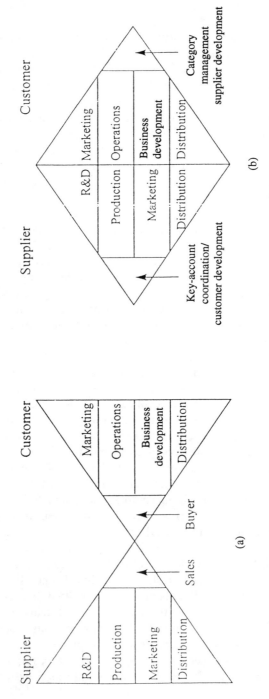

Figure 12.7 (a) Traditional buyer–supplier relationship. (b) Building stronger partnerships through multiple linkages

crucial facts available on computer networks – the infrastructure of the knowledge highways. Inbuilt expert systems can prevent people making errors by checking decisions against recognised or preferred solutions.

The way in which computers are radically changing the way we work is well captured in another quote from *The Economist* (1992). It refers to credit management at American Express, but the potential application to logistics management and the fulfilment of orders comes across very clearly.

> "The latest addition to the 'knowledge highway' is designed to help with overdue accounts. It leaves humans in charge of collection but protects them from error at every step. The system automatically pulls together all the information needed to analyse an account. Previously analysts had to make 22 enquiries on average – to computers spread across the whole of the company – each time they looked at a problem account. Now they typically make only one. The computer keeps track of which state or national laws may affect the account. It helps to generate a dunning letter. It files all the paperwork. And it automatically reminds the analyst if the account needs to be looked at again."

Also, and very importantly, there are qualities of people who will be in demand in the future as we change the way in which we work. From the same *Economist* article we read the following:

> "Thanks to such automated assistance, American Express is gradually changing the sorts of people it recruits to manage credit. Instead of hiring people good at number crunching and applying complex rules, it is turning to people who know how to deal with people."

Simply viewing logistics in terms of process will not be the only key to the future success of companies, but it could well be one of the most important ones. Some would argue that the ability to develop and implement information systems, in support of order fulfilment is just as vital. Others might place emphasis on developing buyer–supplier relationships. High levels of mutual commitment and extensive sharing of information can do much to improve logistics effectiveness as many of the motor manufacturers have demonstrated in recent years.

However, the essential point about BPR is that it reorientates the activities of companies and so can accelerate developments in performance. Crucially, BPR gives companies the potential to revolutionise existing processes, rather than make incremental improvements. This is the key to achieving breakthrough results and sustained success.

By focusing upon logistics as a process innovation can bring dramatic results as Hammer and Champy (1993) illustrated in their use of Ford as a case study. Ford employed 500 clerks in its accounts payable department to reconcile differences in three documents (purchase order, invoice and receiving documents) used in component supply to its assembly plant. By electronically distributing purchase order details and eliminating the invoice the number of data errors in the process declined significantly, allowing Ford to reduce the headcount of clerks by an impressive 75%.

CONCLUSIONS

What, then, can we conclude about the implications of BPR for logistics? First, it is clear from the experience of the BPR pioneers that order fulfilment is one of the core business processes and one which affords many opportunities for significant improvements in performance. Second, in order to achieve impressive results through BPR, it is vital to search hard for imaginative solutions. This requirement naturally has major consequences for the kinds of people employed in the field. And lastly, the very role of logistics seems set to change as a result of the application of BPR techniques. As we have seen, in the transition from physical distribution management to logistics the role changed from one of operations management to coordination and planning at the strategic level. By emphasising the management of process, BPR seems set to give a new steer to logistics management. In all probability, very few companies have yet fully grasped the implications of this important next step in the development of logistics. For those that take the initiative, the potential prize is a gain in competitive advantage by being able to serve customers better – a vital ability in an era when flexible fulfilment requirements dominate our thinking in logistics management.

Part Four

Perspectives from the "Enabling" Disciplines

Chapter 13

Enabling Functions

Colin Armistead and Philip Rowland

INTRODUCTION

This part of the book introduces the perspectives on business process re-engineering of the "enabling" functions:

- Finance
- Human resources
- Information technology

plus

- Business dynamics

which is emerging as a method with great potential for re-engineering projects. This chapter summarises some of the key messages contained in the subsequent chapters as well as highlighting issues which we have identified in the course of our research and work.

SUPPORTING, ENABLING OR DRIVING?

Traditional Place in the Organisation – "Minding the office"

What we have chosen to call the enabling functions traditionally enjoyed a place in most organisations which was well defined with a clear boundary between what "that" department did and what was the preserve of the rest of the organisation. On the whole Finance looked after budgets, accounts and oversaw investment, Human Resources or Personnel looked after hiring, firing, pay and disputes and the people in the IT department built computer systems. Of course, this is an oversimplified view but it illustrates how these functions looked after specific items pretty much in isolation even though the impact of what they did was often far-reaching. In crisis, of course, staff from these functions would get more deeply involved in day-to-day concerns at the coal face or in formulating strategy but the essential purpose of their activities was to "support" the business, i.e. make sure that everything ran as it should and that the money was accounted for.

One thing most of these support functions had in common was that the majority of people working in them were in offices, usually corporate headquarters. Not only were the functions disconnected from the business because of the demarcation in their roles but due to their geography they were usually physically remote from the business as well. These divisions were often illustrated by the near-contempt for staff in these functions shown by other staff and the endless list of jokes about boring accountants, two-faced personnel managers and nerdish computer staff were just one manifestation of this.

Improvement Initiatives and Re-engineering

Despite these jokes many of the staff in the "supporting" functions began to play significant roles in helping the other functions move their business forward. In *Finance* Professor Keith Ward's Chapter 14 highlights a number of techniques used to good effect in such a role such as zero-based budgeting, value analysis and activity-based costing. Indeed Professor Ward describes these methods as "Previous incarnations of BPR". In *Personnel* there was a shift of responsibility for employee-related concerns to the operating areas with the Personnel function, now renamed the Human Resources function in many cases, providing advice to managers rather than always dealing with issues themselves. The *Information Technology* staff closeted in locked data centres with the company computer during the 1970s saw a revolution in the 1980s with the launch of the PC and their domain is now firmly with the user.

These changes have meant an evolution from being "supporting" functions to becoming "enabling" functions as the roles of staff in these areas has increasingly become one of empowering others to perform their tasks more effectively and efficiently. In addition to this new role these functions have some specific strengths in business improvement, both in skills and power base:

- *Finance* – strong analytical training and usually holders of the cash
- *Human Resources* – strong "people" skills and usually control of training

• *Information Technology* – strong analytical skills and control over the computer systems

In addition, staff in these functions often have cross-functional perspectives which those in the operating areas do not have.

While staff in enabling functions can draw on these strengths to be powerful "enablers" there is also a "flip side" as with most strengths. All too often the enabling functions, especially IT, are seen as the "drivers" of re-engineering efforts. This is not altogether surprising. Technology really is transforming both business and the way we live, bringing whole new markets to life, or should we say "virtual" life in the case of the Internet? The problem is that technology rarely, if ever, brings any significant benefits with it but can easily cost a great deal. While IT staff may have many skills which can be usefully employed in a re-engineering effort neither they nor their enabling functions "cousins" should become "drivers" of the business. This should firmly remain a function of those in strategy and marketing.

Finance

The impact and potential of BPR on the Finance functions is outlined in Chapter 14. This combines insights into management accounting techniques with the new focus on processes and demonstrates that BPR may be used to concentrate the organisation on adding value as much as to identify opportunities for cost reduction.

From counting beans to designing the farm

The need for financial information is clear. Without it no organisation could contain its costs successfully over time, be accountable for its money or guarantee payments to its suppliers and creditors. For private sector organisations a lack of control would also mean lost profits and failure to enhance shareholder wealth, undoubtedly resulting in sale, possibly to a hostile bidder. We have outlined above the shift from this traditional "supporting role" to a more "enabling" one based on advanced techniques for identifying value which Keith Ward traces in his chapter. BPR has brought this role into even sharper perspective and while the finance function has itself undergone re-engineering projects to streamline its own workings it has also provided a vital lever to those seeking to maximise the organisation's ability to deliver value and cut out the waste.

Integration

The BPR revolution has extended the movements begun under the momentum of the Quality movement. Finance began to treat business managers as "customers" who were to be served as much as controlled, perhaps even more so. In time this integration into the business units has increased the autonomy of the local management and led to changes in the way finance professionals view their career progression. Chapter 14 extends this trend to highlight the potential for many finance functions to be integrated further, including automation as part of the process, bringing with it further challenges in the organisation of the finance function.

Personnel and Human Resources Management

Martin Hilb's chapter on the impact on human resources of BPR (Chapter 15) highlights the importance of the function not only in helping the change process but also in ensuring the organisation can be managed along process lines after re-engineering. An organisation's pay and rewards structure is a key pillar to organisational performance and it must be realigned to enable effective process working. Martin Hieb highlights an approach based on analysing performance level, time and value added to determine pay for performance and promotion for ability. He urges organisations to aim not to be "lean and mean" but to be "lean and happy", at least as far as its people are concerned. We have observed some, albeit rare, organisations where indeed this "lean and happy" air prevails contributing to a virtuous circle of performance and fulfilment.

Laying the foundations for the future

Many of the "interventions" which the Human Resources department is required to make are to ensure that the future world of process working will be supported by the underpinning "people" mechanisms of the organisation. Recruitment, training, career development, pay and rewards and other terms and conditions can undermine process-oriented organisations by fostering different motivations and behaviours as well as failing to provide the necessary skills and experience.

During the re-engineering project the Human Resources or Personnel function must not only facilitate the change by dealing with people issues, managing union discussions and overseeing communications but must also plan the changes which will effectively become the foundations for the future working of the company.

Information Technology/Information Systems

In Chapter 16 Chris Edwards and Joe Peppard begin by tracing the roots of the term "Business Process Re-engineering" in the search for more effective use of IT. The impact of BPR not just on the corporation but also on the approach to IT planning and delivery is then highlighted, and the importance of IT to many initiatives is re-emphasised. A critical area of importance for managers which the authors highlight is the rise of processes onto the top of management's agenda. It is a clear identification of those processes by which the strategy of the company will be delivered which should drive IT strategy planning. The authors point out other influences on IT planning, including the progress of the IT industry as a whole.

The seeds of failure

Our own work in IT gives this chapter additional resonance. It was in failure that the IT believers found their salvation. It was the disappointments of IT that gave birth to BPR and it is the BPR methodology which is now providing IT with the opportunity to deliver its true promise. Gone are the old problems of "automating the cow paths" (Hammer, 1990) leading to little real benefit. Instead organisations are thinking about what they want to achieve and thinking about how to do it in the 1990s. Starting from this point, many are finding that while IT may be a vital element to their process it may not in fact be the most critical. We would always advocate that the only means to gain real benefits is by improving and aligning different aspects of the organisation including, but not exclusively, IT.

Key to competition in the "cyberworld"

While failure may have spurred the BPR revolution and IT's new-found respectability at the corporate dinner table the growing penetration of IT into the home has also meant IT cannot be ignored by any. IT has traditionally been employed to make the conduct of traditional businesses more efficient or to deliver traditional products in a non-traditional way. With home PC sales overtaking sales to business in many markets and the likes of Microsoft and IBM increasingly targeting consumers, this picture is changing fast. New products and services are being developed for "virtual" markets such as the World Wide Web and the Internet and one only has to look at the number of adverts carrying electronic addresses to realise that a whole new way of trading has come of age in the last few years. The growth of this "cyberworld" means IT increasingly holds the key to competition both behind the scenes and in "connecting" with the consumer.

Business Dynamics

An exciting technique which is gaining increasing support as a powerful tool for re-engineering is Business Dynamics, covered by Martin Davies in Chapter 17. The main premise of this tool is that you must take a holistic perspective of an organisation in order to understand how to effect lasting and positive change.

Complex dominoes

The sight of a long line of dominoes falling one by one has long been used as an analogy to describe "knock-on" impacts of a particular action. While the analogy is not a particularly good one as it does not describe a dynamic system, it does serve to highlight one of the major problems in redesigning the organisation without carefully considering the full effects of the change. In business dynamics a model is created which defines how the organisation as a system functions as a dynamic entity. Cause and effect can be identified and the ways different aspects of an organisation support others can be highlighted.

Informing decisions and process design

A clear benefit of using the business dynamics approach is a better understanding of the workings of the company and a deeper appreciation of some of the consequences arising from particular management decisions. Examples of applications in a drinks and a telecommunications company serve to illustrate the impact it could have. Chapter 17 also provides us with a perspective on some barriers to the use of the approach on a wide basis, the most important of which is the ease of use of the technique. We concur and while experienced proponents of the approach such as Martin Davies can add a hitherto "invisible" but vital perspective on situations and BPR projects, until the approach can be effectively applied by staff after a minimal training period it will remain the preserve of the select few. Advances in computer tools are helping with this problem and it may not be long before this barrier to wider adoption is considerably lowered.

QUESTIONS TO BEAR IN MIND WHEN READING THIS PART

1. To what extent is the role of the enabling functions undergoing fundamental change as a result of process re-engineering and the shift to managing business processes?
2. How important is the participation of the enabling functions in a process re-engineering initiative?
3. What barriers exist to using business dynamics on a wide scale to improve organisational understanding and how could these be overcome?

Chapter 14

BPR – The Impact on and Potential Role for the Finance Function

Keith Ward

WHAT WILL YOU FIND IN THIS CHAPTER?

BPR is about improving added value within processes. In this financial information places a prominent place. In the chapter you will find:

- The need for financial information in the context of changing industry structures
- A discussion of BPR in relationship to other performance improvement approaches including value analysis and zero-based budgeting and activity-based costing
- Approaches to financial measurement for cross-functional processes
- Implications for changing the organisational structure of the financial expertise within organisations

OVERVIEW

This chapter deals with the finance function's role within the BPR process. However it also challenges the common view of BPR as "a cost-cutting and restructuring technique" (*Financial Times*, 5 December 1994). If BPR is used properly it can enable organisations to focus their attention on those business processes which create most added value. However, if this is to be achieved, decision makers require very specific, tailored financial information. Providing such tailored financial information represents a significant potential role for the finance function. Consequently this idea of BPR with an added-value focus is the main thrust of the second part of the chapter.

The first part of the chapter deals mainly with the impact on the finance area of BPR initiatives. This highlights financial information as a core enabling support function within an organisation. A major role for finance is, therefore, to translate the existing financial information into the decision-making support required for the fundamental changes within the organisation which are often needed by BPR. A subsequent role is then to control these new cross-functional processes in order to ensure that the potential financial benefits, which were used to justify the BPR exercise, are actually achieved.

BPR is also compared with previous attempts at similar initiatives (e.g. value engineering, zero-base budgeting, activity-based costing, and value chain analysis). The key difference of BPR from these earlier management tools is the emphasis on cross-functional business processes. This, of course, represents a substantial challenge to finance and accounting departments as most management accounting systems were originally designed to provide functionally based analyses. Even the newer, more strategically focused, accounting systems tend to concentrate on product and/or customer profitability analyses.

INTRODUCTION

BPR is, of course, normally associated with industries which are undergoing substantial changes and is often regarded as the catalyst behind, or prime agent leading to, these changes. However, many industries are being dramatically reshaped in ways which would have occurred even without the invention and application of BPR. It is important to understand these major changes and the types of corporate restructurings that can and do result. They can highlight particular ways in which BPR initiatives may add even greater value than normal when apparently adverse necessity is turned to competitive advantage. In some cases, proper analysis of the reasons behind the apparently dramatic changes may indicate that BPR is not an appropriate response.

It can be argued that in any competitive environment, current sources of competitive advantage will, over time, inevitably become essential factors for entry to, and survival within, the industry. An increasingly important role for management accounting systems is to assist the business in identifying any decline in the value of its existing competitive advantages, so that it can reinvest some of its current high profits in developing appropriate replacements. Thus a pharmaceutical company, such as Glaxo, may create a very strong competitive advantage through the development of a new, patented drug, such as Zantac. During the period of the patent, the company has the opportunity to earn a superprofit on this product, but the patent period is finite and its competitors will all be ready to launch their own versions of the product immediately on its expiry. A key strategic issue for the company is therefore to decide how it replaces this competitive advantage in due course (e.g. by reinvesting in R&D to try to discover more patentable drugs, by acquiring other companies' R&D, by branding its existing product and changing its channel of distribution to over the counter so that this branding becomes more directly relevant to the end user), as shown in Figure 14.1. The good news is that the company should be planning for the disappearance of or significant reduction in its existing competitive advantage over a reasonably well-defined period in a relatively stable environment.

By contrast, some industries are being reshaped due to very rapid, and often unforeseen, changes in the prevailing competitive environment which may be caused by significant movements in the methods or degree of competition within the industry. Thus, quite suddenly, what had previously been a source of benefit and competitive advantage becomes a significant millstone around the organisation's neck, threatening to drag down and destroy the whole business unless dramatic changes are rapidly made. The advent of telephone banking, combined with the already developed infrastructure of automated teller machines (the "hole-in-the-wall" banking machines), threatens to achieve this for those banks with well-developed national networks of retail bank branches. This type of major competitive change can create opportunities for BPR initiatives such as are resulting from several banks actively seeking new uses for their existing retail branches (e.g. turning them into more sales-generating outlets rather than for servicing normal routine banking transactions).

In many cases these original sources of competitive advantage, which previously represented an entry barrier to new competitors, now act as an exit barrier, stopping these businesses from leaving either the industry in total or this particular segment (the retail banks face a very large potential loss if they tried to close down their entire branch network at a stroke) (see Figure 14.2).

Industries subject to dramatic changes in their competitive environment have tended to view BPR as a possible source of salvation, whereas many industries in more stable environments have yet to attempt re-engineering on a significant scale. This appears to be due to the substantial trauma caused by, and effort required for, BPR, so that organisations undertake BPR in reaction to the adverse change in their environment. A more positive way of using BPR would be proactively in advance of predicted changes in the competitive environment; thus potentially creating a competitive advantage from the BPR process. This obviously requires the organisation to be able to predict, far enough in advance, the forthcoming significant changes in its competitive environment.

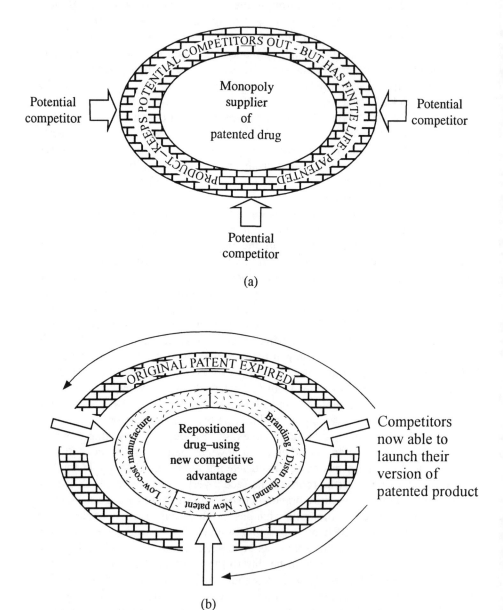

Figure 14.1 Replacing an existing competitive advantage. Competitive position (a) during the life of the patent and (b) after the expiry of the original patent

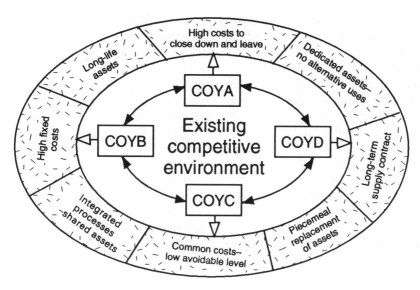

Figure 14.2 Exit barriers

However, an even more dramatic change, which is occurring in many industries, should be predictable if businesses within the industry knew what indicators to look for. As industries move from rapid growth towards the maturity stage of development they go through an almost inevitable phase which can best be described as "vertical disintegration". This results in an accelerating trend towards much more focused businesses within the industry.

Almost inevitably, the ground-breaking companies starting a new industry have to be highly vertically integrated as external suppliers of many essential components and services do not yet exist. Thus it may not be from any clearly defined strategic intent that these companies find themselves involved in such wide-ranging activities; they simply have to be involved in order to produce their product and deliver it to their customers. This type of analysis can be applied to many industries, including oil, cars and computers.

A classic example of such a vertically integrated strategy is the original Ford plant at Baton Rouge in the USA where the pig-iron was delivered at one end and the finished Ford model emerged at the other end. Almost the only components not produced on site were the tyres, but no doubt if the weather in Michigan had been more conducive to rubber plantations this would have been seriously considered as well.

No major car company would consider building such a vertically integrated plant today, as the trend is dramatically reversed, with the focus on outsourcing many components, dedicated assembly plants and even rebadging somebody else's product. Similar illustrations, of course, abound within the oil and computer industries and in many others. Such trends are neither good nor bad, they are simply inevitable and the strategies of businesses within such industries must use these changes positively, rather than attempting to fight against them.

This "vertical disintegration" occurs as the industry grows and its requirements for goods and services become well known by other potential suppliers, as is shown in Figure 14.3. Also as the total demand from the companies within the industry develops, potential economies of scale become attainable for more specialised suppliers, which can target more than one industry player as potential customers.

These more focused businesses may grow out of companies originally involved in the industry or they may move into this specific segment of the industry value chain once the potential opportunity has been identified. As specialists, these suppliers can invest in research and development in order to improve the particular goods or services which they deliver, so that the original players in the industry should benefit by receiving better products at potentially lower costs.

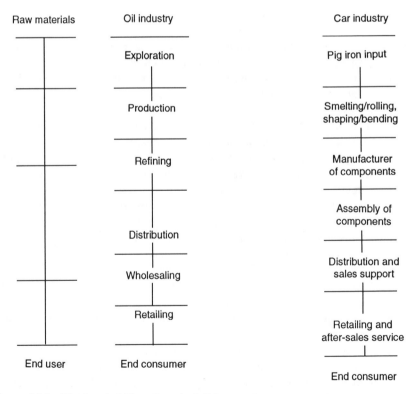

Figure 14.3 The inevitability of vertical disintegration

However, the impact on the future strategy of these originally vertically integrated companies can be dramatic, as it forces them to identify which part of the total industry value chain actually produces their profit. This is a classic illustration of the Pareto effect as, for most companies, it appears to be true that 80% of their profitability is generated by 20% of the things they do. The critical question is obviously, "which 20%?" If this is not established prior to the "vertical disintegration" phase, the company may find that it is left with those areas which add cost, rather than value. Quite clearly a financially focused added value approach to BPR can be of immense value to businesses facing this type of problem, and this is considered later in the chapter. Such industries can, therefore, implement BPR in a very proactive way if they deliberately focus on those processes where they can maintain a competitive advantage and, hence, add most value.

THE CRITICAL NEED FOR FINANCIAL INFORMATION

One of the key statements supporting the implementation of BPR is that traditional functionally based corporations were most suited for a mass market, which was happy to accept a standardised product (whether good or service), which these volume-focused companies were most capable of delivering. Cost reductions were achieved through economies of scale which led to internal segmentation and concentration of roles and functions. Thus individual roles were broken down into smaller and smaller discrete elements in attempts to increase the efficiency with which each function was carried out. This process was often accelerated through automation and computerisation.

An unsurprising consequence of this development was that management accounting systems concentrated on efficiency measures for these increasingly discrete sub-divisions of the organisation. Thus most financial performance measures reflect the relative efficiency of a particular area rather than the effectiveness of the overall organisation or of the key processes within the organisation.

A significant challenge for those organisations implementing BPR is therefore to devise more appropriate financial performance measures, which do reflect the contribution made by the business process. The concentration on functionally based financial information has also meant that many management accounting systems cannot provide the financial information which is required to enable a proper financial evaluation of the proposed BPR exercise to be carried out. By definition, the financial evaluation is being done to support the business decision and hence forward-looking, decision-relevant future cash flow information is required from the finance department. Unfortunately, many management accounting systems are designed to provide primarily historical reconciliations and explanations of what has happened, rather than supporting information for forthcoming strategic decisions.

Even more importantly, as previously stated, most of these analytical systems were focused on the discrete sub-divisions within each functional area of the organisation. As a result it is very difficult to pull together the cross-functional financial information which is required for BPR decisions. These problems can mean that quite major re-engineering and restructuring decisions are being taken without any comprehensive, valid financial evaluation; i.e. the decision is taken as a sort of act of faith, "we have to do it!" A further challenge for finance therefore is to ensure that all BPR initiatives are themselves properly financially justified, and this financial justification must include the often considerable costs involved in the BPR evaluation and implementation process.

BPR WITHIN THE FINANCE FUNCTION

The sub-dividing of the required tasks into their smallest components was particularly well applied within the finance function itself in many organisations. Thus individual accounting staff members, or small groups, were concentrated on incredibly specific and limited clerical tasks in order to improve their "efficiency"; the resulting danger being that nobody felt any responsibility for the effectiveness of the total accounting process or considered its contribution to the value added of the overall organisation. Many accounting departments could be described as being very efficient, while also being very ineffective.

The finance function has therefore been a productive area for the application of BPR, because this has forced organisations to question first, why certain functions are carried out at all and, second, why they are done in this way. However, some of the classic examples of BPR also highlight why a cross-functional approach to the total process is required. A good example of this is the often-cited accounts payable function within any business. The traditional accounting view of accounts payable is that it involves receiving, from suppliers, invoices which require detailed validation before they can be approved for payment. This payment is then made in accordance with the agreed and approved payment terms. For physical goods, this would historically have involved matching together the order, the delivery note and the invoice, checking the price details etc.; all the documentation being passed to the appropriate department for resolution in the event of queries. The accounts payable response to any such query was normally simply to delay the payment until the query was resolved by the other functional area. The supporting documents would often be sent for authorisation to the department responsible and this whole set would then subsequently be used as supporting evidence for the signatory of the cheque or bank transfer. In other words, this type of accounts payable department's function is to tie together and process pieces of paper; this is inevitable because they do not normally have the information, knowledge, expertise or authority to make any actual decisions regarding payments to outside suppliers.

Such a function represents a substantial potential cost-saving opportunity and advances in information technology have enabled the target of "peopleless payables" (i.e. no people in the accounts payable area) to be set by some organisations. Achieving such an apparently aggressive target is actually quite easy if it is viewed exclusively from the functional perspective of the accounts payable department. This department simply stops carrying out its reconciling, progressing, processing and facilitating tasks. This would mean, in the absence of any system changes, that some, at least, of these tasks would have to be carried out in the other departments within the organisation. In many so-called BPR or restructuring exercises, this is in fact what has happened. Many of the functions do still need to be carried out, but they can be performed more effectively by the area with the expertise and authority to make and implement decisions at the same time. Alternatively, more mechanistic functions can be automated; such as the matching together of documents. If fully automated, of course, the physical documents are no longer required as the electronic records can be compared.

A critical element in this type of restructuring exercise is ensuring that the costs incurred in all the other areas of the business are taken into account when the financial justification is computed. Many companies have made great claims for the savings generated from re-engineering their accounts payable functions (and similarly for the accounts receivable areas), but in several cases the partially offsetting increases in workload in other areas of the business have been excluded from the financial analysis. The real financial savings can, of course, still be significant but these are normally derived by: doing without some elements of the original process, utilising other parts more effectively (by relocating the work to the area with the authority to make decisions in order to avoid duplication, transfer costs and unnecessary delays); and using modern information technology to carry out the remaining process more efficiently.

Indeed, information technology is often described as the key enabler of BPR and it is true that many innovative solutions use the power of modern IT. However, if IT is a modern key enabler, the finance function should be viewed as an original *core enabler* of BPR due to its essential involvement in the financial justification of the whole investment in re-engineering key business processes. Using these two enablers in tandem enables the tremendous potential benefits of BPR to be realised by the organisation, but this also requires an emphasis on the value-adding potential of the business processes, rather than on merely reducing their costs.

BPR WITH AN ADDED-VALUE FOCUS

Most definitions of BPR do concentrate on added value rather than just cost reductions; e.g. the definition being used for this book includes "BPR is an approach to achieving radical improvements in performance by using resources in ways which maximise value added activities and minimise activities which add only cost". However, in practical terms the main focus of many BPR projects has been to achieve significant cost reductions, and many commentators describe BPR as a cost-reducing mechanism. One potential reason for this is that it is much easier to measure cost savings than it is to measure improvements in added value. Yet, as the main economic and competitive benefits of BPR come from this focus on added-value processes, it is clearly important that the finance function does attempt to measure these benefits.

This really requires a well-structured approach to BPR within any organisation. Organisations must focus on business processes and on those business processes which add value. This should not result in attempts to break down these processes from an internal efficiency perspective. As is well established, a business process is a collection of activities that takes one or more kinds of input and produces an output that is of value to the customer. Hence the added value of any process should be considered from the customer's point of view. The best form of customer is external to the organisation as the value measure is probably more objective (e.g. the price), but any internal process must result in measurable outputs for identifiable customers, which are outside the areas of the organisation performing the process.

A critical element of the overall analysis and classification of an organisation's business processes is, therefore, the financial analysis of each separately identified process. The total value added of the business is reconciled to the value added by each process so that the key contributors are highlighted; i.e. the sources of sustainable competitive advantage, which can generate superprofits, are clearly identified. This analysis then enables business processes to be placed in one of three basic categories, and each category is then treated in a specific way. The three categories are critical added value processes, non-critical processes which are also not essential to the overall objectives of the organisation, and those non value-adding processes which are essential and necessary.

Critical Added-Value Processes

These processes generate the superprofits of the organisation and are the sources of sustainable competitive advantage. Hence they must be kept in-house and considered as the key assets of the business. Outsourcing of this category of business process would give away the competitive advantage, as many businesses have discovered to their cost. Fortunately, for most organisations, this category represents only a small proportion of their total business processes. The subsequent financial strategy for these added-value processes is the same as for any asset; a financially based decision should be taken as to whether it is worth while to invest more funds in an attempt to increase the value of the asset, whether a maintenance level of expenditure is justified, or whether the asset should be allowed to decline as it is coming towards the end of its useful economic life. Clearly, these critical strategic decisions should be based on appropriately tailored financial information and providing such decision support analyses represents an important future role for the finance function.

Non-Critical, Non-essential Processes

These processes should be discontinued as painlessly as possible by re-engineering the total organisation so that it can happily live without them. A common criticism of restructuring initiatives is that many processes are made more efficient rather than being eliminated altogether. This is why this category of process is considered before those that are essential.

Non-value-adding, but Essential Processes

These processes must be carried out but they tend to add cost rather than value. The obvious strategy is therefore to minimise the cost incurred in delivering the appropriate level of output from the process. A key element in this analysis is the specification of the appropriate level of output, as this will clearly affect the level of cost. Normally this specification needs to be established in the context of the overall strategic thrust of the business and its goals and objectives, and this will be influenced by the impact of this particular process on the critical added-value processes. One potential alternative for these essential processes is outsourcing, if outside suppliers can provide the required level of inputs at a lower cost. It is again important that the finance function is able to provide the required financial comparison on the correct basis, i.e. the avoidable costs which will be saved if an outside supplier is used.

However, there are subtly different ways in outsourcing this category of business process. The normal logic is simply to look for independent outside suppliers to provide lower-cost, equivalent goods and services. A potential problem is that their prices will include their risk-adjusted required level of profits; there is no other reason for them to want to provide the required products. If the organisation tries to transfer the business process up or down the value chain, a more attractive solution may be achieved. Many businesses have established strategies which seek to increase their share of their industry activity. If this involves increasing the share of the total costs incurred in the total supply chain, this can be counterproductive. The organisation should, of course, be trying to increase its relative share of the total added value generated by the industry, as is shown in Figure 14.4. In many cases, this can actually be achieved through transferring tasks, functions and even entire processes to either suppliers or customers.

There are a number of possible reasons for such a transfer increasing the value added by the business. First, the supplier or customer may simply be more efficient at this process and part of the cost saving can be obtained by the transferor through negotiation on price. Second, the business process itself may be broken into two illogical sub-processes (one being carried out, at present, by each party). Thus, combining the process under the control of one organisation may create significant cost savings to the mutual benefit of the organisations

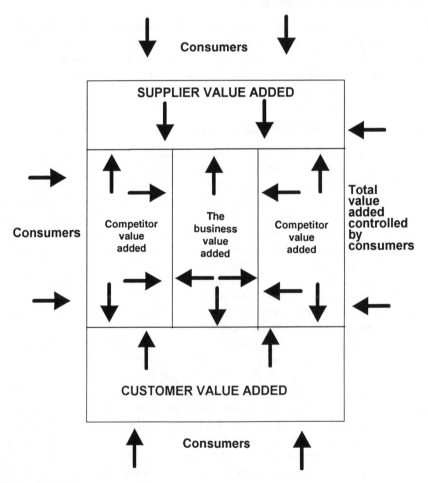

Figure 14.4 The zero sum game

involved. Third, although there may be no cost differences between the two organisations, the price charged may include a lower required return from this process due to a different (in this case, lower) perception of the risk involved. Fourth, the supplier or customer may be willing to charge a price which is less than the full costs incurred because they see some added value from providing this good or service to the organisation. They may see it as cementing a long-term relationship and, as long as the overall relationship produces at least an adequate return, they are prepared to invest in the relationship as in any other asset of their business.

These potential outsourcing alternatives for non-value-adding but essential processes mean that the business should continue to carry out these processes only if there is a sound economic justification for doing so. Supporting these evaluations with objective financial information is therefore a critical role for finance.

Also the BPR analysis should have highlighted several areas within the business where resources should be increased and others where resources can be decreased or withdrawn entirely. These reallocation decisions and their relative sequencing require close involvement of the finance function, and are critical to the overall success of BPR.

PREVIOUS INCARNATIONS OF BPR

Much of this required financial analysis and decision support information is not specific to BPR as it is needed for any major strategic initiative within an organisation. Indeed, it is also often argued that BPR is not really new but is simply a repackaging of existing ideas and concepts. Certainly, people with more than a few years' practical experience in financial management will have seen apparently similar ideas under different titles.

An early related concept was value analysis or value engineering. Its objective was to force businesses to consider whether each incremental level of cost really added more value than its cost. Most of its applications tended to be in the direct product-related area and it was not really used as a cross-functional analytical tool. Thus classic examples of value analysis would be with regard to the packaging of specific products, where each incremental cost element would have to be justified from the point of view of either protecting the product or increasing the customer's propensity to buy it.

A more generally used financially driven concept is zero base budgeting. This is a planning tool which refuses to allow areas of the organisation to justify their expenditure plans for the next planning period by reference to what they spent this period. Instead each area is forced to put forward what resources they would need if they were starting from scratch, i.e. with no existing resources or constraints. This process is very time consuming and some organisations now carry it out on a rolling basis as part of their annual planning cycle; i.e. each area of the business will produce a zero base budget but only once every 5 years or so. Another problem in practice is that the zero base budget proposal may require a drastic change in the way the operations are conducted in future (e.g. move from a field sales force to an office-based telesales operation), if the proposed benefits are to be achieved. It is by no means unknown for the budget to be accepted but with implementation to be made from existing resources (e.g. skill base, etc.); this almost always ends in disaster.

In this respect, zero base budgeting is very similar to BPR; if a BPR analysis comes up with fundamental changes in major business processes, the underlying changes must be implemented if the benefits are to be attained. However, most zero base budgeting exercises were done within existing functions or sub-divisions of the business. In other words, the concept is not used to focus on the cross-functional business processes which are so critical to BPR.

The next development in the management accounting area does try to avoid being constrained by existing artificial divisions and groupings within the organisation. Activity-based costing focuses on the cost drivers within a business and tries to associate (the more technical terms of allocation and absorption unfortunately now have qualitative, almost political, associations themselves) all the costs incurred with their true cost driver. A cost driver is the fundamental reason for the cost being incurred by the organisation, and hence may not be located in the same functional area of the business where the expenditure actually takes place (e.g. the cost driver for the expenditure on producing sales invoices is the number of sales invoices generated by the sales function, but the cost may be incurred within the accounts department). A critical aspect of activity-based costing is therefore the identification of a limited number of key cost drivers, which can be used to explain, control and forecast the main cost movements in the future.

In principle, this concept can be used to get quite close to many aspects of BPR as it is not functionally based. In practice, many activity-based costing systems are used as cost-apportionment systems (i.e. spreading the actual costs across the different areas of the business), but using different bases of apportionment. However, it is now generally agreed that activity-based costing and management (ABCM) represents a fundamentally different approach, which is based around understanding the business and not mechanistically calculating product costings. Indeed very recent developments in ABCM are now referring almost interchangeably to activities and processes. Perhaps the next step is to create Process Based Cost Management.

A related concept also goes a long way towards giving an economic or financial perspective to the thrust of BPR. Value chain analysis builds on the concept of value-added elements and cost-increasing elements in the total value chain of an industry or an organisation. The most far-reaching and innovative application of value chain analysis is achieved by applying it across the whole of the industry, so that supplier and customer value chains are included in the analysis. (This can be compared to the value-added analysis considered earlier and illustrated in Figure 14.4.) Michael Porter (1985) also broke down the value chain within the organisation into different types of direct process and support activities. The application of financial analysis to this framework does start to provide a process-orientated view of value added.

Thus BPR is not altogether new from a financial perspective but it draws together and refocuses the previous incarnations by emphasising the business process over and above the functional areas or other existing organisational structures.

ORGANISATIONAL IMPLICATIONS FOR THE FINANCE FUNCTION

The reorientation of organisations around their key business processes and the consequent internal emphasis on the major added-value processes have significant implications for the future organisational structures of finance departments, and other support areas. Traditionally, the finance and accounting functions for the whole organisation have been grouped together to improve the efficiency with which the required tasks are carried out. Not only did this allow economies of scale to be achieved but it also made career development for finance managers much easier as they tended to progress their careers within this relatively centralised functionally based organisation.

Even, when for logistical reasons, these financial managers are physically located within other functional areas of the business (such as where cost accountants are physically based in the operating areas of the business, e.g. the factory), the main reporting line is to the finance department. (The reporting relationships are often described as being a hard/solid line back to the finance department, with a dotted line responsibility to the area for which support/advice is being supplied. Some finance departments, particularly in those organisations now claiming to be "customer focused", do now explicitly view themselves as suppliers of services with their customers being the other areas of the business.) In the world of the re-engineered process-led organisation, this will need to change.

Many re-engineered business processes include, as an integrated sub-process, the essential financial recording of the details of activities. With the development of financial databases, these details are recorded only once and can then be accessed for any subsequent financial analysis and control activities. However, even these analytical activities are increasingly being carried out as an on-line part of the business process, as are the authorisation elements of the financial control process (authorising transactions retrospectively is not a financial control process!). Thus it becomes clear that in future, the finance and accounting function may largely be dispersed across and within the organisation. In many cases it will be impossible (particularly for clerical input activities) to identify particular individuals as having predominantly financially oriented jobs. Thus the new organisation structure for the finance function may develop as shown diagrammatically in Figure 14.5.

Even if the structural change is not this dramatic, there are clearly significant implications for the training requirements and career development programmes

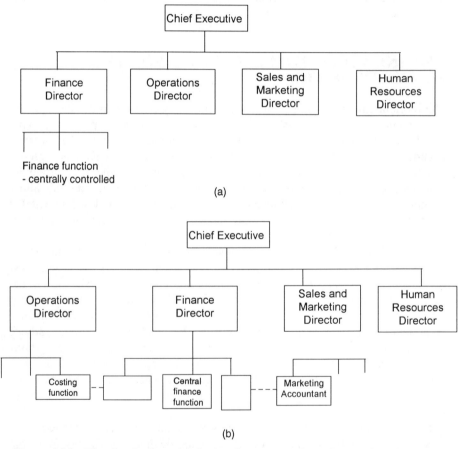

Figure 14.5 The developing organisational structure of the finance function. (a) A traditional functionally based organisation. (b) Devolving finance organisational structures. (c) (facing page) A fully devolved finance function in a customer-focused organisation. The rest of the finance and accounting function is fully integrated within the business processes of the organisation

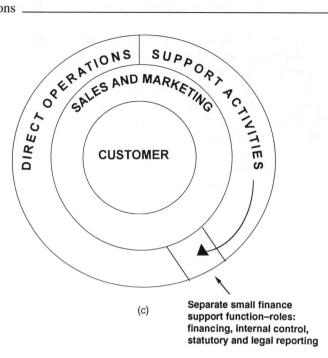

(c)

Separate small finance support function–roles: financing, internal control, statutory and legal reporting

Figure 14.5 *Continued*

of the financial managers (calling them accountants would be particularly inappropriate) in the re-engineered organisation.

CONCLUSIONS

The challenges facing finance and accounting areas in those organisations considering or implementing BPR are considerable. Traditional management accounting systems are focused on functionally oriented measures of efficiency; what are now required are process-based measures of effectiveness. Without such a reorientation it is very difficult for accounting departments to provide the required financial information (i.e. the forward-looking forecasts of changes in cash flows resulting from the revisions to business processes which are being considered) needed to support these substantial strategic business decisions.

Another challenge relates to the application of BPR within the finance area itself, because many redesigned processes integrate the essential financial recording and analysis functions within the normal operation of the business process. Thus the impact of BPR on the finance area itself can be quite dramatic and the management accounting area of the future may largely be dispersed across the organisation. This requires a major rethink in terms of organisational structures, career-development programmes, and required skills for the finance professionals of these future re-engineered businesses.

The most significant resulting challenge facing finance, however, relates to the focusing of businesses on those processes which generate added value. Providing the financial information required to support such fundamental decisions and then controlling the ensuing range of internal and external processes represents a demand for very specifically tailored management accounting systems. At present, most companies are a long way away from such financial information systems.

Chapter 15

BPR: A Human Resources Management Perspective

Martin Hilb

WHAT WILL YOU FIND IN THIS CHAPTER?

It is no secret that the failure of many change initiatives are caused by the failure to address people issues satisfactorily. BPR is no different in this regard. This chapter considers the role of HRM within the BPR process. In the chapter you will find:

- The relationship between HRM and other aspects of BPR
- An approach to BPR and HRM issues
- The areas which HRM must target for successful implementation of BPR including selection, development, appraisal and rewards

INTRODUCTION

Hammer and Champy (1993) describe BPR as a periodic fundamental rethinking and radical redesign of business processes to achieve dramatic improvements in critical contemporary measures of performance, such as cost, quality, service and speed. However, the problem seems to be that re-engineering projects often fail. The reasons for this lack of success seems to be associated with the human factor not being fully considered or understood (Development Dimension International and Scherer & Associates, 1994).

Does this mean that an organisational renewal can only occur either by evolution, i.e. by continuous improvements, or by revolution, i.e. by re-engineering? The answer to quote Scott Fitzgerald is perhaps captured in "The best of a first rate intelligence is the ability to hold two opposing ideas in mind and still hold the ability to function". We might think about organisations in terms of *lean* or *fat* describing their use of resources and *happy* or *mean* describing their cultural view. In times of undersupply and limited competition *fat and happy* organisations may have existed. In more difficult times the tendency was to switch to *lean and mean* organisations. These may have produced the efficiency gains which are often associated with value analysis and downsizing but did not address the cultural state of the people in the organisation. In HRM terms we are perhaps looking more to create organis-ations which are *lean and happy*.

Hsieh (1992) has concluded that "effective renewal requires a contribution of one-time, step-function changes together with a constant ongoing process of evolutionary reconditioning, which enhances learning and helps people to be ready for the next one-time change".

The effect of BPR on an organisation may be very different from previous changes introduced as a result of other initiative such as TQM in the extent of the difference which might be expected. The expectations relating to people and

Table 15.1 Dimensions of change affecting HRM

From	To
Added value to the boss	Added value to the customers, shareholders, human resources and environment
Complex structures	Simple processes
Hierarchy	Network
Centralist tower organisations	Federalist camp organisation of tents
Narrow span of control	Broad span of trust
Supervisor	"COMOACH" (coach + moderator + champion)
Group of scorekeepers	Team of humanistic entrepreneurs
Team of stars at the top	Top star team with cool heads, warm hearts and active hands
Simple specialised jobs	Complex team tasks
Efficiency (activity)	Effectiveness (result)
Top down *or* bottom up *or* lateral	Both top-down *and* bottom-up *and* lateral

the structure of the organisation proposed by Hammer (1994) provides a context for considering the contribution from HRM to the BPR debate, (Table 15.1). It corresponds with Orgland's (1994) argument "... that re-engineering does not represent a breakthrough in management thinking. It is rather a collection of previously existing (but seldom implemented) business concepts and ideas that have been combined in a way that yields a return that is greater than the sum of its parts."

WHAT CAN HRM CONTRIBUTE?

Such changes within an organisation clearly require exemplary Leadership Principles. These are illustrated in the LEGO company by the eleven Paradoxes of Leadership that hang on the wall of every manager's office (Box 15.1).

Human resource management can contribute to core business process re-engineering. We present below a four phase programme we have used in companies to "redirect the ship':

- Phase 1: Diagnosis of the current state
- Phase 2: Redesign of the future state
- Phase 3: Identification of barriers
- Phase 4: Roll-out actions

The company's development can be influenced by these four phases. We see the stages as processing in cyclical form from one to another and recurring.

Box 15.1   Lego's Paradoxes of Leadership (Poulsen, 1993)

- To be able to build a close relationship with one's staff ... and to keep a suitable distance
- To be able to lead ... and to hold oneself in the background
- To trust one's staff ... and to keep an eye on what is happening
- To be tolerant ... and to know how you want things to function
- To keep the goals of one's own department in mind ... and at the same time to be loyal to the whole firm
- To do a good job of planning your own time ... and to be flexible with your schedule
- To freely express your own views ... and to be diplomatic
- To be a visionary ... and to keep one's feet on the ground
- To try to win consensus ... and to be able to cut through
- To be dynamic ... and to be reflective
- To be sure of yourself ... and to be humble

Hence the omission of one phase can drastically influence the company's development. An extreme example, if one phase is neglected, is that there may be no development at all. The four phases can be seen (Figure 15.1) as a move from a disaggregated functionally based organisation which in the worse case has no strategic vision and is characterised by teams of functional specialists who distrust one another. The HRM issues of employee selection and their development is ignored. Performance appraisal is purely on an individual basis which is isolated from corporate goals and bears no relationship to performance.

The future state presents the view of cohesion between vision, leadership and business processes which are supported by the HRM "tents" of selection, personal development, appraisal, reward and human resource development which are targeted to support the achievement of the vision. So what would we expect to see in each of the four stages which are affected by HRM?

Phase I: Diagnosis of the Current State

The diagnosis of the current state should identify the strengths and weaknesses of the present leading team, of the company's strategy, processes, structure and culture as well as of the human resource management especially the quality of selection, appraisal, reward and human resource development. We use a "Corporate Personality Profile Questionnaire" to diagnose the current state (Figure 15.2). Clearly, we are taking the view of matching the HRM development of employees to the mission and strategy and are seeking to achieve structural changes which are compatible with HRM developments.

Phase II: Redesign of the Future State

The future state is illustrated on the right-hand side of Figure 15.1. The company's holistic vision is the basis on which all other leadership and HRM components have to be targeted:

- Structure follows process
- Process follows culture
- Culture follows vision
- Vision follows the star team at the top.

A star team at the top, a holistic vision, a culture of trust, simple processes and federalist structures are the basis of the strategic orientation and integration of the process of selecting, appraising, rewarding and developing intrapreneurs who behave as if the company is their own.

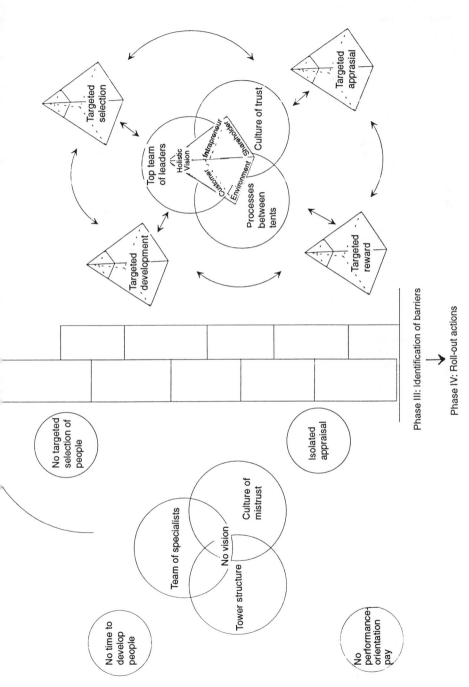

Figure 15.1 Core business process re-engineering: a human resource management perspective

Please indicate how you view the following dimensions of your company as a whole.
Please cross accordingly.

Dimensions Non-existent (=1)	1	2	3	4	5	Highly developed (=5)
1. Mission/strategy						
(1.1) Energy for change (innovation)						
(1.2) Soundly based risk taking						
(1.3) Quality standards						
(1.4) Profit orientation (including cost consciousness)						
(1.5) Customer orientation						
(1.6) Long-term strategic thinking						
(1.7) People orientation						
(1.8) Public image orientation						
2. Structure/systems						
(2.1) Streamlined operations (absence of bureaucracy)						
(2.2) Decentralisation						
(2.3) Simplicity of organisation structure						
(2.4) Shallow hierarchy (few management levels)						
(2.5) Flexible planning						
(2.6) Participative decision making						
(2.7) Effective decision implementation						
(2.8) Constructive controlling						
3. Culture/people						
(3.1) Team spirit orientation						
(3.2) Leadership by example						
(3.3) Common value system						
(3.4) Management of objectives and results						
(3.5) Open internal communications						
(3.6) Intuitive (in-tune) management						
(3.7) Approachability of management						
(3.8) Recognition of efforts						

Figure 15.2   A corporate personality profile questionnaire

Phase III: Identification of Barriers

This targeted future state can only be realised if the potential barriers, which occur by introducing the future state concept, are identified in a further step. On the one hand, barriers in the company resulting from psychological problems of individuals, groups and organisations must be identified. On the other, additional elements must be considered. We have to ask:

- Is the concept realistic?
- Are the processes identified effectively?
- Are there enough financial and human resources available?
- Is the time horizon of, say, a maximum of 12 months realistic?

After having identified all relevant barriers, the next phase can be initiated.

Roll-out Actions

We have to take targeted actions in order to overcome the barriers as well as to realise the future state concept. We believe that HRM should take actions which will help to minimise the barriers to change. The following seem to us to be the most important for targeted actions.

Targeted selection

We suggest the following Pre-selection Principle which we have introduced in some re-engineered companies. Whenever possible, vacancies should be reviewed to establish the possibility of eliminating the position either fully or in part by:

● Enriching other jobs with important elements
● Automating as much as possible the routine responsibilities and
● discontinuing the unnecessary portion of the position.

Targeted appraisal

"When employees are performing process work, companies can measure their performance and pay them on the basis of the value they create" (Hammer and Champy, 1993) for customers, employees, shareholders and the environment. The focus of performance measures has to be based both on objectives (and results) as well as on the added value created for various relevant stakeholders (based on the holistic vision). To measure the performance in a more objective way, we have introduced a 360° feedback programme where appraisal is carried out from above and from below. In the case of a manager, contributions for the appraisal come from a variety of sources – senior managers, staff, team members, other internal customers and, if appropriate, external customers.

Targeted reward

In re-engineered companies "substantial rewards for outstanding performance take the form of bonuses, not pay raises" (Hammer and Champy, 1993). We have introduced variable compensation programmes in re-engineered companies based on the following consideration of three main dimensions (Figure 15.3):

● Performance level
● Time horizon
● Added-value dimensions

The higher the level of responsibility, the higher the variable part and the higher the long-term part of total compensation. Re-engineering companies aim

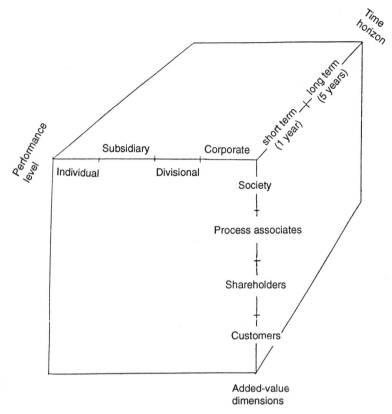

Figure 15.3   A bonus concept for re-engineered companies

to allocate a major portion of their bonus to all "process owners and associates" (former bosses and employees) according to Customer, Shareholder, Process Associates and Public Satisfaction. They pay for performance and promote for ability.

Targeted human resource development

"Today's organisation is rapidly being transformed from a structure built out of jobs into a field of work needing to be done" (Bridge, 1994). There are recurring characteristics that companies encounter in re-engineering core processes (see Hammer, 1994):

- Several specialised jobs are combined into one multidimensional task.
- Planning, decision making and executing are part of one task.
- The phases in the process are performed in a natural way.

- Processes are no longer standardised but have multiple versions.
- Processes are installed where it makes most sense.
- A broad span of trust is replacing a narrow span of control.
- An empowered process representative provides a single point of contact for the whole process team.

In such a process team culture, human resource development does not indicate primarily off-the-job training or climbing up the hierarchy but choosing one of many career paths to expand one's breadth of mind and to master more challenging processes in the future. These may be through:

- Job rotation
- Job enrichment
- Promotion
- Realignment
- Outplacement
- Outsourcing
- Project team activity

These routes for career advancement are not mutually exclusive and an individual may pursue more than one simultaneously.

CONCLUSIONS

According to Orgland (1994), up to now "the literature on organizational change has focused on either top-down change, bottom-up change or a combination of the two". Horizontal process redesign has been neglected. On the other hand, authors on business process re-engineering have focused on horizontal process redesign, and largely neglected the importance of a top-down direction and bottom-up performance improvement (e.g. Davenport, 1993b; Hammer and Champy, 1993). Finally, the literature on strategic management has traditionally focused on the top-down element (e.g. Ansoff, 1984), neglecting both bottom-up performance improvement and horizontal process redesign.

Orgland (1994) developed a new model (Figure 15.4) based on the fact that "fundamental change in complex organizations can only be effectively initiated, managed and sustained by considering all the three 'forces' of change: top-down direction setting, horizontal process redesign and bottom-up performance improvement."

What are our conclusions? First, only a combination of the three phases of the change process can be the basis for an effective BPR. Second, re-engineering makes no lasting benefit if we use a one-dimensional "helicopter approach to consulting": flying in, making a lot of noise and leaving behind not only a

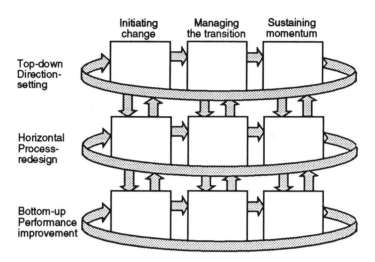

Figure 15.4   Fundamental strategic change in complex organisations

big bill but also a lot of frustrated people. Effective business process re-engineering including the human resource management perspective does not mean "lean and mean!" but "lean and happy!" Achieving this goal means targeting the HRM activity to support other changes which may occur as a result of the move from a functional bound organisation to one adopting a process management approach.

Chapter 16

Implications of Experiences with Business Process Re-engineering for IS/IT Planning

Chris Edwards and Joe Peppard

WHAT WILL YOU FIND IN THIS CHAPTER?

Information Systems and Technology was the startpoint for BPR as organisations searched for ways to derive real value from this resource. IS/IT remains a critical element in many re-engineering projects and managing by process is an area which management needs to consider carefully. This chapter examines:

- The relationship between IT and BPR
- The evolution of Information Systems Planning
- BPR and process management implications for Information Systems Planning
- An approach to Information Systems Planning in a process-based organisation or a BPR project
- The changing role of the IT group

INTRODUCTION

While the origins of business process re-engineering may be difficult to identify precisely, the label for the phenomenon was coined during a research project undertaken to examine the role which IT would play in organisations during the 1990s (Scott Morton, 1991). There are many aliases for this concept, including business process transformation, core process redesign, business transformation and business process redesign. As is no doubt clear from this volume, there are also many flavours of this concept. In this chapter the term business process re-engineering is used to capture the notion of the redesign of organisational process to achieve significant performance improvements.

Researchers involved in this project observed that many leading organisations were implementing information technology in ways which were radically different from the traditional focus on seeking efficiency benefits (Rockart and Short, 1989; Davenport and Short, 1990). Instead of merely automating existing methods of working, progressive organisations were using technology to perform work in innovative ways. A central feature of this phenomenon was the transformation of the way in which an organisation worked internally rather than simply to automate how it already worked.

This phenomenon of BPR also emerged at a time when many scholars were lamenting the inadequacy of existing organisation structures for the demands of today's competitive environment. At the centre of these arguments was a challenge for management practice and an attack on the fundamental principles underlying the design of organisations. Structures such as "the shamrock organisation", "the virtual organisation", "the modular corporation", "the intellectual holding company", and "the network organisation" have all been suggested as new forms of organisation for competitiveness (Miles and Snow, 1987; Handy, 1989; Davidow and Malone, 1992). Many of these new forms are critically dependent on IT and without IT they are impossible to implement (Lambert and Peppard, 1993). At the same time, the dominant logic of business is also being challenged. The concepts of core competences and outsourcing have challenged the traditional concentration on horizontal and vertical integration and the focus on positioning the organisation within an industry.

A common thesis running through these emerging themes is the notion of process, suggesting that it is perhaps through a focus on *process* that these new forms can be implemented. A hallmark of re-engineering is a focus on organisational processes. Competencies are seen as business processes that are "strategically understood" (Stalk, Evans and Schulman, 1992) and through processes strategies are rendered "explicit and precise" (Scherr, 1993). Organisations typically outsource processes "for which the firm has neither a critical strategic need nor special capabilities" (Quinn and Hilmer, 1994).

Yet viewing IT as an enabler of new process architectures is to perhaps miss the profound implications which the process paradigm has for managing information. In this chapter we suggest that early views and debates of the role of IT in BPR must give way to a more considered focus on managing information and, in particular, the implications that lessons from BPR studies have for IS/IT planning. We argue that through considering BPR within the IS/IT planning process, IT can make a greater contribution to the competitiveness of the business.

In order to develop our position, this chapter begins with a survey of different perspectives on the role of IT in BPR, identifying the deficiency of the limiting, yet pervasive, technological focus. We then examine the evolution of IS/IT planning and the management of information. The chapter highlights how a focus on process can enhance the management of the information resource in an organisation. We present a refined model of IS planning incorporating the lessons of three decades of IS planning together with experiences with BPR and discuss its implications for the process of information management in general and information system planning in particular.

A SURVEY OF IT AND BPR

Since the phrase "business process redesign" was coined there has been an on-going debate concerning the role of information technology (IT). BPR as a phenomenon was observed and labelled by the Massachusetts Institute of Technology (MIT) *Management in the 1990s* Research Program, which focused on examining the role which IT would play in organisations during the 1990s (Scott Morton, 1991). The MIT researcher used the term quite precisely to describe the use of IT to transform the way in which a company organises itself for work internally rather than simply to automate the way it already worked. Venkatraman (1991) saw BPR as one level of what he referred to as "IT induced business reconfiguration", although in a recent paper the word *induced* was replaced by *enabled* (Venkatraman, 1994), a subtle but significant distinction.

A similar de-emphasising of the central role of IT has also been espoused by Hammer. His initial definition specifically defined BPR as "using the power of information technology..." (Hammer, 1990). However, in his book with Champy (Hammer and Champy, 1993) the reference to IT was omitted from this definition. Contrast this with Davenport (1993b), who in acknowledging that "information and IT are rarely sufficient to bring about process change" (p. 95) proceeds to assert that "...the use of IT for process innovation [is] a virtual necessity" (p. 44). In this regard, a number of authors have used the term *information technology enabled* business process redesign to specifically refer to the use of IT to change organisational processes for substantial improvement (Teng, Grover and Fiedler, 1995; Grover, Tang and Fiedler, 1993; Talwar, 1994).

The general consensus is that IT is seen as an enabler (although there appear to be different definitions of enablement from "doing" to "supporting") and a creator of new redesign opportunities. IT permits new ways of working and organising which are not possible manually (Davenport and Short, 1990; Hammer, 1990; Tapscott and Caston, 1993). The key argument in support of the enabling theme is the lack of sustainable competitive advantage from IT (Cecil and Goldstein, 1990; Galliers, 1992). Business advantage through IT is relative and in most industries you cannot now exist let alone excel without it (Scott Morton, 1991).

Despite this, both hardware and software vendors have not been slow in promoting BPR as a way of unlocking the potential of IT. They are capitalising on the disappointment which managers have with their IT investments and the general consensus that they are not getting "value for money" from these investments. Economists speak of a "productivity paradox" to describe the huge investment made since the early 1980's in technology while at the same time the productivity of the white-collar worker has remained static. However, in a recent paper Quinn and Bailey (1995) argue that the productivity paradox in services has been overstated.

Predictably, surveys of the role of the IT organisation in BPR have reported that it plays an important, if not central, role in each stage of a re-engineering effort (Bjorn Andersen and Cavaye, 1994; Butler Cox Foundation, 1991; IS Analyzer, 1993; P-E Centre for Management Research, 1993). These roles include educating other members of the re-engineering team about leading-edge information technology and how it can be appropriately applied to business processes, selection and use of business process and data modelling tools (Meirs, 1994), and to build the systems that are envisioned by the re-engineering team. However, there is also a clear message that the re-engineering initiative should not be led by the IT organisation (Edwards and Peppard, 1994).

BPR has highlighted the need to first get the process 'right' before implementing IT (Hammer, 1990; Earl, 1992; Rai and Paper, 1994). Technology itself does not give any sustained competitive advantage; advantage is derived from the process capability which it supports. However, some software vendors argue that with technologies like workflow, existing processes can be automated prior to redesign and capitalising on the power of the software, the process can be re-engineered at a later stage (Tong, 1994).

One of the major inhibitors for any re-engineering initiative are "legacy systems". With a few notable exceptions (Hsu and Howard, 1994) this issue has received little attention, highlighting the urgent need for research. Perhaps this lack of attention is due to the fact that that the "clean sheet" approach to the redesign of processes also assumes *inter alia* that systems can be redesigned through a similar approach. The reality is that organisations have large investments in IT and major rewrites to existing systems can endanger redesign efforts by becoming too large to contain. As Heygate (1993) points out "time after time, the potential value to be unleashed through redesign remains stacked up behind IT bottlenecks, months if not years after implementation should have been complete."

One of the arguments often put in favour of the re-engineering business process is that outdated practices which have been rigidified through a succession of IT investments can be obliterated through BPR. Yet the paradox is that these processes may themselves become rigid and inflexible through the use of the very technology that will enable new process blueprints. This suggests that BPR and IS/IT strategy must somehow be integrated without mimicking the chequered history of IS/IT planning. Re-engineering challenges not only how companies organise themselves but also the traditional paradigm for managing information and by consequence, implications for the IS planning process. IS/IT strategies must be integrated within the context of a re-engineering. A number of authors have attempted to address this issue (Galliers, 1995; Grover, Tang and Fiedler, 1993; Teng, Grover and Fiedler, 1995; Talwar, 1994), but their analysis has been at a conceptual level. In the next section we examine the development of IS planning and highlight particularly the assumptions which underlie traditional planning approaches. This will provide the context to bring to bear lessons from BPR.

THE EVOLUTION OF INFORMATION SYSTEMS PLANNING

The computer has been used as a tool for processing data in most large organisations for the last 35 years. Scholars have traced the development of the computer from a variety of viewpoints: some emphasise the developments in electronics whereas others focus more on the implications for business. In technology terms the "mainframe" has moved to "client–server" environments and in business application terms "data processing" has moved onto "information enabled processes". It is generally recognised that the evolution of applications passed through a number of stages or eras and behind each of those was an unspoken model of how the applications could best be developed for that era. These models were based upon a set of assumptions, some of which appear to have proved true whereas history suggests others might be somewhat less robust.

A number of stage models have been developed as a means to understanding the past and to assess a particular firm's evolution in its use and adaptation of IT. Those of Nolan and Gibson (Nolan and Gibson, 1974; Nolan, 1979), Galliers and Sutherland (1991), and Wiseman (1985) are well documented and have provided a basis for others to develop and refine (Ward, Griffiths and Whitmore, 1990). The process by which planning for the deployment of IT was conducted in a particular era was a consequence of the objectives and the assumptions underpinning that era, and also a driver of how the actual applications were developed and hence the benefits delivered.

Each of the different eras tended to concentrate upon particular groups of issues. Early eras focused upon the development of applications, emphasising the choice of programming languages, selection of hardware and other technology-related matters. Later eras introduced the concept of IS planning and involved all those issues associated with deciding *what* information and applications are required in a particular business using the term IT planning to refer to those issues associated with deciding *how* systems are to be developed and implemented in a particular organisation. The focus of IS planning in the latter stages has been on determining the applications to be developed in support of the business strategy and categorising these in relation to the contribution they each make to delivering that strategy. Table 16.1 summarises the evolution of the applications perspective of IS planning.

This table illustrates the stages through which organisations have passed in their use and adoption of IT. Of course, particular organisations have progressed through this framework at different speeds and even today some organisations may still be in earlier stages. For most organisations stages A, B and C are now a matter of history. While responsibility for IS planning initially rested with the finance function it latterly became an individual activity undertaken by users of personal computers in the organisation. In fact, such activity could hardly be called planning in terms of how we now understand the concept.

Many organisations claim to be in stage D although for the majority this is a debatable point. The thrust of this stage is to integrate IS planning with business strategic planning, reflecting a view that technology not only allows companies to develop applications that support existing corporate strategies but also influences the direction of the business itself. For example, the availability of robust on-line systems capable of dealing with vast numbers of transactions very quickly has facilitated the growth in direct banking and direct insurance.

Top-down (Ward, Griffiths and Whitmore, 1990), middle-out (Henderson and Sifonis, 1986), multiple (Earl, 1989) and eclectic (Sullivan, 1985) methods have been developed to incorporate both business-driven and creative approaches in the search for significant opportunities for gaining benefits from the technology. Techniques borrowed from strategic management, such as five-forces analysis, value chain analysis, critical success factor analysis and customer resource life cycle have been incorporated within the IS planning processes in order to assist in identifying IS opportunities. Such tools, while useful for strategy design, do not translate directly into guidance for strategy execution. More recently, strategic alignment models have been proposed in response to the continued inability of organisations to realise value from IT investments (Hendersen and Venkatraman, 1993). These models conceptualise and direct IS planning based on two building blocks: strategic fit and functional integration. They aim to ensure that not only is IT aligned to the business strategy but it also underpins organisational operations and its IT infrastructure.

This perspective results in an elevation of IT as part of the firm's strategy rather than just a response to it.

All these stage D approaches arise from a vision of IT being a significant enabler and even contributor to business strategy. Over the years, consultancies and business schools have encouraged this viewpoint although some of the supporting empirical evidence of success is hardly forthcoming. It is not that unusual even today to hear of American Hospital Supplies Analytic System/ Automated Purchasing (ASAP) information system (Harvard Business School, 1986; Venkatraman and Short, 1993), American Airlines, SABRE system and Thomson Holidays TOP system being cited as examples of competitive applications, although these examples are at least fifteen years old. What is surprising is that more recent examples have not been found. In fact, the authors and colleagues have categorised all IT applications into a number of generic categories.

The approaches suggested in stage D are underpinned by a number of assumptions some of which deserve detailed consideration and questioning given the experiences of organisations in this era. To embark on a stage D IS planning process assumes that at least some of an organisation's management view information as a strategic resource worthy of their time and effort in managing. If the instigator of the IS planning process is very senior in the organisation then this view can be conveyed to others in the early stages of the IS education process, prior to IS planning proper, but its acceptance cannot be guaranteed. A recent survey reported that 67% of senior managers treated IT as an administrative expense and support activity only (Price Waterhouse, 1993). "We've heard all this IT stuff before" is a view which is still widespread. The belief of an informed and motivated management group is an unsatisfied assumption in many organisations. Despite the criticality of information for most organisations senior management are not involved in the process of developing IS strategies. Responsibility for IT is devolved to the IT professionals and the IT organisations. Interestingly, the corollary is also true; a recent survey reported that very few IT directors get involved in the business strategic planning process (Stephens et al., 1995).

The assumption that an organisation's managers can come together to discuss the organisation's information system requirements and to work together meaningfully for the good of that organisation as a whole is not always reflected in reality. The Chief Executive has the ability to organise such meetings, and may even attend to show support, but before too long the discussions often becomes embroiled in technical detail and he or she will move on to other matters. The success of a group or groups set up to operate across the functions is questionable when all other organisational matters such as remuneration, promotion and power structures are dealt with on a functional basis. Galliers, Pattison and Reponen (1994) report on the experiences of IS planning within a workshop setting and Earl's (1993) study of applying

Table 16.1 Perspectives on IS planning

Stage	Title	A model of the development process	Technology employed	Assumptions	IS planning approach
A	*Data processing* grew to support organisation "efficiency"	User specify to the technical staff their requirements in business terms from which the technical staff develop the system. Additionally techniques of "Organisation and Methods" (O&M) and "Systems Analysis" confirm and add to the requirements. Business and technical staff then jointly implement the system.	Punched-card equipment followed by mainframe computers and latterly minicomputers.	1. Users know the data they require 2. User needs are virtually stable through time 3. Technical staff understand managers' stated needs 4. Managers can agree between themselves if they have differing needs 5. Technicians have the ability to deliver the defined systems 6. Electronic based processing methods are less expensive than manual ones	Systems for attention were identified by briefly assessing the total costs of existing processing methods. As many of the existing systems operated in the financial function many of the new systems were therefore financially focused. In practice, IS planning consisted of identifying the costs and/or the inadequacies of existing methods and prioritising the resultant proposed systems. Piecemeal development of applications. Latterly the beginnings of technology planning through integration.
B	*Management information systems* developed to support managerial "effectiveness"	Largely, such projects developed from analysis and presentation of data that had been collected for data processing purposes and hence such applications tended to utilise existing data. Users specify to the technical staff their requirements in business terms. Technical staff develop the system. Requirements analysis techniques barely existed and previously used O&M and Systems Analysis techniques were not particularly appropriate. Business and technical staff jointly implement the system. (*Notice the similarity with A in how the development process was intended to operate.*)	Mainframe computers latterly with visual display units on managers' desks.	1. Managers know what information they need to enhance decision making 2. Stability of these user needs through time 3. Technical staff understand managers' stated requirements 4. Managers can come to an agreement if they have differing needs or the underlying data need to vary for each of their needs 5. Managers substantially use this kind of information in decision making 6. Better information leads to better decisions being made 7. Managers really care about collecting better information 8. The data that are available are suitable for the purpose	Development resources were still largely controlled by the finance function and hence other functions had to "persuade" Finance of the worth of such projects. IS planning was virtually non-existent; it was more a process of arbitrary sharing of development resources.

	Stage	Description	Technology	Assumptions	Commentary
C	*Personal computing* to support managerial "effectiveness"	Users decide what they need in terms of information for managing. The managers develop the application locally using technology they believe is appropriate. The managers then use the application locally and update it to reflect changing requirements. (*Notice how the centralisation tendency has swung in the direction of decentralisation.*)	The personal computer and later networking	1. Little synergy exists between users in terms of the applications required 2. Little synergy exists in terms of the data required by different users 3. Information Technology is simple enough for non-IT staff to understand and apply 4. Users understand their job in relation to organisational objectives and hence the applications developed align with the objectives 5. Better information leads to better decisions	Anarchy had arrived! Planning of any kind was despised even to the extent of utilising similar equipment. IS planning resided at the level of the individual. Even IT planning did not exist at first.
D	*Strategic information systems* to gain "competitiveness" by "integration"	Users come together to agree and jointly define requirements. Strong links are made with the organisation's objectives and discussion focuses upon how Information Systems can support and perhaps enhance the organisation's performance. Technical staff then develop the applications. Projects are led by managers to emphasise ownership. (*Notice the re-emergence of centralisation in an attempt to link individual activity to the business strategy.*)	Mainframes integrated with, and supported by, personal computers	1. Organisations have a business strategy 2. The business strategy is reasonably stable through time 3. Information can underpin organisational objectives 4. Technical staff can efficiently and effectively develop large applications 5. Users can work together effectively, as a team to specify the organisation's needs 6. Managers view information as a key organisational resource to secure competitiveness 7. IT can enable organisations to integrate effectively 8. Integration of functions by using information leads to organisational benefit 9. Users and IT work to common time horizons and users are willing to wait for IT to develop applications	Senior managers from different functions came together (either physically or via consultants) to apply techniques such as value chain analysis and critical success factor analysis in an attempt to pinpoint applications that could provide competitive advantage. They then appointed managers to pursue development of the application in an attempt to retain business control.

Strategic Information Systems Planning in 21 UK companies makes interesting reading. Indeed, Earl's research highlighted, among other things, that methods could fail if the process factors of IS planning receive inadequate attention.

The assumption of the existence of a meaningful business strategy being followed by the organisation is open to question. Many strategy scholars have become disillusioned and concerns have been expressed about the direction of strategy research and practice. Prahalad and Hamel (1994) have suggested that the concepts and tools of analysis may need basic re-evaluation, arguing that many of the assumptions embedded in traditional strategy models may be incomplete and/or outdated as we approach the new competitive milieu. While the prescriptive business strategy literature proposes frameworks to aid in the strategy-formulation process, descriptively, empirical research clearly indicates that strategy is often emergent, incremental and crafted as opportunities and threats arise (Mintzberg and Waters, 1982). Whittington (1993) has developed a framework which classifies approaches to strategy based on whether the process is deliberate or emergent or whether the outcome sought is profit maximisation or more pluralistic objectives. The implications of the emergent view of strategy are profound for IS planning: for example, if an IT development plan is based upon an outdated strategic direction for the business what support and active involvement can it expect to receive from senior management? Surely outdated IS plans can never deliver benefits to the organisation, except by good fortune. More problematic is developing an IS strategy when the business strategy is being crafted on a daily basis!

The timescales that IT adheres to in developing applications are often not acceptable to the business which operates in a dynamic environment and hence may be forced into much more rapidly changing planning cycles. This is further exaggerated as strategy is continually emerging. The result is that applications are developed long after they are required. In some instances business users may be unwilling to wait for IT to provide support and instead begin to develop applications themselves. Such an approach does not encourage integration, which to some is the very key to success, and leads to the development of disparate systems.

Some of the applications resulting from an IS planning process are inevitably going to be large and complex having many sub-parts and interfaces. The ability of many IT organisations to deliver such applications must be in question. Even the limited information on systems failure in the public domain suggests that systems delivery capability is a significant issue. Examples include the experiences of the London Ambulance Service, Wessex Health Authority, the London Stock Exchange Torus System and the Performing Rights Society. Other failures are catalogued by Currie (1994) and Sauer (1993). Reality is likely to be worse than the information in the public domain would suggest, as organisations would seldom want to publicise failure and hence the failure statistics could well be significantly understated. There is also the issue of legacy systems, referred to earlier, which have tremendous implications in developing any new application. The fact that an IT group is perceived as incapable of delivering strategic applications to the required timescale could well deter some organisations from undertaking IS planning to search for opportunities in the first place.

An assumption in both the techniques of IS planning (e.g. value chain analysis, critical success factor analysis) and its application (forming cross-functional teams) is that the opportunities will cross functional boundaries and that such opportunities will lead to substantial business benefit. It might equally be argued that opportunities will exist in particular functional areas and that these should be pursued in preference to the cross-functional opportunities. If this latter argument is true all the need for cross-functional tools and teams and integration is unnecessary and the same or perhaps larger benefits could be secured with less effort.

In summary, just as the frameworks of the past have faded, leaving few tangible benefits but much greater understanding, IS planning is now being subjected to critical questioning. A key indicator of change is the behaviour of leading organisations: if they are turning to new ways of securing the best from IT then it is worth taking stock. The literature and practice developing in the process re-engineering movement combined with the enhanced technology capability is suggesting exactly that. After all, Lederer and Sethi (1988) found that only 24% of applications recommended for development via a formal IS planning process were ultimately developed as organisations needed to carry out further substantial analysis post planning. Some have even suggested that the whole process of IS planning may be a cosmetic exercise (Flynn and Goldeniewska, 1993). If stage D IS planning is based upon assumptions that have been shown to be questionable or even invalid, what will replace it?

BPR PROVIDING A NEW DIRECTION FOR STRATEGIC IS/IT PLANNING

To this point we have briefly traced the development of BPR and its relationship with IT and considered the evolution of IS/IT planning to date. It is our primary contention that BPR can provide a new direction for managing information, and more significantly, it requires a new approach to IS/IT planning. One can trace its history with some degree of certainty and provide objective evidence substantiating claims. However, this is never possible with the future: to some extent, it is always a matter of speculation. Of course, value lies in influencing the future and shaping organisations to exploit opportunities: unfortunately one can never shape the past.

The experience of companies in stage D have given us a number of pieces of the jigsaw which, when combined with enhanced technology and the business climate for change, enables us to get a glimpse of what stage E might look like. Today we see organisations striving to gain greater benefits from their information systems and the media constantly and repeatedly bombarding organisations with the "information provides advantage" message. The technology today in both hardware and software terms, is certainly more powerful than that available only a few years ago and these substantial performance improvements appear to be likely to continue for some time yet. Organisations appear to have the desire to succeed and the way of making it happen: the key is in developing a framework for organising the ingredients to secure the benefits. Even the direction for this is appearing: the move in many organisations towards a process orientated perspective of business operations.

It is management's concern with process which underpins our vision of stage E (Table 16.2). A lot of the famous, supposedly competitive-edge, information systems in fact represented a long-term investment in business process capability. SABRE, for example, was built as a means of helping American Airlines keep track of its own fares, reservations and scheduling (Hopper, 1990). The advantage of ASAP lay in the long-standing systems and processes that supported ASAP, not in ASAP itself. American Hospital Supplies had already a significant capability in distribution, order-entry and inventory control. It was not until a few years later that AHS realised it could use the system as a marketing tool. The real strategic advantage was in IT enabling and supporting an already sophisticated process capability.

In fact, the traditional IS/IT planning process can result in fragmented systems being developed which may not in fact be aligned with processes. Figure 16.1 illustrates an application portfolio resulting from traditional IS planning approaches and contrasts this with the process which these applications support. The focus on applications as supporting opportunities can obscure the real focus of supporting the underlying process. According to Stalk, Evans and Schulman (1992) organisational competences are processes which are strategically understood and processes themselves are seen as rendering strategy explicit (Scherr, 1993). Competences are embedded in processes, enabling the process capability referred to above. The recommendation of Feeney and Ives (1991) for "looking within the organisation, to discover those unique attributes that can be leveraged by IT" is similar in sentiments to the current thrust in the strategy literature which focuses on an organisation's resources (Wernerfelt, 1984).

Implementing IT to support these applications can be problematic, resulting in the development of disparate systems, which is exactly what IS planning seeks to move away from. The underlying belief is that integration can be achieved at the technical level i.e. by specifying individual applications IT would somehow result in integration and that somehow the technical architecture could be defined through determining piecemeal applications.

Table 16.2 An emerging perspective on IS planning

Stage	Title	A model of the development process	Technology employed	Assumptions	IS planning approach
E	*Information enabled processes used to enhance the focus on the customer and clarify the role of IT*	Senior managers identify their organisations' processes and associated activities. Data used in a process are defined by conventional data modelling techniques but employed at the level of the process. Applications are defined from the activities that constitute the process. User managers develop applications to support activities using common data and a common technology base. *(Notice how this provides a balance between data management which is centralised at the process level but application development is focused at the activity level and hence is organisationally more relevant to the manager.)*	Client–server technology with software underpinnings from a variety of directions (object orientation: application repositories; rapid application development tools, data warehouses and data marts, etc.)	1. Processes and activities are understood by management both in concept and use 2. Managers see information as an important resource to be managed and will devote time to this 3. Managers have the ability and inclination to use rapid development tools 4. Data are significantly more common to processes than to the organisation as a whole 5. Managers can work as a team focusing upon a particular process 6. Managers understand how processes and activities contribute to organisational objectives 7. IT alone does not provide competitive advantage: it is the process capability that it enables and supports.	The emergence of IS planning as a component of process management. IS planning procedures become integrated with process planning and process management. Information management in total becomes part of managing the business.

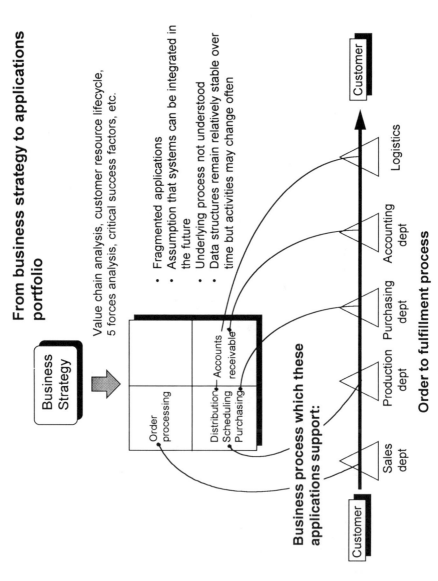

Figure 16.1 From fragmented application to holistic process

Pyburn (1991) has argued that in most of the important examples of strategic IT use, it is technological architecture, not one single application, that provides the real competitive benefit. Similar sentiments have been expressed by Brophy and Monger (1989) who assert that specific IS investments often do not give sustainable benefit but it is the linkage of the various stand-alone investments which gives the real benefit. Using the case of computer integrated manufacturing (CIM) they illustrate that overall benefits are only derived when the total product life cycle (design to production) is linked.

A PROCESS-BASED APPROACH TO IS/IT PLANNING

In this section we outline an approach which is based on research in the domain of IS planning and experiences with BPR (see Figure 16.2). To aid clarity of explanation an on-going example is developed and included here in italics.

An organisation can be seen as a collection of business units each of which consists of a number of processes. A "process" represents a consolidation of the outcome of stakeholders identifying their expectations of the business unit. Indeed, processes are often expressed in terms not recognised by the organisation, for example, individual employees seldom reference the process they work on rather they focus on particular individual activities (steps A and B in Figure 16.2).

Imagine a commercial bank with business units of "retail banking" and "corporate financing". Within the retail banking business unit stakeholders would consist of customers, the corporate unit, employees, etc. Some expectations of customers may be a reasonable pricing structure compared to other banks, ease, speed and courtesy in performing transactions, and security of the invested funds. Processes resulting from these expectations may be a product pricing process, a customer transaction interface process and an investment process. As only one stakeholder has been considered, no consolidation with the expectations of other stakeholders has occurred but one could reasonably expect this to happen if all stakeholders and all expectations were analysed.

This identification of processes as a consolidated list of "why we do things" (i.e., to satisfy stakeholder(s)) is hardly revolutionary (Peppard and Preece, 1995) but its application suggests it is a valuable exercise if only in identifying and verifying the stakeholders' expectations. Indeed, Hammer (1990) recommends organising around outcomes. For customers, these will be the reasons why they choose to do business with a company as opposed to a competitor and are normally related to quality, cost, flexibility, delivery reliability and/or speed. Minor extensions to this basic task could include

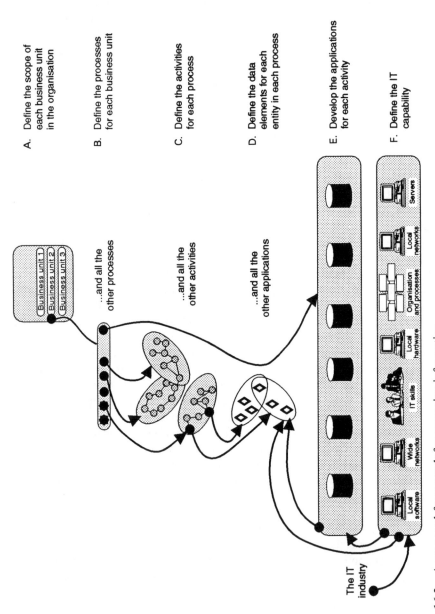

Figure 16.2 A proposed framework for managing information

adding the identification and verification of stakeholder "delights" to expectations in an attempt to further understand the stakeholders' requirements.

From the processes of an organisation the activities can be developed: these are the ways in which the processes are to be operationalised. An organisation has a choice in how the processes are to operate and this should be explicitly examined and considered at the highest level. Some activities may exist to service two processes and it may be decided to operate these together for efficiency reasons. Many issues impinge upon this decision to combine activities, but examining these is less relevant here. In reality organisations already exist and are doing "things" and hence activities already take place. Perhaps a stage in process redesign may be to identify all the "actually are" activities at the macro level and consider how these relate to processes. Another way is to disregard the present and to consider how the organisation desires to operationalise the processes and then how these "should be" (the clean-sheet approach) activities relate to the present "actually are" activities. An organisation may or may not decide to allocate individual processes and activities to particular managers but, given a desire to encourage empowerment and accountability, it appears sensible to extend the clarity that has developed through process analysis (step C in Figure 16.2).

To return to the bank and the "customer transaction interface process": this could be operationalised by obtaining high street properties and locating staff and on-line processing equipment in each and encouraging customers, via advertising, to visit. Another way may be to create a central telephone enquiry point supported by automatic telling machines in large petrol stations around the country to issue and collect cash: a third may be a combination of both. Bank management will need to consider each of these and decide the appropriate activity implementation for them in their circumstances.

For many years the technique of data modelling has attempted to develop the entity related data by focusing upon a business or a business unit and to organise this into a database. In the formative years of data modelling, disk hardware and the database methods were somewhat limited and the techniques were difficult to apply. It was propounded that management involvement was central to data definition but all too often the techniques became a tool employed by IT staff. This occurred for a variety of reasons, not least of which was the considerable time and effort required of management in defining the database.

A compromise position may be that data entities and data definitions be defined at the level of process (D in Figure 16.2): certainly common data definitions will be required within a process. The management team, focusing all their attention upon a particular process, should wish to be deeply involved in the definition as every single element of the discussion is of central importance to them as process managers. This contrasts with the same methods employed at the organisational level in which often a substantial part of the discussion is barely relevant to particular individuals, particularly in a functionally based organisation. It is quite likely that some elements of the data will need to be common through a number of processes, and this can be dealt with by jointly defining the data for common entities, but this tends towards the problems previously cited and assumes that process redefinition moves forward on all processes together. Developments in database software allow additional items to be added to existing definitions to satisfy the needs of a second or subsequent process. This effectively removes the need for all processes to develop the data definitions at the same time and re-engineering of particular processes can move forward at the speed appropriate to that process.

Returning to the bank example, the entities underpinning the customer transaction interface process would consist of items such as "customer name", "customer address", "account number", "account balance", etc. From these, data definitions could be developed using the existing tools of information engineering.

We turn our attention to the technology infrastructure that will underpin this framework (F in Figure 16.2), mainly the hardware and communication technologies which are becoming more standard, if not quite "open", as each year passes. UNIX or NT-based client–server, the Power PC, TCP/IP are all promulgating this standardisation. In spite of the many frameworks employed by companies to ascertain their IT investments, we would suggest that investment decisions are driven by the IT industry. Most IT groups today appear to be working towards the same or very similar storage, communication, processing and other technologies. Indeed, the argument often proposed for outsourcing is premised on the fact that IT is now a commodity. Those that are not doing so have a desire to but are constrained by decisions of the recent past.

Our fictitious bank will be moving towards essentially the same IT infrastructure as other organisations. For example, the technology infrastructure underpinning the ATM network on the garage forecourts would use equipment and software very similar to that of competing banks.

It is suggested that those individuals managing and working on a process will have access to the same delivery technology utilising the same set of software for local development of applications and access to the same data jointly defined.

The remaining link in this framework is the development of applications. Historically, applications have been large, requiring many months of development time, integrated and developed mostly by IT staff, which may involve code cutting or tailoring packages. The word "application" is used here to mean a small module that performs a single task and likely within the development potential of an average computer literate manager of tomorrow. For those managers not desiring this role, information assistants may be employed to develop the applications for that particular manager. However, it is clear that such staff work for the business and not IT.

Applications will be developed using the infrastructure provided (clients and object repositories and rapid application development tools) and using data from the previously defined process of which the activity is a component. Applications that change the data, as against merely performing analysis, will undoubtedly need to undergo some quality testing procedure prior to applying, likely controlled by the IT group for the good of all. Repositories of applications developed in using the standard hardware and software will be maintained to facilitate even more rapid application development by building upon the quality-checked work of others. In essence, the control of applications will largely be under the control of process managers with responsibility of activities and can proceed at a speed and urgency dictated by them but to an agreed standard (E in Figure 16.2).

One can imagine the manager of an activity in our fictitious bank using the standard hardware and software to extract data from the database, and presenting it in a form that precisely suits him. Other suitably empowered activity managers may develop applications to add new customers to the database or change the data in some other way.

It is quite clear that the model proposed above is perhaps many years away in some organisations, but as the primary schoolchildren of 1980s, brought up using MSWord and Excel, become managers they will not be content to leave information management largely to the IT staff. They can and will want to be involved with managing and exploiting information: "managing" means managing all the resources not avoiding or sub-contracting information management to specialists.

Just as the frameworks of the past were underpinned by critical assumptions, the one here is no exception. To mention the more important ones: the assumptions of organisations understanding processes and activities need close scrutiny and that of the average manager being able to develop small applications using IT tools is questionable. Add to this the requirement for standard hardware and software technologies, the migration issues involved in implementing this approach and the new role of the IT group, essentially being the custodian of IT infrastructure, may lead one to suspect the model is pure fiction. However, question each of these a little more and one can begin to see that they are already occurring. For example, today many managers can download data and analyse them to produce information using tools like Excel and Forest and Trees. Evidence exists to suggest the possibility of parts if not the whole of this model being implemented today.

The central issue that will assist in evaluating proposals such as this is the extent to which it will help organisations in using information to accomplish goals. The logic underpinning this framework is that BPR techniques will ensure that organisational goals are embodied in process goals and the subsequent link to activity is very clear. This is quite reasonable as this goal clarity is one of the aims of BPR. If the link to activity is clear then that to application should be similar, as those responsible for processes and activities are also those developing, or having developed, the applications.

The days of the big IS steering committees are numbered! Information empowerment of managers is nearly with us: however, only time will reveal the benefits of such an approach. This model has many implications for the IT group in its role of IT infrastructure custodian and the skills it will need to develop in the years ahead but this matter is a matter outside the scope of this chapter.

IMPLICATIONS OF THE PROCESS PERSPECTIVE

Over the past 35 years the history of IT in organisations has been a chequered one. Two contrasting yet complementary perspectives have contributed to this situation. On the one hand has been the inability of the IT group to deliver systems which support the business strategic direction. On the other has been management's reluctance, particularly senior management, to become involved in IS/IT planning. The traditional IS planning process itself has also been a contributor. We have argued that the emerging process perspective of organisations is a step in integrating these divergent views and we have developed an approach which captures the research findings and experiences with both business process re-engineering and IS/IT planning.

It is not our view that an IS/IT planning framework to support process-oriented organisations will ever be applicable in all organisations nor will it be applied instantly in any. The pain of migration and change may be substantial and may deter its application.

In its current form, this framework has a number of implications for both business managers and IT professionals. It challenges traditional assumptions underpinning the roles which each play in the organisation.

Redefining the Information Role of Management

Management will no longer merely specify information requirements but will now also develop their own applications. They, in essence, become an integral part of the delivery mechanism which was previously the preserve of the IT professional. With rapid application development (RAD) tools, graphical user interfaces (GUIs) and object libraries it is now possible to build applications in a short time. Evidence confirms that such an approach already exists in a limited form with the downloading of corporate data from mainframes and the data's subsequent local manipulation using spreadsheets.

In effect, this represents a change of role from planning information systems to managing information and has profound implications for management. Training and development initiatives must now focus on giving management the ability and confidence to be managers of information. They must understand the nature of information and how it can contribute to the process of managing. Technical skills, already possessed by some managers, will have to become more pervasive and will become a necessary constituent of supporting the management process. This now becomes a critical management capability.

Such changes should be welcomed by management as this approach may well provide the final ingredient of managerial empowerment. Total empowerment must include the ability to specify *and* develop the necessary applications they need in support of their particular managerial role.

Processes are Critical and Management must Understand Them

Processes define how the organisation will deliver the business strategy and this is consistent with emerging developments in the business strategy arena. Management must clearly understand how their activities operationalise processes and how information relates to activities. The message from BPR research suggests that it is imperative that this chain is clearly articulated.

Process and Activity Analysis is the Beginning of Identifying Applications

In the approaches to information systems planning which are currently deployed there is a gulf between the business strategy and the resultant applications. Analysis tools, such as critical success factor (CSF) analysis and value chain analysis, aid in analysing this gap but not in bridging it. The proposed perspective highlights the need first to identify the processes which underpin the business strategy, define the activities and then specify the information requirements which will enable these activities to be performed. These are the pillars upon which the bridge will be built.

Centrality of IT Capability

Emerging research (Ketkar, 1994; Weil, 1993) coupled with the experiences which companies have had with BPR highlights the centrality of the IT capability. In order to allow the rapid development of applications, this capability must be in place to enhance the speed and integration of development. This IT capability includes:

- *Organisation and skills* – these are the way the IT resources will be developed and organised in the IT group
- *Data* – the storage of data in a secure and resilient environment
- *IT infrastructure* – the hardware, networks and system software used

- *IT management process and methods* – the essential "cement" that allows the technology, organisation and skills to be used to provide the capability.

The annual survey of IS executives who are members of the Society of Information Management (SIM) identified IT infrastructure as increasing in importance (Niederman, Brancheau and Wetherbe, 1991). Building a responsive IT infrastructure was ranked sixth in importance and was the only new issue in the top ten issues raised. More recently, IT executives reported that designing and providing infrastructure services will be the top job of the future IT executive (Price Waterhouse, 1993).

IT infrastructure in itself does not yield organisation benefit. It merely provides the organisation with the *capability* to develop applications rapidly and it is these applications which provide the benefits (Parker and Benson, 1988). This will have direct implications for how IT investments are, first, determined and second appraised and evaluated.

The Changing Role of the IT Organisation

The rationale for the existence of the IT group will be to provide the IT capability described above. This might sound simplistic and obvious, but many recent writers suggest that the IT group should begin to focus more on information and its contribution to the business. In fact, the whole of the hybrid manager story is one that centres around developing IT managers and staff who are very business aware. The framework outlined in this chapter suggests that IT managers should focus on managing IT and business managers should focus on managing the business and the information needed to achieve that.

Despite the fact that the IT group are the custodians of the IT capability, this does not necessarily mean that IT professionals can totally become "techies" again. Venkatraman and Loh (1993) consider the changing nature of the IT function whereby it moves from managing a technical or product portfolio to a "relationship portfolio". They suggest that the IT function should focus on managing its relationship with its "customers" (in the business) and its "suppliers" (in the IT industry). It is likely that all the technical aspects of the IT capability could be potentially outsourced to service providers, although the management and responsibility of providing IT services will always remain in-house. Negotiation, communication and legal skills could well become as important to the IT professional as technical ones.

Technical competences are likely to remain a core requirement of the IT organisation. A recent survey (Todd, McKeen and Gallupe, 1995) of IS job advertisements from 1970 to 1990 raised questions concerning the implicit understanding by academics and practitioners alike of the need for business knowledge on the part of systems analysts and other IS professionals. The survey suggests that technical competences are still the critical competence for IT groups.

A Flexible Data Architecture is Critical

New technological developments mean that a corporate-wide data architecture need not be defined in totality prior to beginning its development. It is now possible with data warehouses and data marts to define the data required for an individual process and then extend the definition of the data to include new attributes that are required for a second process. In fact, with recent developments in middleware, it is possible for data for a single process to exist on disparate platforms.

Allen and Boynton (1992) examined two extreme approaches to meeting the objective of flexibility and speed as well as low cost and efficiency in delivering systems. With what they call the low road, there is a high level of decentralisation of IS with only data definitions and standards and communications facilities being provided centrally. With the high road, on the other hand, there is total centralisation of IS with complete control of technology, applications, resources, etc. residing at the centre. The framework proposed here conforms to the low road.

Separation of Activity Content and Activity Sequence

With its strong process focus, BPR highlights the importance of decoupling data, activity content and activity sequence, as illustrated in Figure 16.3. Early IT-based systems, particularly those developed in stages A and B, incorporated both the data and the processing engine within the one software system. This

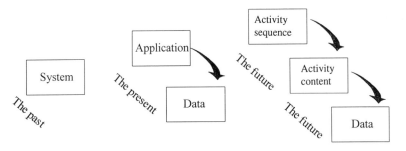

Figure 16.3   Separation of activity content, activity sequence and data

was partly due to the limited capability of early programming languages but also to the narrow functional focus of the development exercise. Developing information systems was a complex process requiring expert skill and knowledge in programming. As a consequence, maintenance becomes a critical problem, as is clear when one examines the amount of time which the IT organisation spends on the upkeep of legacy system, particularly those developed using early technologies.

More recent developments in database technology make it possible to decouple the data from how the data are applied and used within the business. Such advances make it possible to focus more on the development of application in support of business requirements without too much concern for the underlying data. That is not to suggest that data are not important. On the contrary, companies spend vast amounts of resources developing robust corporate data models. Integrity of data is all-important. Many so-called strategic systems are built around this architecture.

The current focus on process and particularly on the flow of work through an organisation, central to the doctrine of BPR, highlights the need to emphasise activity sequence and content of an application. The traditional notion of *the application* is redefined to decouple the activities involved in the application from the sequence through which work flows. In terms of BPR the work flow management system helps to set up a model of activities, which requires a thorough understanding of the process and functions. It can be used to model new relationships and processes, to implement solutions, and to revise them over time to be more efficient and effective. However, in order to enact this model, processes must first be identified.

Business Process Re-engineering Begins with Re-engineering the IT Group

Organisations that have been through the re-engineering experience often cite IT inflexibility as a significant obstacle to the re-engineering exercise. In an attempt to assist the organisation with re-engineering the ever-helpful IT department provide fixes, interfaces and pseudo-integration to deliver applications which underpin the re-engineered business. However, such fixes may solve current problems but they create inflexibility in the business. Each subsequent round of fixes, interfaces and pseudo-integration make the business ever more inflexible. Perhaps one day some businesses may become so rigid that they are unchangeable.

The framework outlined in this chapter is contrary to this: organisations should begin by re-engineering the IT department to provide the IT capability which will translate into business flexibility. This is not just for the present but also for the future. Perhaps medium- and long-term advantage from IT will result from such business flexibility.

IT Strategy is Driven by the IT Industry

It is an interesting observation that organisations spend much time developing IT strategies which in conclusion appear to be very similar to each other. For example, are most organisations not working towards a client–server architecture, common set of end-user applications, outsourced IT supply, and re-usability via some form of object orientation? We would suggest that IT strategies are greatly influenced and dependent on available technologies. The consequence of this is that the IT industry effectively drives a company's IT strategy and this may be a reason for the many successful examples of IT outsourcing. There is the suggestion that in many companies the IT organisation has always been "culturally outsourced" (Ward and Peppard, 1995).

IS Planning is Tactical, Not Strategic

Perhaps the final and most profound implication for IS planning from experiences with BPR is that IS planning may not be strategic. What is strategic is the definition and provision of the management capability and IT infrastructure that will allow applications to respond very quickly to changing organisational needs. IS planning in terms of developing applications may not therefore be a strategic exercise but a tactical response to process demands. This is an area where more research is warranted.

Chapter 17

Business Dynamics: Business Process Re-engineering and Systems Dynamics

Martin Davies

WHAT WILL YOU FIND IN THIS CHAPTER?

This chapter introduces and demonstrates business dynamics as a tool for reengineering. The following issues will be discussed:

- The history of system dynamics
- The "language" of systems dynamics
- The relationship of systems dynamics to re-engineering and process management
- Using business dynamics
- The future of business dynamics as a practical tool for managers

OVERVIEW

This chapter explores the relevance and application of system dynamics to business process re-engineering. My contention is that system dynamics offers a consistent body of theory and knowledge with potential to make a powerful contribution to the field of business process re-engineering. The purpose of this chapter is to justify this view and to set out my understanding of current challenges and opportunities associated with this important subject.

The application of system dynamics to business problems is not new, but the past eight years has seen significant developments in both theory and practice. Fuelled by advances in research and supporting technology, this has seen a shift away from a classical *operations research* approach, where use of the method has been in the hands of specialists, towards direct use of the technique by managers or owners of a "problem situation". This has been combined with a discovery of the importance of the "mental models" about the world which people hold, and recognition that a major part of the value in using system dynamics derives from the shared understanding and quality of insight developed during the process of model construction itself. These views link strongly with the idea of learning, centred approaches to business improvement and innovation. Thus in Senge's (1990) *The Fifth Discipline* we see the idea of system dynamics, in its modern form, placed at the heart of organisational learning theory and practice. To reflect these developments I use the label "Business Dynamics" as an umbrella term to refer to the application of system dynamics to business and management-related issues.

It is now over 30 years since Jay Forrester (1961) published *Industrial Dynamics* marking the advent of system dynamics. Since then the field has flourished developing its own international society and journal *The System Dynamics Review* and has researchers and practitioners working in areas as diverse as medical epidemiology, development economics, management of ecosystems, urban development, social policy, military planning, conflict management, not to mention most areas of business.

To those closely involved with system dynamics this spread of activity seems little cause for surprise. On the other hand, to those discovering system dynamics for the first time it seems more surprising! A flood of questions spring to mind; if these ideas have been around for 30 years and are so good why haven't I heard of them before and why aren't we using them already? The only conclusion: perhaps the ideas aren't so good(?). But then if the ideas are no good why would so many people be using them and working on their development? Answering these questions provides a key to understanding the opportunities and challenges associated with business dynamics.

SYSTEM DYNAMICS

The origins of system dynamics lie in that branch of management science concerned with the application of feedback control theory to exploring the behaviour of physical and social systems (Richardson, 1991). As the name suggests, system dynamics is concerned with understanding the evolution of a system's behaviour over time. The distinct viewpoint adopted by system dynamicists is that the behaviour of a system is determined by its internal *structure*. By using a simple language to describe a system it is possible to characterise its behaviour over time. In turn this provides a basis for comprehending the sorts of behaviour that might be exhibited by such a system in the real world, as well as providing a framework for identifying and evaluating potential improvements.

The use of the term *structure* in system dynamics has a particular meaning. In addition to referring to the organisation of tangible resources it also encompasses the organisation of intangible resources. Thus, system dynamics recognises the critical role played by the information and policy framework within a system in determining its behaviour. And a major part of a system dynamics investigation will be concerned with detecting and surfacing the guiding policy framework (both explicit and implicit) that govern decisions within a system.

The approach adopted by system dynamics practitioners involves constructing a representative model (or models) of a system under investigation. By enabling insight as to the drivers of system behaviour these models provide a basis for comprehending the sorts of behaviour that might be exhibited by such a system in the real world. According to the nature of the system under investigation, it then becomes possible to identify and investigate potential improvements.

Depending on the nature and purpose of the system, investigation of a variety of different types of model may be used. These divide into two broad categories: qualitative and quantitative (Wolstenholme, 1990). For a detailed introduction to the concepts of system dynamics and their application read Wolstenholme (1990). However the description given here is sufficient to appreciate the relevance of system dynamics to business process re-engineering. Qualitative models take the form of a graphical map showing the major relationships that drive system behaviour. These provide a descriptive presentation of system behaviour and are effective for developing shared understanding among groups of people or for communicating the results of findings. Quantitative models enable a pictorial representation of a system to be transformed into a numerical form. Tools are then available to simulate the performance of the system over time. This approach allows the possible evolution of the system to be explored over any time period of interest. For example a model of a company's telephone call reception and management system could be used to investigate the possible impact of customer demand on delivered service level minute by minute throughout a day; or we might evaluate the implications of a company's market strategy on market share over a five-year period; or we might be involved in an investigation where we want to explore the possible impact of demographic trends combined with government planned health funding policy over a 100-year timeframe.

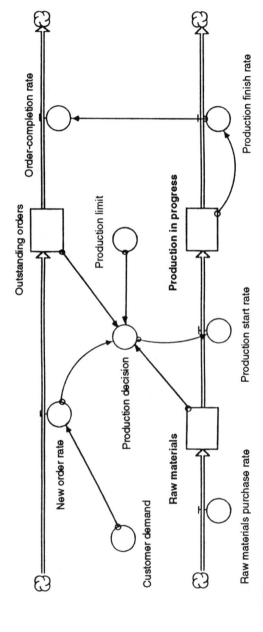

Figure 17.1 A system dynamics map

THE LANGUAGE OF SYSTEM DYNAMICS

Any system, whether natural, artificial or a combination of both, can be described as an arrangement made up from a combination of four building blocks. These are *Stocks* (or Levels) representing accumulations of a resource (e.g. customers, staff, orders, goodwill, etc.); *Flows* (or Rate Variables) representing the rate of flows that increase, or decrease, the level of stocks; *Converters* which process information about stocks and flows or represent sources of information external to the system, and *Information Links* depicting the relationships between stocks, flows and converters.

Therefore, in the example shown in Figure 17.1, which depicts part of a system concerned with processing customer orders and manufacture of a product, we can describe the system as follows. A stock of *Outstanding Orders* is increased by a flow *New Order Rate* which in turn is driven by information about *Customer Demand*. A flow, *Raw Materials Purchase Rate*, increases a stock of *Raw Materials*. The stock of *Raw Materials* is decreased by a flow *Production Start Rate* which in turn increases the stock of *Production in Progress*. A *Production Decision* is taken based on information about: the *New Order Rate*, the extent of *Outstanding Orders*, the availability of *Raw Materials*, and *Production Limit*. This *Production Decision* determines the flow *Production Start Rate*. The flow *Production Finish Rate* is determined by information about the extent of *Production in Progress*. Information about the *Production Finish Rate* drives the *Order Completion Rate*.

In this way, the language provides a complete description, in graphical form, of the workings of a system (the cloud-shaped symbols at the end of the flows mark the boundary of the system under investigation, and converters with information outputs but no inputs, such as Customer Demand or Production Limit, represent sources of information external to the system or parameters of the system). This in turn provides a basis for describing the behaviour in qualitative terms, alternatively a start point for production of a quantitative model that can be used to simulate the behaviour of the system over time.

LOOPS, FEEDBACK AND DELAYS

The dynamic behaviour of a system is determined by its feedback structure and the influence of delays between changes in one part of the system and their impact in another part. There are two feedback mechanisms: reinforcing (positive) and controlling (negative).

Figure 17.2 shows a single reinforcing loop. *Sales* of a quality product result in an increase in the *number of satisfied customers* which in turn increase *new customer purchases* so resulting in increased *sales*. This description gives rise to the idea of a "virtuous circle". (We also recognise that some processes might

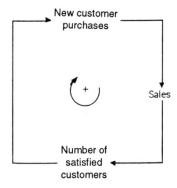

Figure 17.2 A single positive loop

work in reverse as a sort of "not-so virtuous spiral" leading to reinforcing decline!) Loops of this type will exhibit some form of exponential growth or decline.

Figure 17.3 shows a single controlling loop. These exhibit a balancing or self-correcting behaviour and can be read as follows: an increase between *target sales volume* and current *sales* gives rise to an increase in *sales gap*. The increase in *sales gap* results in an increase in the level of *sales incentivisation and promotions* which in turn increases *sales* so closing the *sales gap*. The "o" symbol adjacent to "Sales Gap" in Figure 17.3 is to indicate an "opposing" effect; that is, an increase in "Sales" serves to reduce the "Sales Gap".

Changes do not give rise to instantaneous effects. For example, in Figure 17.3 it will take some time for any increase in sales incentivisation or promotions to produce an effect on sales. Thus, in not recognising the delay, it is possible that we might increase the level of incentivisation and promotions above that needed to close the gap, so subsequently exceeding our target. Delays give rise to the characteristic overshoot, undershoot and oscillation that are encountered in many business processes but most commonly known in the vagaries of the "business cycle".

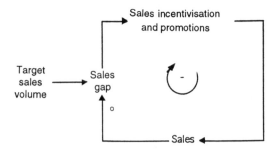

Figure 17.3 A single negative loop

APPLYING SYSTEM DYNAMICS

In practice a system will contain many loops. It will be a combination of positive and negative loops and will contain a number of different delays. Thus its behaviour over time will be a complex addition of effects as on occasion one loop dominates, while at another time some other loop, or combination of loops, will move to have a major influence.

From this it can be seen that understanding why a system responds in a particular way in a given circumstance, or predicting the effects resulting from a specific change, becomes an impossible task without some form of assistance. The application of system dynamics equips us with a tool that enables us to construct representative models of a system under investigation, simulate their behaviour over time, reproduce problematic behaviour, evaluate the impact of changes, and test and share our understanding of how a system works. In so doing it helps to overcome our mental limitations in coping with complexity and, through use of simulation to compress time, allows us, using a "what if" process, to access and comprehend glimpses of possible futures that we might observe in the real world.

This technique has broad application to any investigation where we are concerned to understand behaviour over time and, as such, we find examples of the application of system dynamics in many different areas.

Relating Business Process Re-engineering and System Dynamics

At the heart of business process re-engineering is the notion of a *process* as a set of related activities concerned with fulfilling some purpose. This idea of a "purposeful whole" leads directly to a need for an integrated view and understanding of how different elements of people, technology, information, time, money, and other resources combine to enable a process to fulfil its purpose. The potential for business dynamics to make a powerful contribution to building such a view becomes immediately clear.

Dependent on our specific concern, a variety of tools and techniques are available to assist us in conducting business process re-engineering. A number exist that support continuous and discrete time simulations of detailed business processes. These are often used as part of in-depth operational research studies into specific issues; common applications include transport and logistics as well as some manufacturing processes. Likewise, a number of flow diagramming tools and techniques (e.g. IDEF, IEF, SSADM, etc.) exist for documenting processes as part of process design or improvement initiatives, or to support the creation of information systems.

It is helpful to consider how the use of business dynamics fits alongside these other techniques. My own experience of having used many such different techniques is that no single one is best suited to all circumstances, and in this respect business dynamics is no exception. The use of business dynamics will be especially relevant where we are concerned to understand the performance of a process over time. And if we wish to bridge a knowledge of process structure with an appreciation of managerial assumptions about process workings, and to understand the dynamic impact of the explicit and implicit control mechanisms at work, then, to the best of my knowledge, business dynamics is the only technique available. This then defines the area of relevance for business dynamics.

PROCESS STRUCTURE

In using business dynamics we can consider a process, in general terms, to be represented as shown in Figure 17.4, where thicker single-headed arrows indicate the flow of deliverable resources (i.e. those representing the purpose of the process), and thinner double-headed arrows depict the flow of supporting resources.

From a dynamic perspective, our attention naturally falls on the structural fit between the workings of the process and the interfaces between customers and suppliers and the requirement for coordination with related processes. At the next level of detail we can consider the different process activities as falling into groups concerned with acquisition, transformation, distribution, and management of resources. This results in an expanded view of our general process as shown in Figure 17.5.

The importance of process management activities now becomes clear. For, in addition to the standard coordination and control activities, if the process is to be viable it must encompass the necessary *learning* activities to enable it to adapt to its changing environment. Understanding this general form, and its relationship to a dynamic viewpoint, is central to the application of business dynamics. In terms of business process re-engineering three approaches are

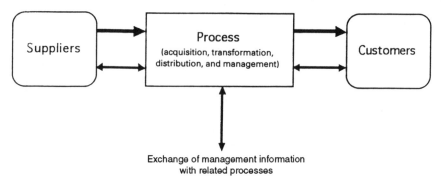

Figure 17.4   A general process definition

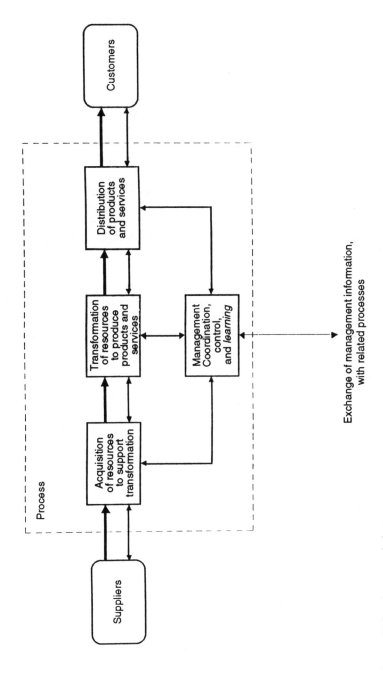

Figure 17.5 An expanded process

revealed: *redesigning the decision processes, redesigning the physical process,* and *redesigning information channels* (van Ackere, Larsen and Morecroft, 1993).

UNDERLYING CONCEPTS

The essence of using business dynamics is to understand the behaviour over time that may be generated by a given organisation of resources. We are interested in an integrated view of both tangible and intangible resources, and the role played by management. We wish to understand the impact they have on the behaviour of the system.

The impact of management can be divided into two broad groups. The first relates to implicit consequences that flow from their decisions about the organisation and availability of tangible resources, and specification of organisational roles. The second group relates to impacts that stem from the policy frameworks they establish, performance measures used to guide an organisation, and finally the day-to-day flow of decisions they take governing operation of the organisation. Examples falling into the former group might include decisions to make all products on one production line; the division of sales and distribution operations into regional areas; alternatively, limits on the availability of production capacity, working capital, or staff. Examples in the second group vary across a broad spectrum but could include a policy of incentivising salespeople on total amount sold, or a decision to restrict recruitment in the face of falling demand. The distinction between the two groups can become blurred but is important. In a sense it can be likened to the notion of "fixed" and "variable" costs; while in the long term all costs can be considered as variable, in the short term many costs will be fixed. So it is with *structure*. In broad terms the first group concerns impacts that flow from the way the organisation is set up, i.e. "the way the business works", while the second concerns "the way the business is operated".

The point to note from this discussion is our concern with the role of managers. The beliefs they hold about "how the business works" ultimately shape the decisions they take to develop and steer the organisation. From a business dynamics perspective, we can view the activity of management as a process of conversion of information into action (Forrester, 1992). Information about the current state of affairs is interpreted as a basis for determining future actions. The problem is that we are not good at comprehending the full range of consequences that flow from our actions while, at the same time, we have to work with partial, uncertain and conflicting information. And further, as research has consistently demonstrated (Hall, 1976; Sterman, 1989; Paich and Sterman, 1993), where causes and effects are separated in space and time, and where there are significant delays between our actions and their effects, we are not good at appreciating the implications of our actions. Thus, what happens is that we tend to formulate our actions based on the immediate stream of events that surround our activity and lose sight of the broader picture and longer term. However, this is to miss an opportunity; the high points of leverage for management rest in understanding *structure*, and herein lies the strength of business dynamics.

As Figure 17.6 shows there is a trade-off between accessibility and scope of impact. The pressure to solve "today's problems today", power, politics, culture, attitudes: "there are no problems only solutions!"; our natural desire to reap the fruits of our own labour, a preference for local solutions to local problems, an inclination to action, all favour management solutions reacting to the immediate events of the day using existing policy frameworks. In any case it is simply too difficult to grapple with the deeper issues! However, the impact of such actions are limited, they are restricted by the imperatives of the underlying structure.

What we learn from applying business dynamics paints a different picture. As managers seeking to influence the future behaviour of organisations the major scope for impact lies in the decisions we take about *structure* and the interaction between deep structure and policies in use. Intuitively this seems obvious: "if in doubt reorganise!" Unfortunately, unless we understand the dynamic implications of decisions about *structure*, any decisions we take may, although well intended, be flawed. Insights at this level are difficult to access requiring us to pool the understanding held by different individuals and to deal with the complexity of pictures that often span organisational boundaries. By providing a framework, and supporting tools, for exploring such behaviour the

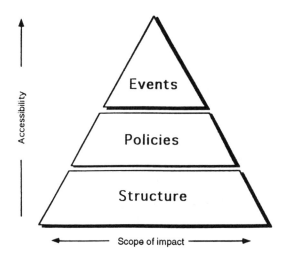

Figure 17.6 The importance of structure

application of business dynamics helps to overcome this problem by making such understanding more accessible. All this suggests a shift in emphasis in the task of management from "operating" towards one of "designing" (Keough and Doman, 1992); that is, choosing and setting the most appropriate *structure* to fulfil a particular purpose.

A common theme in the different uses of business dynamics is a desire to discover and implement more effective structures for fulfilling a given purpose. That is not to say that there is one "right" structure for every circumstance (each particular structure will have its own characteristic strengths and weaknesses) but acknowledges, for a given purpose, that some structures will be better suited than others. But we find it is simply not possible to explore the full range of implications of choosing a particular structure from a static viewpoint. Thus business dynamics provides a useful addition to our management "toolbox" by equipping us with an ability to move beyond a static understanding to explore the implications of a dynamic picture. Such a viewpoint leads us to a more disciplined framework for weighing the difference between long- and short-term benefits flowing from any structural change. Due to feedback structure and delays we find that many dynamic effects are counterintuitive and work against the intended outcome. By absorbing this reality as part of the dynamic viewpoint we can appreciate the balance of short- and long-term implications. This leads to the idea of a change impact grid as shown in Figure 17.7.

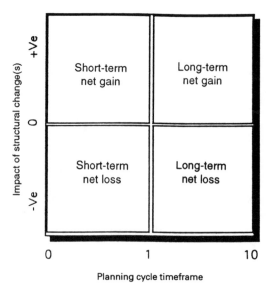

Figure 17.7   A structural change impact grid

This depicts a division between net gains resulting from change in the top half and net losses in the bottom half. The left-to-right division draws a distinction between short- and long-term timeframes. By incorporating candidate changes within a business dynamics model, and tracking its resulting evolution over time, it becomes possible to evaluate the net gains and losses associated with that change. From this we can identify a number of general scenarios as shown in Figure 17.8.

For changes that result in clear short- and long-term net gains or losses, classical "win/win" or "lose/lose" situations, we have an easy task. However, in a majority of cases the picture we discover is more complex. We may well find that a notionally sound change (for example, encouraging and allowing employee overtime in the face of a sudden surge in customer demand), which results in net short-term gains (ease of delivery delays with little increase in overhead), subsequently results in long-term losses (lower quality and increased staff attrition and loss of expertise) which outweigh the short-term advantage; a story of "glory today" but either not foreseeing or choosing to ignore the consequences for tomorrow. Alternatively, a change which initially appears unattractive (increased non-billable time and investment in staff development) due to short-term net losses actually results in significant long-term net gains (increased market attractiveness of consultants due to novel capabilities) which more than compensate for the initial short-term losses; the idea of a "price worth paying" but often in practice a "path not taken" either due to short-term constraints or alternatively a narrow evaluation of options.

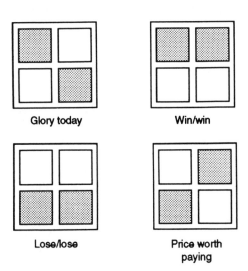

Figure 17.8   Evaluating the impact of structural change

The above examples may seem obvious with hindsight but this makes them no less important, for although the ideas of "short-termism" and "things getting worse before they get better" are generally accepted in practice the implications are often ignored. And, by providing for the pooling of individual knowledge, development of shared understanding, and the discovery and communication of counterintuitive effects, business dynamics provides a powerful and practical tool for helping managers grapple with such issues.

USING BUSINESS DYNAMICS

Applications of business dynamics can be found in all areas of management, revealing three distinct modes of use: problem investigation and solving, design, and learning.

Problem Investigation and Solving

The startpoint here will usually be some existing concern involving problematic behaviour over time. Examples might include: falling market share, or profitability; highly volatile sales; or increasing customer dissatisfaction. The first step will be to construct a model, either qualitative or quantitative, that seeks to explain the behaviour. Once such an explanation has been developed the next step will be to identify and evaluate opportunities for improving the situation. The resulting explanatory model can then be used to help communicate findings from the investigation and to help build commitment to and formulate plans for implementation of any resulting changes.

Design

In this mode business dynamics models are used to assist in designing and evaluating new organisational processes. Examples might include: investigating the configuration of activities in a new telephone sales operation, designing a new production system, or exploring alternatives for the launch of a new product. The approach taken here will be to construct representative models and to use them in a "what if" type of way to explore the implications of adopting different designs. The resulting models can then be used in a variety of different ways to help move forward from design to implementation. They can help in clarifying and quantifying the different resource requirements. They can be used to check assumptions about the response of the process in the face of different demand patterns. They can be useful in identifying information system requirements and helping to define operating procedures. And they might be used to track the validity of design assumptions during the early stages of operation of a new process.

Learning

The objective here is to use business dynamics to help in developing understanding about complex behaviours. Some of the more recent novel applications of business dynamics have occurred in this area. Examples include: exploring market growth strategies, developing an understanding of the limitations of different operating strategies, appreciating the balance of short-term versus long-term trade-offs in an existing process, or exploring long-term policy implications. The approach adopted is to construct a sort of management flight simulator, often referred to as a "learning micro-world" (Senge and Sterman, 1992), and to encourage people to explore this as part of a structured learning experience. By providing individuals with an objective it is possible for them to test out their assumptions about the most effective management strategy. In seeking to explain any differences between the results they expect and the behaviour produced by the model, insight is gained into the counterintuitive aspects of dynamic behaviour and the validity and consistency of their own internal "mental models" about the process.

Early applications emphasised creation of large-scale, detailed, models of whole business systems as a basis for predicting future business performance. These applications proved costly and required significant specialist expertise. In addition, the fallacy of seeking to predict the future, and the fact that results were not accessible to managers, served to diminish perceptions about the value of the method. However, improvements in modelling technology, growing recognition of the importance of the process of model construction itself, and discovery of the power of the method in linking individual beliefs ("mental models") about the workings of a process to the reality of the organisational setting has resulted in a steady increase in useful applications. More recently, many successful applications have involved the use of relatively simple models focused on specific issues.

A selection of examples highlights the diverse potential for use of business dynamics. Recent supply chain applications include an examination of resupply practice and information flows for a JIT Kanban system (Byrne and Roberts, 1994) resulting in 25% savings in a manufacturer's stock holdings, on-going research into the dynamics of capacity-constrained supply chains (Evans and Naim, 1994), and the use of business dynamics to support re-engineering of value processes for a sales operation (Thurlby and Chang, 1994). Examples from other areas include scenario modelling of the future demand for telecommunications services (Barnes *et al.*, 1994) and an examination into re-engineering of career plans (Davis, 1994). Table 17.1 provides a summary of example business dynamics applications in each of the main management disciplines.

Two recent cases highlight different uses of business dynamics. These contrast the use of quantitative and qualitative approaches and show how

Table 17.1 Example applications of business dynamics

Enterprise	• Examining the viability of business start-up plans
	• Evaluating policy frameworks for grant support for SME development
	• Investigation of regional development policy
Finance	• Examining the evolution of working capital requirements
	• Evaluation of company growth plans
	• Assessment of investment proposals
Human resource management	• Evaluation of recruitment and staff development policies
	• Training capacity management
	• Examining the impact of remuneration schemes
Information systems	• Evaluating information system benefits
	• Exploring information system requirements
Operations management	• Product and service delivery system design and improvement
	• Operating policy investigation and improvement
	• Supply chain evaluation and improvement
Sales & marketing	• Investigation of new product launch strategies
	• Evaluation of pricing policies and product promotions
	• Assessment of long-term market development
Strategic management	• Evaluation of business plans and scenarios
	• Assessment of strategic development plans
	• Investigating the impact of performance measures on organisation performance

business dynamics acts as a catalyst for integrating issues. Both demonstrate how use encourages the implications of issues in one area (e.g. changes in the nature of market demand) to be linked through to concerns in other areas (e.g. human resources and finance). Related to this it can be seen how the process of model construction itself aids in the process of building a shared understanding of key issues among those involved.

CASE 1: BUSINESS PLANNING AT FOOD CO.

Background

Food Co. manufactures and sells an established range of well-known branded products. It has a record of innovation in new product development and marketing while being acknowledged as one of the leaders within its sector with a quality reputation for excellence.

This case involved the application of business dynamics as part of an investigation into the management of finished goods stock. The investigation took place against a background of other major improvements in supply chain management. These included reconfiguration of distribution operations and the interface between sales and the factory, and a programme to replace the existing sales order processing system with a new integrated information system. This new information system would for the first time link sales and distribution directly through to production forecasting and planning, and ultimately enable the automatic generation of production orders for the factory.

Production took place mainly at one site although for selected products, and to meet peaks in demand, regular use was made of contract suppliers and packers. Distribution was based around a centralised warehouse system. Most orders were shipped direct from a centralised store. Some smaller orders were distributed through a regional network although all inventory was held centrally. The future trend was towards all shipments direct from the centralised store.

The business was characterised by a highly fluctuating demand pattern. Partly driven by seasonal factors, the pattern for individual products was also known to be significantly influenced by promotional activity. Combined, these effects emphasised the importance of effective business forecasting and planning and the need to be able to adapt production output to fit the varying demands placed upon it.

The importance of new products and promotional activity had grown over the past few years. This had resulted in a pattern of increased product variety and shorter promotional runs of particular products. Rather than a high volume of sales from a small number of different products, the business was moving to a situation where a growing percentage of sales were taken up with lower volume sales on a greater variety of products (see Figure 17.9). This trend was thought likely to continue.

The existing production capability had been driven by a previous strategy geared up to meet a requirement for a high-volume, low-cost, low product variety, production demand. This resulted in a mismatch with current business requirements. To offset this, effective use of contract suppliers and packers had assumed a growing importance. At the same time, there had been significant changes in distribution. The shift towards centralised warehousing had seen total storage capacity reduced and there was a continued pressure to justify stock levels at a minimum consistent with meeting the needs of the business.

While the internal drive had been towards improved business practice through simplification, streamlining of processes, and integration across critical interfaces, the overall business logic coupled with marketplace developments had resulted in an external demand of growing complexity. Given this reality, over the years Food Co. had developed a highly sophisticated and capable business forecasting and production planning process. This manual process,

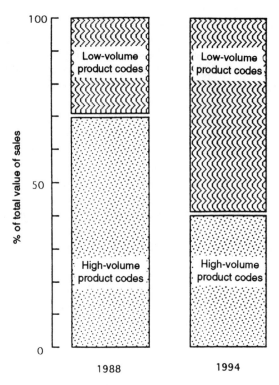

Figure 17.9   Long-term trends in sales profile

based on a multiple time-horizon rolling schedule, provided a basis for agreeing and fine-tuning the weekly production schedule. However, as part of planned new information systems it was envisaged that this manual process would become largely automated.

The Investigation

Work started by building, based on discussions with key managers, an overall picture of the production and supply system (see Figure 17.10). During a subsequent workshop session, involving senior managers representing each business area, the principles of business dynamics were introduced and the picture of the business system was further extended and analysed to identify factors impacting dynamic performance. By considering the actual order and stock profiles for a representative product it then proved possible to collate a combined picture of different managers' perceptions of key drivers. The results of this qualitative evaluation then formed a basis for specifying a subsequent phase of more detailed investigation.

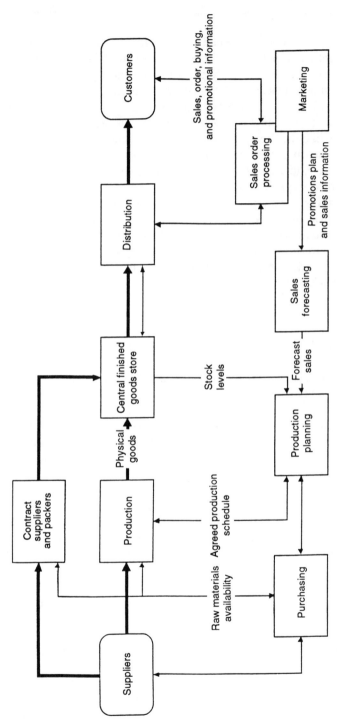

Figure 17.10 Food Co. business system

The initial workshop helped to develop a common view among the management team of the key drivers of dynamic behaviour. Out of this came recognition of the role currently played by finished goods stock in meeting the external demands placed on the business. Finished goods stock was seen to fall into two categories: "structural" and "service". The "structural" component represented the amounts of stock implicit in the way the business was being operated, while the "service" component was seen as that necessary to provide for uncertainty in demand faced by the business.

Given the extent of other business initiatives underway it was decided to focus the next stage of investigation on the stock profile of a few key products. To support this a quantitative system dynamics model of part of the production and sales system was constructed (Figure 17.11 shows part of this model). Using this model combined with stock management theory, knowledge of the existing approach to production planning, and historic information on actual order and stock patterns it became possible to investigate the dynamic behaviour of stock levels.

Findings

Both phases of investigation revealed important insights. The qualitative investigation demonstrated important dynamic effects associated with promotional activity, in addition to the different roles played by finished goods stock. In talking with managers about causal impacts stemming from promotions a difference between their effect on trade and end-consumer sales became clear. The major impact of some promotions was transfer of value to trade, whereas in others the promotional benefit was of value to end-consumers. Promotions to trade were seen to have little or no effect on total end-consumer sales. The dynamic effects of such promotions were to cause a surge in sales to trade as they loaded stock levels to take advantage of the promotion. However, given the minimal impact on end-consumer demand, the resultant net effect on the business was a period of reduced sales to trade as trade stock levels were once more run down to more normal ones. Although this effect was known about, the full extent of its impact on peak storage capacity requirements and fluctuations in stock levels had not been appreciated. Using business dynamics provided a framework for discussion of this important issue and a startpoint for evaluating the relative costs and benefits of different promotional strategies.

The phase of detailed investigation revealed important gaps in knowledge about, and deficiencies in, the existing approach to production forecasting, planning, and management of stock levels. Central to these were the nature and use of information about customer service levels. The tacit assumption by management was that stock levels were managed at such a level to deliver an acceptable level of customer service. However, investigation revealed only

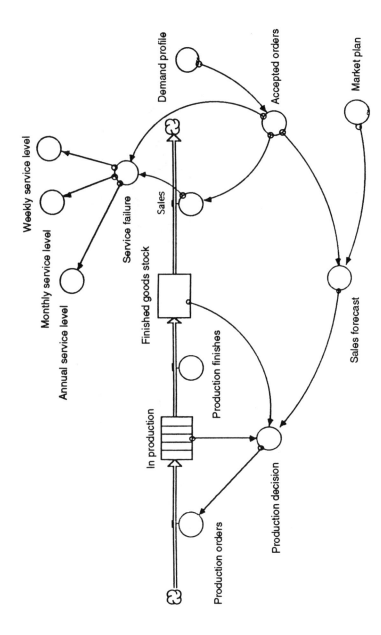

Figure 17.11 Business dynamics model for Food Co. investigation

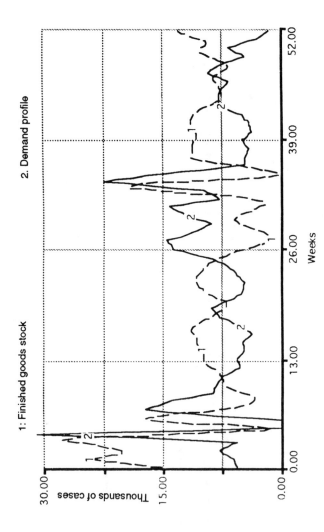

Figure 17.12 Example stock profile

limited collection and use of information about unconstrained customer demand. Since the primary measure of customer service level was against "accepted orders" it was not possible to determine to what extent, if at all, the existing approach to management adversely affected service levels or total sales. However, by profiling stock into "structural" and "service" components, and by simulating a business dynamics model with the actual demand pattern (see Figure 17.12 for a typical simulation profile), it became possible to explore in a "what if" way the possible impacts of different approaches to forecasting and production rules on inventory levels. Comparison of these results with actual stock levels led to a conclusion that there was no evidence, given the pattern of demand, to support a view that actual stock levels on the items investigated were excessive. Business dynamics thus provided a solution for evaluating the effectiveness of the existing approach to production planning, in addition to enabling evaluation of the possible business impacts on customer service levels and storage requirements of introducing the new automated approach to forecasting and setting of production orders.

Conclusions

The application of business dynamics in this case provided an important contribution to an existing programme of process improvements. The construction and interpretation of an integrated picture enabled management to develop a shared view of the dynamic drivers affecting the total supply chain. Most importantly, the use of a quantitative business dynamics model, in one area, identified critical aspects in other parts of the business. This in turn led to identification of important risk areas related to existing implementation plans for process improvements. Finally, the use of a qualitative business dynamics model highlighted the need to investigate further the impacts and benefits associated with promotional activity and to better understand the costs and benefits associated with different production rules.

CASE 2: TELCO. OPERATOR SERVICES

Background

Telco. Operator Services is a centralised resource providing telephone operator services, (including emergency 999, directory enquiries and general operator assistance) for Telco.'s different customers. Significant problems were being experienced with poor delivered customer service levels and excessive staff attrition within the group. An internal audit team was invited to examine the problem. As part of their investigation they made use of a qualitative business dynamics model to capture and structure understanding about the different issues, and as a basis for communicating their findings.

Investigation

There were differing views as to the source of problems being experienced by the operator services group. By using a business dynamics map to represent different perceptions of the intended management policy, and problems being experienced, it was possible to build a shared understanding of the underlying causes as a basis for exploring and agreeing improvements.

Figure 17.13 shows a version of the map produced during the investigation. The intended management policy was based on a budget determined by a forecast demand for operator services. The budget was set on the basis of new line sales, and a calculation of operator call volume for the number of lines. This calculation used historic data on the pattern of operator service demand associated with a line. The budget determined a target for the number of required operators which in turn governed the rate of new operator recruitment. An increase in the number of operators was seen to have a positive impact on the delivered service level. Increases in actual demand for operator services were seen to reduce the level of delivered customer service. The management response to drops in delivered customer service level was to increase the budget for provision for services so allowing for the recruitment of more operators. In turn after a *delay* this increase in budget had a positive impact on the recruitment of new operators.

The intended management policy was thus described by the negative loop depicted at the centre of Figure 17.13. This can be read as follows: "A fall in delivered service level results in a rise in budget for provision of operator services which in turn, after a delay, results in a rise in the recruitment rate of new operators, which leads to an increase in number of operators so leading to a rise restoring the delivered service level." Increases in the actual demand for services were setting off a cascade of other effects. In addition to driving an increased budget, falls in delivered service levels were causing an increase in operator stress. These increases in stress were serving to reduce operator productivity at the same time as increasing the operator attrition rate. Increases in the operator attrition rate were having a number of adverse effects. While clearly reducing the total number of operators, they also drove a requirement for increased recruitment. Thus as well as recruitment associated with expansion of demand, a growing percentage of the total recruitment burden was associated with replacement of operators who were leaving. Other effects of an increased operator attrition rate were reductions in the average level of operator expertise and in the quality of supervision. Both these factors served to impact productivity adversely. The quality of supervision was further reduced by increases in the recruitment rate due to the need for supervisors to be involved in the recruitment process to select new operators.

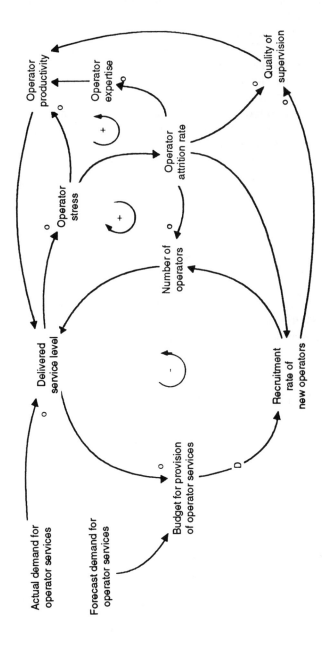

Figure 17.13   Telco. qualitative business dynamics map

Discussion of the map revealed an imbalance between the impact of the intended management policy and that of the vicious circle of decline driven by increases in operator stress. Standing back from the immediate situation the underlying cause was revealed as a disconnect between the forecast and actual demand for services. This focused management attention on the need to understand better the nature of demand services and away from tackling the immediate symptoms associated with increases in the operator attrition rate. Subsequent investigation revealed that changes in the pattern of sales invalidated the assumptions being used to set the budget. An increasing number of new sales were for cellular mobile lines. Users of these lines had a very different pattern of requirement for operator services. By understanding better, and forecasting, the demand for services management was able to build agreement on process improvements for the provision of operator services, and control of resourcing.

Conclusion

This case provides an example of using qualitative business dynamics. There was no need to build a quantitative model in this situation and in any case the prevailing culture would have made this difficult even had it been desirable. Aside from the consultant who led the internal investigation, no other participants had prior experience of business dynamics. Those directly involved found the map a useful way of structuring and sharing their understanding and as a basis for communicating the need for change.

OPPORTUNITIES AND CHALLENGES

One of the prime insights from using system dynamics is that well-intended policies often result in counterproductive long-term outcomes, and being able to comprehend the reasons for disconnects between the intended result of policies and their ultimate impact is one of system dynamics' major contributions to knowledge. My own view is that bridging a managerial understanding of process behaviour with process structure is an important and neglected area of business process re-engineering, and although a considerable body of research in system dynamics has concerned this topic (Hall, 1976; Sterman, 1989; Paich and Sterman, 1993) this has yet to be successfully related to work in business process re-engineering.

In general, the main areas of opportunity for the future development of business dynamics stem directly from recent developments in theory and practice. These include expansion beyond limited use as a specialist operations research technique, recognition of the importance and value of the process of model construction, acknowledgement that business dynamics can be used in a qualitative mode, improvements in modelling technology, and use in helping to support learning-centred approaches to business improvement and innovation.

Challenges for the future development of business dynamics centre on ease of use, integration with other methods, and education. They are best summed up in a comment made to me that "system dynamics is easy to know but impossible to apply". The problem is that the core ideas of business dynamics are deceptively simple; however, exploiting them requires a fundamental shift in the way in which we think about the world and approach problems. This highlights the importance of education. And while progress in the development of qualitative techniques and the idea of system archetypes (Senge, 1990) has gone some way to overcoming these difficulties, much remains to be done.

Some of the most novel opportunities for business dynamics centre on the use of learning microworlds as a basis for helping in translating new insights into changed managerial behaviours. Extensive research at MIT based around a "claims learning laboratory" for insurance company managers reports significant short-term benefits as part of training (Senge and Sterman, 1992) although the long-term benefits have yet to be fully assessed. Other research into the long-term evolution and survival of companies and the relationship with managerial learning has potential implications for the development and implementation of strategy. A detailed review of the evolution of two London-based insurance companies over a 20-year span using a business dynamics model suggests that understanding the limit of sustainable growth for a company may be of vital importance (Doman *et al.*, 1994). Also, experimental research using a calibrated business dynamics model to explore managerial learning trajectories has important implications for testing management assumptions on process behaviour (Hall, 1994). Linking such techniques as part of the routine business planning cycle, by combining representative business dynamic models of a company's key processes within an executive information system, is one possible extension of such ideas. A good review of business dynamics in this area can be found in *Modeling for Learning Organizations* (Morecroft and Sterman, 1994). Finally, method development will continue to be an important area of activity since being able to integrate the use of business dynamics alongside other techniques is critical in many applications. Recent experience in seeking to combine methods reveals the need for an integrating methodology (Hocking and Lee, 1994). Other research points to the potential for standard business dynamic building blocks for use in investigating manufacturing processes (La Roche, 1994).

CONCLUDING THOUGHTS

At the beginning I set out some questions for us to keep in mind about the extent of use and importance of business dynamics. As to the relative obscurity of business dynamics I believe two factors are significant. First, its broad applicability results in expertise being spread among many different management disciplines. Second, until recently, there was a strong perception that it was a specialist method of little relevance to practising managers.

Looking to its importance much has been learnt during the past 30 years. The key message is that business dynamics should not be seen as a panacea, but rather as an integrating theme. It is not an "instead of" but an "as well as" method and its use is not the sole province of specialists. Effective use requires the active participation of managers, policy makers, and problem owners, and without such its full potential will not be realised. With these factors in mind, the challenge for researchers is to make the knowledge of business dynamics more accessible and its practice easier. The challenge for managers is to recognise the importance of understanding dynamic performance and their responsibility for the design of effective organisations and policies.

Used appropriately, business dynamics has the potential to make a powerful contribution to the improvement of management. As the technology and systems we create become more sophisticated, as the number of dependencies between (and within) our organisations increase, I believe we will recognise an increasing need for the insight which its application reveals. Business dynamics offers a proven and powerful set of tools for supporting business process re-engineering.

_____ Part Five

Case Studies

Chapter 18

Introduction

Colin Armistead and Philip Rowland

There are a series of case studies in this part of the book. In selecting them we have tried to satisfy a number of requirements. We wanted cases which illustrated the improvement programmes in a range of different types of organisations in both the public and private sectors. We also looked for cases of different lengths to allow for flexibility in use. Finally we wanted cases which could be used in a comparative way.

We suggest you use the cases in a variety of ways depending on your own individual learning needs. At a first level you may wish to read through them to gain a general appreciation of what has been done and how people in different organisations reflect on the experience. On the other hand, you may wish to examine a particular case in more detail either on your own or as a member of a learning set. To help to structure your approach to the cases we suggest a number of questions. The first set are what we would see as generic questions which could be addressed to all the cases. The second set are specific questions which we think are particularly applicable to specific cases. The third are questions which allow you to compare cases. If you are analysing the cases in detail we would expect you to be using the ideas and frameworks which have been outlined in the preceding chapters and the Appendix at the end of this book.

GENERIC QUESTIONS

We think it useful to group these questions under four headings addressing the issue. Why do it? Who is involved? What approaches can be taken? What problems are encountered?

Why do it?

1. Why do organisations chose BPR and a process orientation as an improvement methodology?
2. Why is BPR chosen instead of continuous improvement?
3. What benefits do people hope to achieve from taking a business process management approach?
4. Is BPR and subsequent management by process appropriate for small to medium-sized enterprises?

Who's involved?

1. What is the role of senior management in BPR and how important is it?
2. What is the interaction between process, people and technology?
3. To what extent is the role of the operating functions undergoing fundamental change as a result of process re-engineering and the shift to managing business process?
4. How important is the participation of the operating functions in a process re-engineering initiative?
5. To what extent is the role of the enabling functions undergoing fundamental change as a result of process re-engineering and the shift to managing business processes?
6. How important is the participation of the enabling functions in a process re-engineering initiative?

What approaches can be taken?

1. What are the main steps in a business process re-engineering project?
2. What's the role of the process owner in managing process re-engineering and the new organisation that results?
3. What project management approaches have been used to control re-engineering projects?
4. What barriers exist to using business dynamics on a wide scale to improve organisational understanding and how could these be overcome?
5. How might measurement systems change in moving to a process-based organisation?

What are the main problems?

1. What are the main problems in undertaking a BPR project and the transition to a more process-former organisation and how can these be dealt with?
2. What defensive behaviours surfaced in the companies and how was this overcome?

3. How can managers gain an effective understanding of their core processes without becoming "bogged down" in the details?
4. How does an understanding of culture help managers in re-engineering and the shift to managing by process?
5. What considerations must management address when shifting to a more process-orientated management structure?

CASE-SPECIFIC QUESTIONS

The following are questions which we see as being relevant to individual cases.
Mitel Telecom

1. To what extent is there evidence of Mitel Telecom applying the principles of managing by process?
2. How significant is the role of the managing director in the shift to process orientation?

English Nature – Realising the Vision

1. What were the pressures for change in English Nature and how did the management team respond?
2. What additional problems is English Nature likely to face as a public sector organisation?

Re-engineering Customer Support in Hewlett-Packard

1. How did the role of customer service and support change for Hewlett-Packard as a result of the re-engineering project?
2. How did Hewlett-Packard integrate considerations of process, people and technology?

St James's Hospital and Lucas Engineering Systems – A BPR Collaboration Case (A) – Elective Admissions – Urology
Project A

1. What are the costs and benefits of implementing a BPR project in a major hospital such as St James's?
2. Imagine you are a patient in St James's. What might your concerns be about the project and how might the hospital's management cope with these?
3. How important will a modification to the hospital's culture be in the re-engineering project?

Re-engineering the Post Office Supply Chain

1. What are the strengths and weaknesses of the Post Office's approach to managing the project? What suggestions would you make to improve the approach?
2. How would you justify the project being customer driven?

Making the Valuable Difference: Successful BPR at National Vulcan

1. What evidence might there be that National Vulcan would be classified as "driven" in the strategy framework outlined in Chapter 9?
2. Describe the benefits from each major change in National Vulcan's project.

Cigna: Changing the Culture

1. Assess Cigna's approach to cultural change using the cultural web model outlined in Chapter 6.
2. To what extent is Cigna moving towards a more "empowered" workforce?

Reflections on a BPR Project

1. How might management respond to the fears and concerns expressed in the chapter?
2. How would you construct a communications plan to motivate staff?

Apollo Fire Detectors

1. What might the next steps for Apollo Fire Detectors be after the improvements in manufacturing?
2. How might Apollo harness the learning in manufacturing to improve other parts of the business?

COMPARATIVE QUESTIONS

Undertaking re-engineering requires a knowledge of the issues which usually occur as well as an ability to identify the unique company or project-specific issues. Comparing and contrasting different cases helps in this process and we suggest you spend some time in thinking about the differences and similarities highlighted in the cases. We suggest a few questions which you may wish to use.

1. You are a consulting team pitching for the project at St James's Hospital. You have been on an initial visit and have been asked by the CEO to present your approach to the hospital's board, drawing on three examples of recent projects. In particular, the CEO is interested in how the financial benefits of such a project can be evaluated and how the natural resistance to change can be overcome.
2. Compare and contrast the roles of the CEO in Mitel Telecom and National Vulcan.
3. Benchmark the approaches to analysing customer deliverables in the Post Office and Hewlett-Packard. In particular, you should focus on the approaches each has taken to relating customer requirements to the delivery processes and discuss the strengths and weaknesses of each approach.

Chapter 19

English Nature—Realising the Vision

Graham Hutton

(This case is reproduced by kind permission of English Nature and CCTA)

English Nature is a non-departmental public body financed by grant-in-aid from the Department of the Environment. It has more than 700 staff and an annual budget of almost £40 million. It manages some 140 National Nature Reserves, advises on the management of around 3700 Sites of Special Scientific Interest involving about 23000 owners and occupiers, has management agreements with owners and occupiers of special sites worth about £7 million per annum and gives a further £2 million in grants to other bodies.

Recently, English Nature has had to undergo a period of profound change in the way it manages its business. The trigger for this change was external, not internal. Before change was thrust upon them by Parliament, the managers of English Nature's predecessor, the Nature Conservancy Council (NCC), believed that they were already satisfying customers concerned with nature conservation. But NCC were not satisfying the government – the customer for NCC's advice. Nor were they satisfying the owners and occupiers and many other people outside the "conservation community" whose choices and decisions affect and are affected by conservation of the natural heritage.

Fuelling the process of change at all times was the organisation's vision of where it wanted to be and what it aimed to do. The Board defines this vision as follows:

> "English Nature will give the lead in sustaining and enriching England's natural heritage for all to enjoy now and in the future. We will share our knowledge, understanding and practical experience to inspire, enable and empower people to achieve this with us. The service we deliver will be founded on a strategic approach to the conservation of wildlife and natural features."

This chapter describes how English Nature developed its vision and how it radically transformed its organisation and business processes to realise it.

THE SITUATION FACING ENGLISH NATURE

English Nature was formed on 2 April 1991 following the passing of the Environmental Protection Act (EPA) in 1990. Almost all the staff were transferred from the Nature Conservancy Council (NCC) which had been set up after the Second World War to provide a sound scientific foundation for nature conservation in Great Britain. The EPA separated the Welsh and Scottish operations from the English and merged the Nature and Countryside bodies in the smaller countries into the Countryside Council for Wales (CCW) and Scottish Natural Heritage (SNH). In England, the Countryside Commission remained a separate entity from English Nature. A Joint Nature Conservation Committee was established to coordinate UK-wide issues and provide much of the scientific underpinning for conservation.

The changes came as a shock to the management and staff of the NCC. It was a science-based organisation whose philosophy was expressed in the 1984 report on *Nature Conservation in Britain*, a report highly respected in the science and conservation community. The culture was that of scientists, not of managers and administrators: the staff had their own views on the aims of NCC which provided many with the opportunity to "do science" much as if they were working for a university or voluntary organisation. These attitudes made NCC well respected among those who shared the views of its staff. But it made it unpopular with the many other stakeholders in conservation territory. Not least of these were the government ministers who had to reconcile conflicting interests, notably in Scotland and Wales. NCC's Peterborough HQ was regarded as being out of touch, its Board was divided, its aims were much debated but not agreed and accepted, and it was seen to be inefficient. A consultant was asked to research staff attitudes and the survey produced as a result stressed the need for leadership and communication.

Reorganisation of the statutory bodies did not actually re-engineer the business processes, but it did create the conditions which made radical transformation in English Nature possible. The government appointed a new external Chairman, a peer with impeccable scientific and political credentials, and promoted an insider with considerable management skills and a strong scientific background to be Chief Executive in the summer of 1990. Together, they were to provide the management drive and leadership that English Nature needed, beginning with the Board itself.

WHAT ENGLISH NATURE WANTED TO ACHIEVE

The Board of English Nature produced a statement of their philosophy, for the new organisation whose birth was now imminent. During an intensive 24-hour workshop away from the office, the Board succeeded in agreeing a one-page statement (see Box) which each signed individually. Subsequent discussion with English Nature's Council produced only minor modifications. The

---

English Nature's Philosophy

We believe that the natural heritage matters to everyone.

Parliament has given us obligations and powers; in fulfilling our public duties we shall observe this statutory framework.

Our purpose is to promote directly and through others the conservation of the wildlife and natural features of England within the wider setting of the United Kingdom and its international responsibilities.

In support of this we are committed to:

- Teamwork as a means of achieving our purpose in a positive and authoritative, yet flexible, manner.
- Developing the potential of all our employees – which is essential to our success.
- Encouraging the free flow of information and ideas upwards, downwards and across the organisation.
- Setting clear priorities and implementing them through informed decision making.
- Achieving efficient and effective use of resources through the operation of planning systems.
- Creating trust and understanding in our dealings with others.
- Helping people to make choices and decisions that favour nature conservation.
- Enhancing our reputation for advice and practice based on quality science, solid experience and balanced judgements.
- Encouraging people to appreciate the country's natural heritage.

We are determined that our efforts for this heritage will benefit everyone now and in the future.

English Nature's statement of Philosophy

---

philosophy is positive; the negative attitudes of the NCC which had sought to regulate owners and occupiers to conserve nature are absent.

When the statement was circulated to all the staff, there was intense debate. Management had given a clear lead, only to find that many staff were concerned that they had not been involved.

The new structure still reflected the old organisation; it was to take three years to achieve all the changes necessary to develop a vision statement into a transformed business. But English Nature had by now re-engineered its most important business process: management. Leadership and communication provided the foundation on which to build the re-engineered business.

HOW ENGLISH NATURE WENT ABOUT IT

The new management asked for a review of its Information Systems strategy as part of the refocusing exercise. During this review, the organisation developed a process for strategic planning which required the IS strategy to be derived from the business strategy. But there was no documented business strategy in place. So the IS strategy group persuaded the Management Board to lock itself away and concentrate on producing one, using the new strategic planning framework. The outcome was a new and challenging strategy for the organisation.

The Board now had to lead the implementation of its strategy. But leadership is not about simply telling people – they must become involved and make a contribution. The Board itself had undergone a team training exercise which had built up the members' confidence in and understanding of each other. It recognised the value of the experience and set out to develop similar team work throughout English Nature. Workshops were to be part of the process of team building as well as an essential step in the development of a comprehensive strategy to achieve the vision expounded by the Board. During the next nine months, one third of the staff were involved in week-long branch and section workshops using similar strategic planning models to that used by the Management Board.

At this stage, English Nature had transformed its philosophy statement into a vision and a set of "mandates" for the business units holding workshops. There was a common workshop guide and a consultant as facilitator, challenger and source of external ideas. At the start of each week a Director came in to talk about the developing English Nature strategy and at the end of it the Chief Executive attended for a presentation of the results. The results often reinforced the Board's initial strategy, underlining the point that the structure was wrong and that the group at the workshop was not therefore an appropriate "business unit". Before the workshop, the question of who should attend was usually difficult to answer.

However, the very process of participation acted as a catalyst for staff to become more receptive to the culture of change. It allowed individuals to consider their role in more detail, to experiment with new ideas – and to challenge existing expectations. It permitted them to understand that there was significantly more potential and flexibility under the new regime, and this realisation in itself resulted in the loosening of some of the organisational rigidities.

Those who attended took the results – a view of their strategy and how it contributed to corporate strategy – back to their colleagues and tried to summarise a week's experience in a few hours. The message sometimes got across, but the cultural change brought about by participation as a team in a strategic planning workshop could not be spread to non-participants by such limited contact. Some of the senior staff involved now believe that they should have involved almost everyone in the full workshop exercise.

There was no "Change Plan" document – a cultural change in itself, because scientists have always liked documents. The units carried on with their plans to make the changes discussed at the workshops.

At the same time, all the 1000 or more initiatives which resulted were gathered centrally and analysed. The Board considered this analysis, additional material from other research, the output of several focus groups and many individual comments. As a result, they hardly changed the vision, but the business definition and expression of the values of the organisation were improved. The strategy was then expressed in terms of mandates and founding messages, supported by a set of key products and services. The first version of the strategy document was circulated in December 1992 and an agreed, little-changed version was published the following May. It showed a business whose shape was based on its values: a smaller Board; general managers to put the strategy into practice; and customer service teams to deliver benefits to the customers.

The Board knew before the workshops started that it would have to reshape the business. The strategy determined how they would do it. But there remained anxieties about who would fill which roles in the reshaped business. The HQ and regions hierarchy was to go, and with it many posts. The organisation would be flatter and few coordinating units would survive. Many HQ functions have become internal service branches with service-level agreements (SLAs) with their customers, the (external) customer service teams. The SLAs have both hard and soft indicators.

Having got the commitment, it was possible to remove many of the constraints. An "audit of restrictions" showed that many were self-imposed. Convention and practice could often be ignored. There is no need, for example, to have one layer of management for each civil service grade: two managers between the most junior staff and the Chief Executive is sufficient. Civil servants traditionally think in terms of the similarities of roles at particular grades, not of the differences between the individuals who fill them. For example, the staff inspectors from HM Treasury have an organisation handbook which, of necessity, treats people in the same grade as if they were as interchangeable as money of the same denomination. But in another radical change in culture, English Nature's new shape called for good people to be general managers and team leaders, irrespective of grade.

WHERE ENGLISH NATURE IS NOW

English Nature has a clear and agreed vision and some transformed business processes through which to realise it. Changes in processes demanded changes in structure which are now complete, but not without blood on the carpet. A few people have taken early retirement, others have left because they were unwilling to support the strategy. The percentage distribution of staff between divisions has changed as Table 19.1 shows.

The systems and procedures are now changing in line with the new strategy and shape but this further re-engineering will take some time to complete. Work is underway on implementing the IS strategy. The decision to defer work on that strategy until the business strategy was complete has been vindicated. The new strategy has transformed English Nature's approach to nature conservation from regulation of the public to partnership with customers.

Most evident is the change in the standard of behaviour to colleagues as well as to customers. The following are quotes from the strategic planning workshops (Dair, 1993):

"This is the first time since I joined the organisation that frustration and cynicism have been beaten down by opportunity and hope."

"A greater understanding of the Management Board's vision, goals, values, etc. A more imaginative approach to planning. It made me more aware of the problems associated with managing change."

"Now we can stop bitching and get on with the job."

Table 19.1

Division	April 1991	April 1994
HQ	38%	4.5%
Regional Office	26.7%	
NCST		1.4%
Specialist Support Teams		31.6%
Local Area Teams		62.5%
Local Office	35.3%	

WHERE ENGLISH NATURE IS GOING

There are still some obstacles to overcome. English Nature still has to work within Treasury rules and cope with an annual grant-in-aid, as well as the procedures of its parent department the Department of the Environment. For the foreseeable future, budgets are therefore in the traditional civil service style. In addition, the rebalancing of effort in favour of local area teams is incomplete and there is more talk than action on some schemes.

But there is a lot of light at the end of the tunnel. Although internal changes will take time, this does not preclude external changes. The government could decide to bring together Countryside and Nature in England, as it has in Wales and Scotland. If it were to do so, English Nature now knows how to manage change on such a scale – most specifically how to deal with the restrictions limiting its ability to serve its customers. With continued commitment from the top and an unwavering focus on communication at all levels, there is every reason to believe that vision will indeed become reality – and sooner rather than later.

Chapter 20

St James's Hospital and Lucas Engineering Systems Ltd—A BPR Collaboration Case (A) – Elective Admissions – Urology

Valerie Bence

(This case was researched and written by Valerie Bence at Cranfield School of Management. The purpose of the case is to stimulate class discussion and should not be taken to represent good or bad management practice. The case was written with the help of the Harold Burmeister Scholarship 1995, created by the Centre for Organisational Studies, Barcelona. The author gratefully acknowledges the help given by staff at St James's Hospital, Leeds, during the research for this case. The case is reproduced by permission of Cranfield School of Management, copyright 1995.)

INTRODUCTION

St James's University Hospital in Leeds is one of the biggest teaching hospitals in Europe and one of the largest acute service units in the NHS. Granted Trust status in April 1991, it employs over 5000 people and sees 450 000 patients a year. Operating income from the internal market totalled £125.8 million (1993/4) with 70% of the income coming from the contract with Leeds Healthcare. For 1994/5 the Trust has negotiated contracts with 12 Health Authorities and 130 GP Fundholders.

St James's provides services both locally and to the wider Yorkshire community against the background of national, regional and local objectives and priorities required to meet the ever-changing demand on services. In spite of increases in activity by the hospital, admissions and waiting lists are increasing, reflecting this increasing demand (see Table 20.1).

Health Authorities want the best value for money service, best use of resources and high patient throughput. In addition the government wants 2% more activity in the financial year 1994/5 plus a 1% cost-improvement programme.

In view of the constraints and demands placed on the hospital and their commitment to improving both quality and value for money, St James's began an innovative collaboration in 1991 with Lucas Engineering Systems Ltd (hereafter LES), the aerospace and automotive group. Initial contact between the two organisations was made during a Working Party on Electronic Data Interchange and the National Health Service. A member of St James's Supplies staff encountered work done by LES, who were keen to investigate the transferability to the public sector of some of the techniques that have led to increased efficiency in car manufacturing plants. Lucas, a leader in such systems, had developed their methodologies during their restructuring in the late 1980s and were now looking beyond the manufacturing sector.

After an initial meeting, good working relations were established and possibilities were discussed of transferring the methods used in industry to within the hospital organisation in order to improve the efficiency of working processes.

LES gave a presentation to St James's at Board level. This overview was not project-specific, but did interest the Board enough for LES to be invited back to do a two-day workshop for senior hospital managers. This would investigate

Table 20.1

| | Admissions | | |
	1991/92	1992/3	1993/4
In-patient	17 444	17 198	15 641
Day cases	16 136	21 893	27 237
Acute	36 459	37 793	39 490
Waiting list		8 723	8 820
Total	70 039	76 884	82 368

possible areas for collaboration using the Lucas approach to the management of change (involving business process redesign). The aims were:

- To review LES redesign methodologies
- To discuss whether and how these principles could be applied to specific change projects at St James's and/or complement current initiatives
- To discuss relevant case examples of the application of the methodologies in order to identify tangible benefits.
- To make specific decisions on how to progress the change programme.

Following the workshop, the Board gave the go-ahead for work with LES and proposals were invited from within the hospital for possible projects. Careful selection was necessary since there had to be an element of cost saving to pay for the project, which would hopefully go on to generate revenue for St James's. There were also issues surrounding Trust Status (management changes); the Patient's Charter (performance measurement); and customer care (quality) to consider. Selection criteria were developed based around the need to choose something with a good chance of success; that would test the thesis that these systems could be transferred from industry; and that was health related and financially viable.

It did not take long for a number of potential projects meeting the required criteria to be identified. Both partners were learning from each other and while in most areas it did appear that manufacturing techniques for process change could be transferred, it was becoming apparent that there were to some extent a "separate set of rules" for the NHS. This was because of the nature of the organisation, internal and external constraints and the pace, extent and speed of change. Two projects were identified with different objectives. A reorganisation of the Purchasing and Supplies function would hopefully meet the cost-saving requirement, whilst a reappraisal of the admission procedure was more of a cross-functional experiment, but both involved systems investigation and a process approach. Thus the final decision was:

Project A – Elective admissions (not emergency)
Project B – Non-pharmaceutical supplies – Purchasing and Supplies

This case follows Project A.

Two groups of hospital staff were selected (on voluntary secondment) to work full-time on the projects. It was made clear early on what the starting base was, what the aims were and why they were doing it. The projects began with a week's off-site training in order for LES to familiarise St James's staff with the theories and methodologies to be used and for the teams to look at timescales and deadlines. There was a definite date for the projects to end, with well-defined milestones. Both teams would have weekly progress meetings with their managers, plus presentations on findings and monthly meetings with the hospital's Director of Organisational Development.

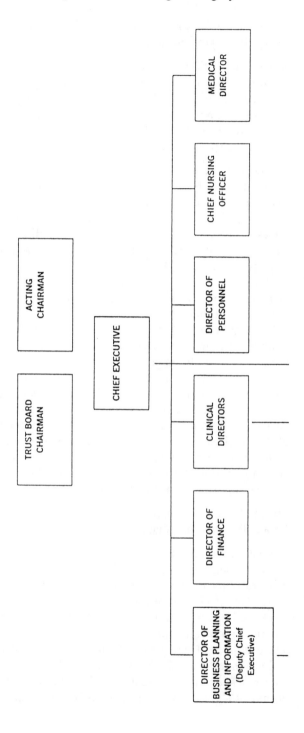

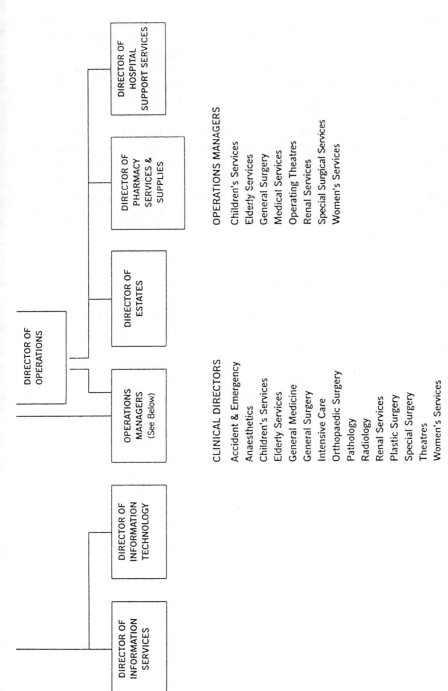

Figure 20.1 St James's University Hospital Trust: corporate management structure (July 1994)

Producing the hospital's Application for Trust Status acted as a catalyst for many changes and part of this involved spelling out how much and how far medical staff would become involved in hospital management. The 15 Clinical Directorates (similar to Business Units) evolved from this and covered all aspects of clinical activity at the hospital. They are headed by clinicians with day-to-day management undertaken by full-time Operations Managers. (See organisational chart in Figure 20.1.

Following project selection and staff training, specific process issues were refined in discussion with Clinical Directors. However, it is important to remember that St James's went into the exercise knowing what the particular process problems were but not knowing what the outcomes would be or how the process of change would evolve. Both projects represented a potential risk with large investments committed in time, money and people – and the hard work was just beginning.

PROJECT – ELECTIVE ADMISSIONS

The main aim of this project was to streamline the patient admissions process. With the hospital in the midst of reforms this was something that had already been identified as needing attention.

As a teaching hospital providing services both locally and regionally, St James's admits patients acutely (through accident and emergency, via GPs or other hospitals) and electively (from GP and hospital referrals) primarily for cases placed on a waiting list in a surgical speciality. The NHS gives national guarantees of a maximum wait of 24 months for any procedure (18 months for hip and knee replacements and cataracts) and St James's aim is to achieve a maximum waiting time of 18 months for all conditions. Although working under cost constraints, St James's were already investigating ways to both cut waiting-list time and reduce cancelled operations. There were a number of problems in the waiting list system, key concerns being:

- *Balance of admissions* – beds required for elective surgery can often be occupied by other patients, notably overspilling from acute areas.
- *Links between departments* – the process is cross-functional and involves different central functions: outpatients, medical records, diagnostic departments, wards, theatres, admissions office, etc. This leads to problems in the scheduling and tracking of information.
- *Waiting list* – waiting-list management is critical, not least because of the political dimension.
- *Contract delivery* – the admission of elective cases is a key concern to the hospital's customers (Health Authorities, GPs and patients themselves) as

the hospital is contracted to deliver set numbers of operations in any financial year.

- *Quality* – many quality issues are tied up in this system, e.g. cancellation rate, use of operating theatre resources, etc. The requirement is for a smooth and efficient admissions system that would improve the service to patients.
- *Internal concerns* – the issue of elective admissions is a key concern to clinicians and staff within the hospital, particularly the surgeons.

PROJECT OBJECTIVES

The team developed project objectives and this enabled them to decide which aspects of the admissions function to focus on, in order to

- Improve the process for planned admissions
- Reduce the steps necessary to procure an admission
- Ensure that planned admissions are not cancelled
- Improve communications
- Make sure the hospital satisfies the internal market and delivers to contract
- Maximise the effective use of hospital resources.

Maximising resource use should result in reduced waiting-list times, improved customer satisfaction and speed of throughput, etc. The project should be revenue neutral with the aim not to save money but to improve the quality of service to patients by cutting down on cancelled admissions and operations. Dismantling the central admissions function in order to change the system hospital-wide was impossible, so it was decided to focus initially on one department (Urology) of one Directorate (General Surgery). This Clinical Director was in favour of changes and agreeable to taking the next steps. The Operations Manager was a key player but was not part of the task force as such.

The project team consisted of

- A full-time leader (a Nursing Sister)
- Three full-time members of St James's staff (from medical records, theatre and path labs)
- Two Lucas engineers

They were allocated a Seminar room off the Urology ward for 3 months and worked under considerable time pressure.

An initial recommendation of the project team was that all Urology patients should be co-located onto a single ward, rather than be split over two. This was actually achieved during the project, which acted as a catalyst, but was initiated by the Operations Manager as a separate issue. Previously, Urology patients had been located on two different wards (Wards 8 and 14) – one for 5-day

Urology patients (with patients from other surgical specialities) and one for the main 7-day acute patients plus 14-day Oncology patients. A single ward (14) was set up prior to implementation of the main project. This was moved to Lincoln Wing which would also house the new Natural Group (Consultants secretaries and administration staff) as well as all Urology patients in

$$8 \times 5 \text{ day beds and approx. } 20 \times 7 \text{ or more day beds}$$

One early problem was over measurement and evaluation – what and how to measure, in order to test whether things did in fact improve. A paradox emerged – the "better you are, the worse you get". Since making the hospital more efficient brings waiting lists down, this in turn leads to more referrals, more patients, therefore longer waiting lists. Eventually the proposed measurements were cancelled operations (both before and after admission); length of patient stay; theatre utilisation, etc. For example in 1991 585 patients were admitted to the Urology ward – 12% of these had their operations cancelled after admission (no available theatre time) plus a further 300 were cancelled before admission.

As a result up to one-third of patients for non-urgent surgery found their appointments/operations were being cancelled. During the Diagnosis Phase, the team discovered that one of the reasons for this was that between a consultant saying a person needed an operation and their arriving at the operating theatre, responsibility changed hands 59 times as it passed through ten departments!

The team endeavoured to find their way through this maze of handovers and found that one of the main reasons for cancellations under the old system was no bed available at the last minute, due to a lack of communication between admissions and theatre scheduling. Admissions were sending for twice as many patients as they could cope with and around 50% would be cancelled or unable to come in. The project team aimed to improve these figures by investigating process changes and they began work on a three-phase project.

PHASE 1: DIAGNOSIS (APPROX. 6 WEEKS)

The admissions process as it stood had to be identified. Elective admissions only were investigated, as this was the only case with control over numbers. Details of the present system and operational objectives were studied and the team drafted many questions and interviewed relevant managers and staff in order to plot current processes and identify constraints and problem areas. For example, many GPs referred only to specific consultants and this resulted in persistent over- and underloading. There were also several versions of the waiting list, with admissions, the consultant's own list and the Urology department – the link being the consultant's secretary.

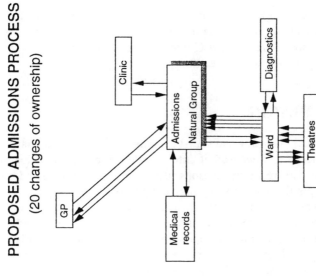

PROPOSED ADMISSIONS PROCESS
(20 changes of ownership)

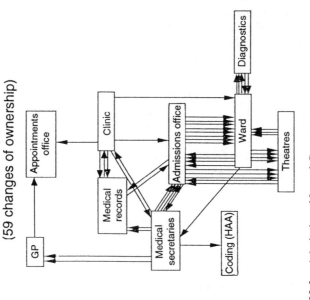

ORIGINAL ADMISSIONS PROCESS
(59 changes of ownership)

Figure 20.2 Admissions Natural Group

The project team were conscious all the time of having to work within the Patient's Charter, i.e. they had to make sure that the hospital continued to perform within certain guaranteed measures such as the maximum waiting-list time.

Processes were mapped and handover points identified (see Figure 20.2) and the team now had a grasp of what the problems were and ideas on how to tackle them. They reported back to the Clinical Director and St James's management with their ideas on the way forward.

PHASE 2: DESIGN

Having collected interview and statistical data, including benchmarks, the team took the concept and worked it into a detailed proposal. With key issues identified and with recommendations made for the areas to be addressed they could now begin the task of designing new processes.

The aim was for a more efficient use of two major resources – beds and theatres. The new processes would involve planning ward admissions in parallel with the planning of operation theatre bookings. This had never happened before. Previously someone would look at the empty beds for the next day, say six, and send for perhaps ten patients. Not all would be able to come and some would be cancelled. There was no collaboration with operating slots before admission.

The recommendation to be looked at in detail is the forming of a Natural Group for Urology Admissions. This was based on LES's previous experience in manufacturing, of forming "cells" or groups, to operate new systems. By physically removing sufficient resource (in this case individuals) they became generic to the system rather than purely functional – they became the *Urology Admissions Natural Group*.

Previously this department's admissions had been administered by the relevant central functions, e.g. central admissions, outpatients and theatre. Within the admissions office Urology had been the responsibility of a member of staff dealing with all kinds of general surgery admissions. The formation of a Natural Group meant that members of staff had to be moved (physically) from their existing posts to new locations. This led to much negotiation over changing roles, both for them and for people remaining within the central function; hours, responsibilities, etc.

The Natural Group concept was accepted by the Clinical Director who already wanted to overcome existing barriers. However, other managers (mainly administration) identified a number of implementation difficulties. For example, contract information – within central functions all information is gathered in one place for invoicing etc. – could pose problems if it was to become spread over the Directorates. However, it was hoped that the formation of this Natural Group, which would concentrate on the process as a whole rather than on individual functions, would fulfil the main aims of the project: shorter waiting-list time; shorter stay on wards; fewer cancelled operations.

PHASE 3: IMPLEMENTATION

Implementation of the recommendations took another 3 months, with one member of the project team (from St James's) on hand full-time to advise. The Natural Group was to be located in close proximity to the Urology ward and consisted of:

- An Office Manager
- Three medical secretaries (including the consultant's secretary)
- Two Urology-specific admissions/clinic clerks (from central admissions and outpatients).

Their training was based on the Lucas 5^* plan (again adapted from industry) which designs individual training schedules and helps develop multi-skilling for new staff members. New processes were identified to eliminate handover points, which involved constant negotiations with the central functions and the changing of individual job responsibilities. Measurements for data collection were put into place so that performance could be monitored.

Changeover took place on 2 September 1992, when all patients to the Urology ward were admitted under the new system with its new jobs, processes and responsibilities. From this date the Natural Group controlled all Urology admissions, i.e. keeping records; planning operations; ensuring theatre and bed availability; calling in patients. The 59 handover points were reduced to 20 and by November 1992, only 11 out of 326 operations were cancelled on the day (3%). The aim was still for continuous improvement.

So within the boundaries set, the redesigned procedures for Urology admissions have been successful and have had tangible benefits. This part of the system has been "undone" to such an extent that going back to the old procedure is not an option – the point has been reached for decisions to be made on the next step:

- To stay where they are (new systems in place in one area only) or
- To roll out the new system within the whole admissions function or
- To roll out the new system within the Directorate including Urology or
- To investigate other areas within the hospital that could be tackled in the same way, i.e. initiate new projects using the expertise from these exercises.

Chapter 21

Re-engineering Customer Support in Hewlett-Packard

Colin Armistead, Graham Clark, Paula Stanley and Philip Rowland

(This case was prepared by Graham Clark, Philip Rowland and Paula Stanley, Cranfield School of Management and Professor Colin Armistead, Bournemouth University. It is not meant to illustrate good or bad management practices. The case is produced by permission of Hewlett-Packard. Copyright 1995.)

THE COMPANY

Hewlett-Packard is a US company with subsidiaries world-wide and its European headquarters is based in Geneva. It supplies computers and related products to businesses and increasingly to the home-user market.

The hardware products which require support can be categorised into three groups, effectively relating to the particular level of service required by the customer and to the sophistication of the product itself:

- *Mission critical* – High specification equipment, typically installed in Financial Services' organisations where the whole business is reliant on the machine working, for example Dealing/Trading departments. Typically "solutions" as opposed to commodities are being supported. For these customers a 2-hour on-site presence is guaranteed and a 4-hour fix is aimed for.
- *Commercial distributed* – These are typically products that may be found in

either of the other two categories, but for which the service requirement is not as demanding as "Mission critical", but more stringent than "Office productivity". Service agreement response time is 4 hours.

- *Office productivity* – This segment is typically at the lower end of the market, and is predominantly small business. Home-users are, however, forming an increasing proportion. This segment is predominantly price driven and is a commodity-type market. Service agreements for this segment would typically be next-day fixing of faults. The parts required for the fix are usually known from a fault description given. The fix time is typically less than one hour.

Service agreements, in addition to the standard warranty offered, are sold to customers at the time of product sale. This is where profits are generated due to the chargeable nature of these services.

THE ROUTE TO BPR

Within Hewlett-Packard there is no centralised directive for BPR world-wide, due largely to their culture of devolved responsibility. However, a world-wide task force, on which a UK member sits, does exist, which is assessing tools for BPR. The task force provides the tools used to re-engineer processes and plays a major role in the identification of common re-engineering links across the world.

A philosophy of "quality improvement" has also been a part of the Hewlett-Packard culture for the past eight years. However, more recently they believe that continuous improvement is not enough, and that re-engineering is needed to make the radical gains required.

> "So there is a total awareness I think right throughout the whole company that re-engineering is needed in an awful lot of processes."

The current top-down drive to understand the processes and in particular the linkages between the processes within the business is being driven by the Managing Director of the UK organisation. As an illustration of his commitment, when he makes a presentation about the organisation his first slide is a process slide; this would not have been the case five years ago. The drive to think about the organisation in terms of processes encourages everyone "to pull in the same direction". The re-engineering initiative began in Hewlett-Packard in December 1992.

The UK Delivery Manager defines BPR as: "It's just setting yourself such radical goals that you have to change what you do to meet them."

There are two key processes which have the subject of re-engineering: hardware maintenance and software maintenance. This case focuses on the hardware support business.

PRESSURES FOR CHANGE

There have been a number of factors which have been drivers for the re-engineering projects:

- The *pace of change* within the computer industry is accelerating and the timescales to improve performance have significantly reduced. Hewlett-Packard has improved performance ten times and halved its costs over two years. Previously they estimate that it would have taken five years to achieve this level, and ten years prior to that.
- Changing *markets* into which Hewlett-Packard is selling. Home-users of PCs and peripherals are now a far more important segment than in the past. This segment, its needs and the problems they present are relatively new to Hewlett-Packard.
- *Customer focus and increasing cost/revenue/profit consciousness.* Over the last five years there has been "more of a realisation of who your customers are," both internally and externally. No longer are customers a focus primarily for customer-facing sales staff. In Hewlett-Packard, the focus (and particularly on the internal customers) throughout the whole organisation, combined with the measures of cost and performance have led to the outsourcing of a number of functions/services which previously would not have been considered for outsourcing.

"There's no such thing as business as usual."

There are, however, unwritten limits on how far a department/subsidiary would be allowed to go down the outsourcing route.

- *Quality and performance directly linked.* In the past quality improvements were reviewed "from a policy point of view" and not according to business performance. Over the last eight years the two have become more closely linked. The focus has moved from making changes in isolation to considering their potential impact on different parts of the business, and particularly on the benefits of "Quality" in terms of profitability.

ADDITIONAL PRESSURES ON THE HARDWARE SUPPORT PROCESS

Hewlett-Packard have expanded their existing hardware support processes in line with the widening of their product markets. This has created additional processes in respect of costs, volume and job focus:

- *Costs*: Products requiring support, from the high specification equipment used in financial houses, to small laser jet and desk jet printers bought for £200, were generally dealt with in the same "process fix-it", which was by engineers of similar skill sets going out to customers. The support process used for all three segments was originally designed for the commercial distributed segment. Thus, the costs of supporting the lower-priced printers were little different to supporting the high specification products:

"Historically it's been £300 to £450, just depending on the amount of time the engineer is spending on-site, not necessarily what product it was. So Fred's fish and chip shop could be £300 and our big multinational could still be £300."

Customers were also beginning to complain about prices. Repair bills for £300 on a product bought for £400 were not uncommon.

- *Call volume*: 70% of calls fall into "office productivity" (120 field support people), 20% into "commercial distributed" and 10% into "mission critical" (80 people). Thus, the majority of products sold by Hewlett-Packard fall into the lower price range, and yet the cost of supporting all products, wherever segments are similar.

"When we're selling a box for £250, to fix it for £300 doesn't make a lot of sense."

- *Job focus for engineers*: Increasingly, "account management [was] being dealt with by the individual". As a consequence maintaining links with customers and generating business became an over-riding rather than a secondary consideration:

"So I think we were getting to the point where engineers wouldn't know what they were doing. We'd expanded out of the role to be so broad that people de-focused into an area that wasn't the key reason for existence."
"It's quite interesting the story I tell the engineers. I was a systems engineer but as a PC manager I went out with engineers as a matter of course. You could do five calls a day and never get offered a cup of coffee. This is unheard of for a systems engineer. We don't undo the bag unless we've got a cup! So they got invited in and may or may not be invited in through the tradesman's entrance. Especially in the City. It's like engineers carrying brown boxes and briefcases don't come in the front, they go in the back. You get, "Oh fine, you're the engineer are you? It's over there". And you just fix it and say "Done it" and they say "Oh fine". That's as much partnership we have with our customers? None. We are not selling any additional service there. It didn't matter if we turned up in a Ferrari or a beaten-down transit, no one cares so long as we did the job and left. And with the minimum of interaction almost because they didn't care who fixed the laser jets."

CHANGING THE PROCESS

The Old Process

Calls were received by the response centre and then connected to a Despatcher (Figure 21.1). An engineer would be assigned to the call, who would contact

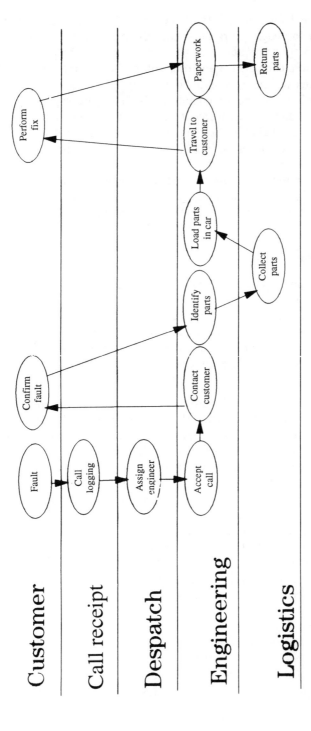

Figure 21.1 Old delivery process

the customer and confirm the fault. For next-day fixes, this could be done before or after the engineer responded to the previous day's calls. He would then identify the parts required, go to logistics, collect the parts, load them in his car, travel to customers, in any order of job and fix the problem. Typically the first customer was not seen until about 10.30 am.

A number of quality improvements to the hardware support process were made. These included improvements in the way engineers could ring the response centre for help, in the parts holding and in the tools the engineers have. With these, engineers were achieving an average of 2.5 support jobs a day.

With the decision to re-engineer came two targets. The first was an efficiency target of six support jobs achieved on average per day per engineer. The second was a cost target, to reduce the cost of calls by an average of 50%.

The New Process

Under the new process calls come to the Call receiving Group where a staff of twelve take approximately 1100 calls per day (of which 50% are hardware related) (Figure 21.2). The average call time is 2.5 minutes. Here the type of response required and the need for technical qualification or remote product delivery is ascertained. Forty-five per cent of laser jet calls are closed at this stage. Over all the PC product ranges the proportion that can be closed is about 32%.

- *Remote product delivery*: for problems that require replacements rather than fixing, the customer is asked the product number on the item and a replacement is posted to arrive at the customer by first post the next day. This replaces personal delivery that would not reach the customer until the engineer arrived with them, some time during the next day.
- *Technical call qualification*: Calls are streamed by priority and are responded to by engineers. The aim is to complete qualification of all same day and four hour and less within 30 minutes. For next-day response calls the aim is to get back to the customer within 2 hours or by 5.15 pm. Calls that are received by technical qualifications, are also logged into despatch at same time. This shortens the time it takes to identify the engineer to respond to a mission-critical or a 4-hour response call. Located next to the call qualification centre is the software expert centre which increases the breadth of the expertise available. Forty per cent of calls can be closed at qualification.

Once the fault has been confirmed with the customer, parts are requested from Logistics, who are asked to deliver them to wherever the engineer wants them. This eliminates the need for engineers to fetch parts. There are thirteen logistics locations around England and Wales. This method of

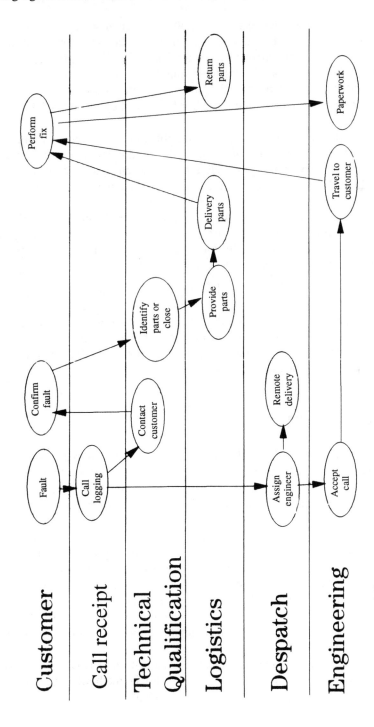

Figure 21.2 New delivery process

dealing with spares is the best that has been arrived at so far. Alternatively, schemes have delivered parts direct to customers but sometimes customers are not there to accept them or have used a major distribution company's warehouse but the sizes of parts were found to be incompatible with those of Hewlett-Packard. Consequently the use of petrol stations has proved to be one good option for collecting parts because they are open 24 hours a day.

- *Next-day response*: Following call qualification, parts are wrapped for distribution. By 7 pm parts are allocated to sub-contractors to distribute around the country. These are delivered to the engineers' homes or drop points. Engineers receive electronic copies of their work distribution. This allows Hewlett-Packard to have a general idea about where a particular engineer is at any given time. Electronic "paperwork" completed at the end of each job enables Hewlett-Packard to know what work has been completed by whom and when. This enables the billing process to take place automatically. Morning delivery vans collect parts not used on the previous day.

The utilisation of engineers' skills sets has been changed in the process. Some prefer to work with one type of response, others prefer a mix of types. Also a separate team of sales and marketing support services has been created to relieve engineers of their role of business generation. Equipped with lap-top computers engineers can complete paperwork soon after the visit and the billing process takes place automatically.

MAKING THE CHANGES

Hewlett-Packard used the Rummler and Brache methodology with the addition of a piloting phase. This included the initial stages of defining the project, its scoping and its goals, forming a team, identifying the "sacred cows", developing a project plan with timescales and getting the agreement to proceed from the sponsors.

A steering committee for the project was formed, made up of senior managers from all parts of the process. This was led by the overall delivery manager. The multi-disciplinary project team was led by a project manager who was an engineer with experience as a field-based manager and as manager of a response centre. A core team of ten includes field engineers, field district managers, response centre managers, call handling people, administrators and people from logistics. Additional consultants including personnel experts were co-opted as required.

The Project Manager and the Quality Manager undertook a one-week facilitator training course on the Rummler and Brache methodology. They then ran one-day training programmes for the project team.

Existing processes were mapped over three days. The links between the processes and the places of "disconnects", errors or duplication were identified. Flipcharts were used to map processes and the ABC Flowcharter used for drawing. Fairly high-level processes were drawn onto three A4 sheets of paper and the 30 major disconnects identified.

After a rest period the team then designed a "should" map, which took them about a week. The approach was not exactly "clean sheet" as the team worked around several built-in constraints and based any new process on some of the existing organisational structures.

Particular problems experienced in redesigning the new process included those of freeing minds from the existing processes:

> "It's a heavy facilitation involved in trying to get people away from the issues of today rather than the issues of tomorrow. And a certain amount of identifying some key people who are going to lead the way."

After redesigning the new process some benchmarking was undertaken with organisations in the same and different sectors, to see if the processes generated matched anything other companies were doing. The new process was piloted using two engineers working out of one district with particularly high-volume and low-value customers and performance was measured. Five delivery mechanisms, different from the first design, were tested. The number of disconnects remaining and the number of new disconnects were established. "You learn as you go, and it's frustrating as hell for a project manager."

Customers were consulted to increase the understanding of the variation in call volume over a day. This was the extent of customers' involvement in the redesign. Once the process was finalised job profiling was undertaken.

Communication was a particular issue for the project team. After an initial announcement and a series of presentations by the Project Manger communication was largely by e-mail and hard copy to others in the organisation. In addition, a number of transition teams were created with representatives from all sectors affected. This meant that people became involved in the project and that good information could be conveyed quickly to all concerned. The project team also tried to communicate through management channels but experience showed that if messages had a negative connotation for a particular manager then it went no further. With hindsight they reflected that they had at times held off communicating in order that they did not communicate the wrong message. "The only one that really works is ... having a group of five engineers and some of us go through it because it's the only way they feel comfortable enough to ask the right questions."

The new process was implemented in the UK by region throughout 1994 and is now forming the basis for world-wide re-engineering. As expected, there are still problems which need to be solved. The uncertainty the new process has created has meant people have felt less able to respond: "Due to the management of change stuff people have frozen up on doing that, and that's caused more problems as well." Increasingly problems will need to be fixed "in the main stream" rather than being referred back to the design team for consideration.

Future improvement projects are being identified to improve the new process. Areas for future development are likely to focus on developing new ways of customer contact other than by answering calls, such as caller ID to route new calls before they are answered and bringing in a fax or electronic front end to the process.

THE OUTCOME

The aim of the project was "not to actually change the deliverable to the customers but rather alter the cost of delivery". Based on figures so far, cost improvements are being realised. However, performance relative to competitors has not improved but efficiency gains are being realised. In addition, almost as a by-product, some improvements in customer service are being realised.

- *Managing costs*: Costs per call have reduced by over 60%. Inventory holding costs have increased but the expectation is that they will fall in the future.
- *Managing customer service*: Where customers require replacement products the use of a postal service rather than personal delivery by an engineer means that the replacement arrives with the customer first thing the following day. There has also been an improvement in the service given to customers by the call qualification activity. Forty per cent of calls can be closed without relying on calling in engineers between existing jobs. Once established Hewlett-Packard has been able to make commitments to customers in the high volume market to be with them at agreed times within a half-hour margin.
- *Managing people*: Inevitably, some employees experienced problems with the changes being introduced. Some managers resisted the change out of fear of being de-skilled and feeling frustrated. This was particularly so for those whom the new process did not fit, or was not what they wanted it to be. Engineers also experienced some difficulties in accepting the changes. Once people became aware of the pilot project it put "a ripple of fear through the organisation". "What happened was that the whole of our same-day engineers all started to get jittery that they were going to be asked to do five calls a day."

Although there is an aim to reduce the existing number of engineers from 240 to 100 there have been no job losses through the redesign of the process.

However, some engineers have moved out from direct product support to new business generation. On reflection the team thought that not enough time was invested in developing release or transition plans for those moving out of hardware support. The effects of uncertainty for some on being told about the move to take place at some point in the future led to an inability to move forward. This resulted in problems with motivation and commitment during the transition phase.

In the high-volume, multiple fixes end of the support processes increasingly contact people are being taken on rather than using salaried engineers The move provides scope to alter the balance of skills available should the product mix require it. It also spreads the existing engineers, traditionally the best available, across the more profitable end of the product support.

This clearer segmentation of working practices has meant that the engineers' roles and the skills required to fulfil the role have changed. Consequently some engineers have in effect become fitters rather than specialists. Conversely, it has provided others with opportunities to specialise in particular areas. Management of these changes was felt to be one of the most difficult aspects of project implementation.

The introduction of appointment scheduling enabled the HP manager to have a greater control of the support process but not without problems: "So it's perceived as Big Brotherish but it's actually very practical."

The use of delivery vans to take parts to engineers' homes and as a result the loss of the morning meeting together became a major issue:

> "It was seen as a major issue that they never saw their colleagues any more. What we did, we said fine, we will build in as much team work as you want, on the proviso that you understand that this is reducing our effectiveness."

Hewlett-Packard also allocated a dummy call for all engineers at the same time, to allow them to meet together in a structured meeting, initially once a week and subsequently every two weeks. Increasingly, engineers are saying that these meetings are not needed as often. In the future they are likely to take place only once a month in normal circumstances.

MANAGING THE PROCESS

As a result of the re-engineering, most situations where escalation may have been required have been eliminated. The process has in-built devolved authority, so that very few events arise where escalation is required; most "problems" can be dealt with as part of the process.

In addition, call qualification by specialist engineers has led to better qualification of the parts required to fix. This is likely to lead to better product design in the future, where error messages should give greater detail about the parts that need replacing.

Hewlett-Packard has built into their process greater capability for flexibility. With call scheduling they have better knowledge about where engineers are at any given time, allowing them to allocate new calls should a quick response be required. The use of contract staff at the lower end of the support market will enable them to shed labour should their product market shift substantially.

Finally re-engineering the process has meant redefining the measures. Traditional performance measures may not be appropriate "because they've been there for a decade". Developing new and appropriate measures was not an easy task: "I don't know what the position is to that, I just think you have to go through the pain and the anger and the anguish of it all."

Chapter 22

Re-engineering The Post Office Supply Chain

Sylvie Jackson

INTRODUCTION AND BACKGROUND

Our involvement in re-engineering began in February 1994 as a result of an initial diagnostic for the future of the Supply Chain in The Post Office. The Supply Chain Review is one of the key platforms for future purchasing and supply strategy. The review commenced in June 1993 and embraces all elements of the supply chain throughout The Post Office Group: These have been identified as:

- Demand Forecasting
- Purchasing
- Contracts
- Inventory Control
- Administration
- Warehousing
- Physical distribution
- Waste disposal and recycling
- Financial interfaces

The Post Office is split into three major businesses (see Figure 22.1): Royal Mail, Parcelforce and Post Office Counters Ltd. Purchasing + Logistics

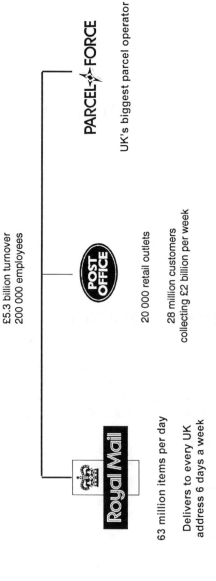

Figure 22.1 Organisational structure of The Post Office. (Reproduced by permission of the Royal Mail)

Services is one of a number of Group Services (e.g. Training and Development, Occupational Health Service, Information Technology, Employee Support (Welfare), etc.) who operate on behalf of all the Businesses and charge out their services.

The Supply Chain Review was instigated by the Director and General Manager of Purchasing + Logistics Services who joined The Post Office in January 1993. He compiled a SWOT analysis within 6 weeks of joining the organisation (see Table 22.1). All the points he identified were confirmed by individuals in the Businesses during the surveys conducted as part of the Supply Chain Review diagnostic.

The initial diagnostic phase of the Supply Chain Review identified the scale involved in an organisation as large as The Post Office (see Figure 22.2). This is perhaps surprising bearing in mind that The Post Office is a service organisation.

The 1089 full-time staff directly involved in supply chain-related activities represents 0.57% of total staff. Additional staff requisition supplies from

Table 22.1   SWOT analysis

Strengths	*Weaknesses*
• Integrated purchasing and supply elements	• Customer perception of poor service, substantial fixed overhead, inflexibility, bureaucratic systems
• Knowledge of the Post Office business	• Strained customer relations
• Purchasing expertise	• Hierarchical structure
• Tight control standards (financial and regulatory)	• Lack of effective communications
• Demand aggregation	• Old and clumsy systems
• Break bulk/detail issue capability	• Lack of third party customer base
• Established distribution network	• Lack of retail expertise
• Some internal performance measures	• Absorption costing and no ABC analysis
• Quality programmes being implemented	• Lack of process oriented performance measures
	• Poor-quality forecasts
	• Poor warehouse utilisation
Opportunities	*Threats*
• Consistent standards for purchasing supply	• Knee-jerk fragmentation
• Increased demand aggregation	• Perceived restrictive legislative framework
• Supplier base reduction	• Lack of responsiveness to genuine customer needs
• Activity based costing	• Inconsistent approach to procurement
• Profit centre status	• Government review
• Government review	• Lack of will and flexibility to change
• Supply Chain Review	
• Third party business, public and private sector	

Bought-in costs (purchase prices)	£1.5 billion
Suppliers	6500
Operating costs	£43.6 million
Inventory	£38.9 million
Stockholding points	**1144**
Staff–Purchasing	308
–Warehousing	781

1089

Figure 22.2 Supply Chain Scale. (Reproduced by permission of the Royal Mail)

internal suppliers and stores as part of their duties. The original network structure is shown in Figure 22.3.

The objective of the Supply Chain Review was "to recommend the most cost effective and efficient processes, network and organisation for optimum Post Office Group supply chain performance which meets customer requirements".

As The Post Office purchases and/or supplies a very wide range of goods and services, it was decided to group them into Product Areas so that they could be managed:

Clothing/Uniforms
Automation/Engineering
Vehicles/Fuel
Print/Stationery
IT/Computers/Office Machinery
Facilities Management
Freight Services (carriage of mail)
Professional Services (consultancy, advertising, manpower, etc.)
Value Stock (stamps, postal orders)

The Review team was made up of representatives from all the Businesses/ Business Units within The Post Office Group. They examined the bought-in cost of goods and services and identified where Purchasing + Logistics Services could add value.

There was no attempt to make any judgements on the possible outcome of the Government Review of The Post Office which was happening concurrently but the proposals allowed some flexibility. As part of the Review, all current operations were analysed to gather information on processes, network, operating costs, inventory, systems measurements, organisation and policy.

The diagnostic report was taken to The Post Office Executive Committee on 30 November 1993. It identified and quantified potential cost savings and

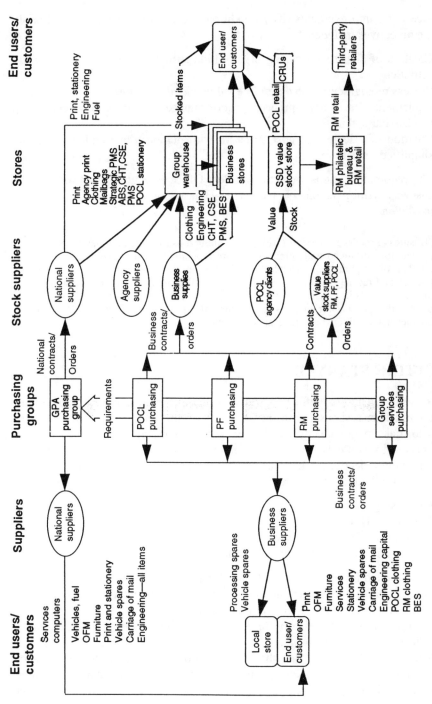

Figure 22.3 Current supply chain structure. (Reproduced by permission of the Royal Mail)

service level improvements. Key conditions necessary to achieve the Supply Chain objectives included:

- Creation of a customer-facing organisation structure to reflect supply chain activities
- Process re-engineering to determine value-added activities
- Implementation of appropriate key performance indicators to reflect Group and Business objectives
- Creation of a lean base cost structure with demonstrable added-value and simplified procedures

As the recommendations went to The Post Office Executive Committee, Eric Evans was writing in the November 1993 issue of *Purchasing and Supply Management*:

> "Business Process Re-design (BPR) has emerged as management has recognised a need for continued and often radical improvements. There are an increasing number of organisations which have looked at the whole of the purchasing process and redesigned significant elements or all of it. Their experience suggests that others should consider BPR. The key is that it provides an opportunity to review the purchasing process rather than the purchasing function. It is this broader perspective which generates the benefits."

GETTING STARTED

As expected, The Post Office Executive Team endorsed the recommendations. The immediate response from the Director of Purchasing + Logistics Services was to make major changes to his Executive Team by introducing "Change Agents" who would be responsible for implementing the large-scale changes which would need to take place. While Finance and Personnel remained untouched, all other posts were scrapped and four new posts were created:

- Purchasing Director
- Operations Director
- Strategy and Projects Director
- Quality and Business Process Director

We also looked for a new Supply Chain Review Project Leader to run Phase II (planning phase) which was due to report with recommendations in June 1994. It took longer than originally anticipated to fill the posts (the Operations Director post was not finally filled until end-July 1994), and this had a significant impact on the project.

It was agreed early on that the Phase II project should be better managed than Phase I. (Failures in Phase I had included no identification of resources required, tasks or critical path and no plan to ensure end date met. Few of the people involved had had project management training, although they had been involved in or had run projects in the past.) The Post Office had adopted the PRINCE project methodology in a number of areas so it was agreed that this should be used. A key factor was that the Information Technology department was using the methodology; and as systems were likely to play a major role, it was appropriate to use the same methodology. Key players for Phase II attended a week-long PRINCE project management course in December 1993.

PRINCE is an acronym for "PRojects IN a Controlled Environment". The methodology evolved in UK government sectors in the late 1970s and is owned by the CCTA (Central Computing and Telecommunications Agency) – linked to the Treasury, although it is a publicly available open product.

The methodology is based on a number of principles:

- Organisation
- Planning
- Controls
- Stages
- Project Based Projects
- Quality

The overall objective is to ensure that the right people make the right decision at the right time.

A project support office was set up in January 1994, and the team developed a structure for the project, even though a Project Leader was not appointed until February. This difficulty should have raised alarm bells early on. One of the first things organisations are told about BPR is to get the very best people working on the project. In practice, it is very difficult (if not impossible) to persuade their bosses to release them. We had tremendous difficulty getting a project leader and when he finally was released it was for a six-month period only, and both he and his boss insisted on his return even though Phase II was not completed.

So why is it so difficult to get people onto BPR projects? It may be that they themselves are not keen to become involved in what could be a politically sensitive project which has unspecified absences from their job with the potential vulnerability from not being in-post and under a powerful patron. In addition, they may have to help their replacement through a lengthy hand-over and/or coaching phase which delays the start of the new project and on their return, they find the replacement has changed everything. Their old boss may not want to go through the upheaval of reinstating the former manger. No one wants to lose an integrated team which has taken a considerable time to move to the performing stage of team dynamics. Additional areas that need consideration are appraisal and objective setting with their links to reward and bonus.

Other considersations could suggest that the managers themselves may change through the experience of the BPR project which could give new expectations and skills, allowing them to view the organisation and themselves in a new light.

A number of individual projects which were already in force were brought together to ensure integration into the overall strategy. These included the First Class Supplier Programme (an accreditation programme), Product Group Teams (new way of running strategic purchasing through cross-functional, cross-business teams) and new areas such as communications, change management, systems, business process re-engineering and the business case (funding for systems and the project).

It quickly became clear that the project was in danger of becoming too unwieldy so it was split into two key areas with different project managers (See Figure 22.4):

- Major individual projects – managed by the Strategy and Projects Director (who had previously led Phase I)
- Integrated Projects – (those dependent on each other) run by a project manager borrowed from Royal Mail for six months (Royal Mail is the key customer for Purchasing + Logistics Services).

As Quality and Business Process Director, I was asked to lead the Business Process Re-engineering Project. As project leader, I set my sights high and decided to re-engineer the whole Supply Chain Process, from suppliers through the organisation to external customers.

We were already operating to tight timescales due to the late start of the project, which put me under great pressure to get started, and this led me to my first obstacle: How do you actually do BPR?

In February 1994 there were only two to three books available (including Hammer and Champy and Davenport) and a few articles. Having read them from cover to cover, I knew what benefits I could achieve, but not what to do. Finally I was offered a methodology by the consultancy who were advising on the overall project, which I gratefully accepted. The overall business process workplan is shown in Figure 22.5. The aim was to go through the detail design loop with as many representatives of the business as possible (minimum 70!) so that there was extensive buy-in and ownership to the plans. Our deliverables were to include:

- List of business processes
- Detailed process designs to include:
  - Key policies and procedures
  - IT requirements
  - Critical success factor action plan
  - Process flow chart
  - Process task definition
  - Impact analysis

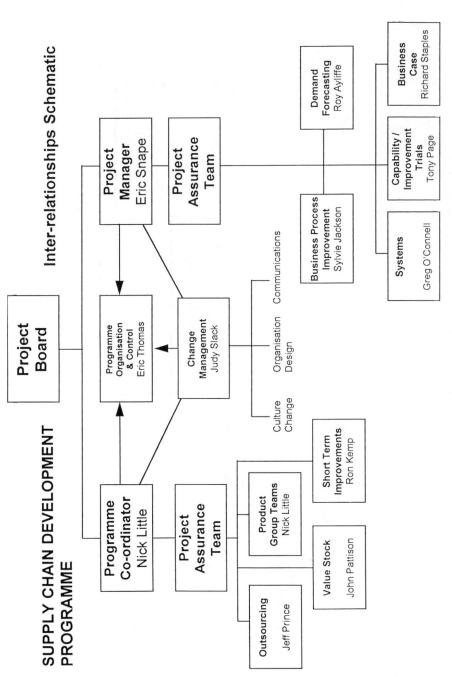

Figure 22.4 Towards tomorrow's purchasing and logistics. (Reproduced by permission of the Royal Mail)

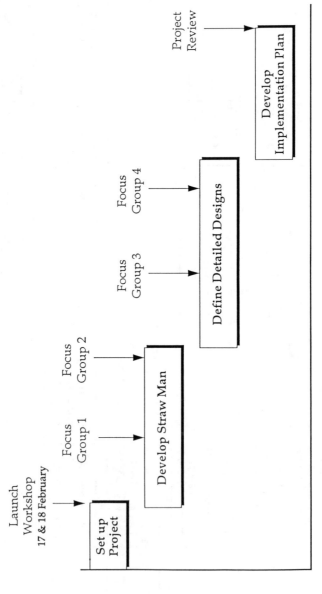

Figure 22.5 Overall BPI workplan: Phase II outline. (Reproduced by permission of the Royal Mail)

- Job descriptions
- Organisation requirements
- Responsibilities and accountabilities
- Decision-making matrix
- Key Performance Indicators
• Organisation Recommendations
• Implementation Plan

Despite the wide range of items purchased and supplied to The Post Office, key principles were that one process should suffice for all product categories, and that anything was possible. I was particularly taken with Mike Hammer's idea of "triage" processes where 90 + % of transactions can be covered by a very simple process and then to just add extra "loops" for more complicated areas rather than building the process to accommodate the most difficult transaction.

BPR or BPI?

A "core" team of approximately 15 people started the BPR project with a two-day session to develop the "straw man" process. The first day was largely a teaching/discussions session to get people up to speed on the Supply Chain Review Project Phase I. It also covered some team building; paradigms and understanding change management, business processes and a mini case study (Rover) on what could be achieved with BPR.

On the first evening, we identified the key process steps in the supply chain (order-fulfilment process)

• Customer needs identified
• Order
• Supply
• Receipt by customer
• Payment to supplier

On the second day we used the IDEF technique to break down each of the process steps to identify Inputs, Resources, Controls and Outputs. (See Figure 22.6 for Customer Need Identified Step.) While this was useful information, it took us a while to realise that there was little to re-engineer at this level and that we would need to look at Level 1 or 2; that is, at how the process was carried out before we would want to make changes.

Levels 1 and 2 were tackled (without IDEF) at meetings with Business Representatives. In view of the tight timescales we were running these meetings virtually every week with no real time to evaluate our process in between. We were under intense pressure for a deliverable because the systems team were dependent on us for a statement of requirements before they could develop a systems specification for the June 1995 report deadline.

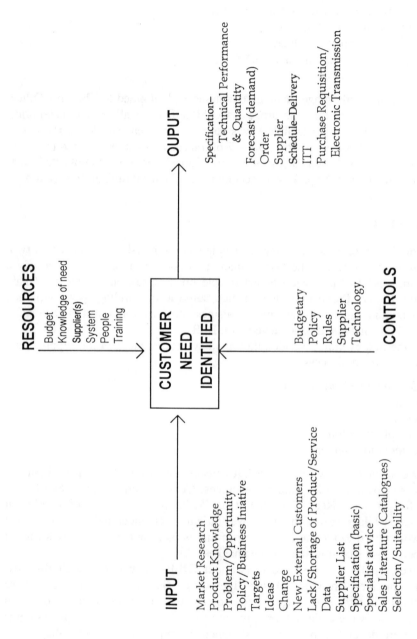

Figure 22.6 Current Need Identified step. (Reproduced by permission of the Royal Mail)

We had great difficulty getting a wide range of representatives to attend the meetings, so increasingly the same faces attended each week. It also became clear after a few weeks that the team were having difficulty with paradigms. They seemed unable to suggest any way of doing things other than the current way and offered the explanation that there must be a good reason for this. Suggestions for alternatives by myself were often met with the response that we would not be allowed to be so radical by either the finance or audit functions.

After requesting advice about any assumptions we should be making, we finally got a response which curtailed our radical thinking as constraints appeared concerning systems, financial conventions and budgetary and authorisation processes to be used. These were all areas where we had hoped to make inroads.

After a few weeks, it was clear we would make no further progress aside from the list of recommendations of changes already identified. Since the process changes were now curtailed to fit in with a specific computer system, one of my colleagues who had systems knowledge worked with the systems team to develop the detailed process plans.

The final report contained a high-level overview/summary; suggested changes; detailed process plans with critical success factors and a risk assessment. While the report was well received and contained extensive recommendations for changes to the process; it was essentially Business Process Improvements rather that Business Process Re-Engineering. (See Exhibit, p. 298, for a summary.).

LESSONS LEARNED

Our first attempt at re-engineering was not as successful as we had hoped. As I learned and read more about BPR, I began to understand where we had gone wrong. First, we had attempted to tackle the whole process when we were not fully empowered to do so. There was no buy-in or ownership to our proposed changes which cut across all the businesses. Lessons learned – do not bite off more than you can chew, and ensure ownership of stakeholders. Second, the constraint of the computer system which was originally bought for its financial capabilities, not its purchasing applications curtailed our project. Its purchasing applications were in fact able to provide the majority of the changes required. Lessons learned – beware heritage information systems, whose cost/life cycle must be taken into account.

Our biggest mistake, however, was not to have a vision of what we wanted to achieve. We had made it clear that the process should be better, faster and cheaper but that was all. Davenport (1993c) suggests that a vision "should specify the processes to be redesigned, the attributes of those processes and quantifiable process improvement objectives". The vision should have been a clear picture of the future which would have forced us to be radical to achieve it.

LEARNING FROM OUR MISTAKES – BPR 2

We had avoided any work on the centralised warehouse during the initial BPR project for two reasons: lack of time and the new Operations Director had not been appointed. By December 1994, he and his direct reports were keen to do work on the warehouse processes. Two alternatives were offered:

1. Map the current processes, via the ISO 9000 procedures then look for any duplication, waste, etc.
2. Look at the warehouse as a whole and aim to tackle the major improvement opportunities identified. The team were cautioned that this could be a major undertaking. There was unanimous agreement to go for the second option and I agreed to facilitate a two-day session to initiate it and give follow-up support.

I had concluded that BPR needs to be approached/have input from four areas:

- Blank sheet of paper approach – if I was starting from scratch, what would it look like?
- Review current process – while I had originally dismissed this as encouraging paradigms, I now realise it is easy to overlook key parts of the process when re-engineering (e.g. legal requirements).
- World class/best practice – by understanding what is world class or best practice performance for the process, it helps develop the vision and give a minimum to aim for or exceed.
- Customer, supplier, organisation requirements – by understanding these requirements, it can trigger innovative solutions, and the new process can be checked to ensure it delivers all the requirements.

We used the above to build our two-day session at the beginning of February 1995, inviting two "warehouse experts" from Cranfield University to join us. They visited the two warehouse sites in advance and talked to a number of managers and frontline staff. Customer and supplier representatives were also invited along.

Day 1 looked at the current situation, and identified world-class performance and processes for warehousing and customer/supplier requirements. From mid-afternoon, we began to describe a vision for the future; painting a clear picture in terms of customer satisfaction; working environment; measurement systems; employee requirements; profit; operations; suppliers; etc.

During the evening of Day 1, the Operations Director and myself tried to group the information gathered, so that we could split into two syndicates (led by each of us) to work up action plans.

The syndicates examined the improvement opportunities and identified those which would give major benefit. Twenty-six specific topics were each given a bullet point key action plan with barriers and benefits highlighted. We identified the quick wins versus longer-term work and a process was agreed to take the work forward before the completion of the two days' work.

The eight people who attended from the Operations Team (four direct reports and one of their managers) volunteered to lead the 26 projects. The "owner" was tasked to progress the project through to completion. Each project was given a mentor (Operations or Quality and Business Process Director) to provide help/support/guidance. The mentor was also tasked to deal with any buffers or barriers the project owner could not resolve. Additional resource was offered by the Quality Team and a manager who had some free time. A full review meeting was booked for the beginning of April 1995. The aim was to achieve as much as possible in 8 weeks.

The 26 projects identified were:

1. Reduce overhead costs administration support
2. Move to a "can-do" culture
3. Raise productivity
4. Suppliers – range of projects, including receipt of goods
5. Perfect order – order fulfilment – 100% accuracy
6. Introduce end-to-end measurement
7. Re-engineer returns procedure
8. Extend opening hours
9. Better, cheaper, faster – improve client relations
10. Client stock level improvements (for Post Office Counters)
11. Obsolete stock procedures
12. Reduction of inventory levels – live stock
13. Better use of accommodation in warehouse
14. Employee skills matrix/training and development
15. Two-way communication
16. Re-engineer complaints procedure
17. Introduce service level agreements with customers
18. Introduce customer satisfaction card/customer care
19. Improve telephone responses
20. Extend pricing menu for different warehouse goods
21. Re-engineer "new product launches" for early warehouse/purchasing involvement
22. Review and recommend new management information requirements
23. Develop action plan to move to paperless process warehouse
24. EDI paperless processing for orders and invoices
25. Invoicing for third-party work
26. Information flexibility

The BPR project became known as WINWIN – Warehouse Improvement Now, Which is Noticeable.

Despite the fact that the eight project owners were given no extra time or concessions, and that the three or four projects were over and above their normal work, the progress has been remarkable. We all left after the 2 days very highly motivated and convinced we could "pull off" the improvements. One of the managers later remarked to me that it was the "best two-day session he had ever attended".

By the review meeting in early April 1995:

- Ten projects were either completed, implemented or due to be implemented: e.g.

No. 3 *Raise Productivity* Productivity scheme developed with bonus-driven achievement, negotiated and agreed for implementation with front-line and managers' unions. Short-term aim to raise by 15% per annum. Already achieved in live store for year 1.

No. 11 *Obsolete Stock Procedures* "Obsolete" excess stock (print and clothing) identified. After liaison with Businesses, agreement given for disposal. Result: 10% reduction in inventory and 4% space released by volume 600 positions (pallet loads).

No. 19 *Improve Telephone Responses* Guidelines/targets introduced for telephone answering, e.g. within five rings, standard response "Good morning .....etc." Monthly monitoring, report to ensure all "customer numbers" are answered to target.

No. 7 *Re-engineer Returns Procedure* Process completely "re-engineered". Customer has replacement sent or credit given with 24 hours (improvement from up to 2 weeks while enquiries were made).

No. 17 *Service Level Agreements* Introduced for all the Businesses and tailored to their requirements. Areas included cover:
Order cycle time: 48 hours
Order fill: 99% (moving to 100%)
Returned Goods: action required – replacement/credit within 24 hours

- Ten projects would have substantial output by July 1995: e.g.

No. 1 *Reduce Overhead Costs* All support staff complete a log for one month to identify percentage of time spent "supporting" core business or purchasing or operations. Analysis to identify non-value-added work and lead to reduction of overhead (likely to be staff).

No. 8 *Extended Opening Hours* Four and a half-day week extended to 5-day week for warehouse by June 1995. Proposals developed for annual hours and increased flexibility to cover work/customer requirements. Need to be negotiated with the unions before proceeding.

No. 14 *Employee Skills Matrix/Training and Development* Appraisal process introduced for front-line staff with all relevant core skills; technical and social identified. Skills matrix developed to show current skills and those where training required.

No. 18 *Introduce Customer Satisfaction Card/Customer Care* Questionnaire postcard developed with customers and now sent out in all print and uniform orders. Report shows 10–20% improvement in satisfaction with uniform orders in first 2 months. No improvement with print orders in first few months but there has been a problem with stock availability. Specific new posts created in uniform and print teams to act as customer care/liaison. Initial customer response suggests this has been well received.

- Six projects would have made inroads towards their "desired state" by September: e.g.

No. 21 *New Product Launches* Worked with Royal Mail and Post Office Counters Ltd to change their processes to ensure Purchasing and Logistics are involved at a much earlier stage and there is input to the specification of the products/support material. Huge potential for major savings on cycle time reduction (new product/service to market) and spend on products/support material (e.g. standard sizes ref forms and labels, etc.). Awaiting first live trials.

No. 13 *Use of Accommodation* Facilities team currently working with MSc student to identify ways to move existing work into two warehousing units instead of three. This will release 30+% space for third-party work and reduce overhead costs for heating, lighting, etc.

In retrospect the initial BPR "failure" was an excellent lesson for us. It gave us time to think through what had gone wrong and do things differently the second time. Our customers (Royal Mail, Parcelforce and Post Office Counters Ltd) are already commenting on the improvements they have seen in the way we do business with them.

NEXT STEPS

Our re-engineering has covered all aspects of the warehouse – and we are making significant progress towards our vision, but the central warehouse is only a small part of the overall supply chain. There are a number of other initiatives progressing well, such as the First Class Supplier Programme (for accreditation and supplier management); Product Group Teams (who manage the purchase and select the best way to supply goods and services) and the Supply Chain Development Programme (which is concentrating on the development of systems for Purchasing and Common Coding).

Moving to managing the supply chain as a process as opposed to a set of discrete functions is proving to be quite a formidable task, not least because of the scale of the supply chain and that it crosses different businesses with different requirements and priorities. However, we remain convinced of the benefits.

Business process re-engineering is not something to be tackled lightly but with the right commitment and vision it can be a great success.

EXHIBIT: BUSINESS PROCESS IMPROVEMENT

INTRODUCTION

The Business Process Improvement Project has been the "hub" for much of the Supply Chain Review Phase II work. The material and recommendations in this Annex report have been compiled through a series of workshops which aimed to get input and agreement from all areas of the Post Office Businesses.

AIM OF BPI PROJECT

Improvements:

- *Time*
  - Reduce cycle time
  - Release time by abolishing/reducing non-value-added activity
- *Cost*
  - reduce costs
- *Quality/customer satisfaction*
  - Reduce errors
  - Improve performance of suppliers by better feedback

Clearly some recommendations will impact on all three areas, e.g. Introduction of "system" for end user ordering

- Single entry of data
- Reduction in cycle time
- Reduction in resource requirement (people)
- Reduction in errors (e.g. keying of information)

Business Process Model for the Supply Chain

Core processes are those which are core to the provision of customer service. Wherever possible, the only steps within the core processes are those essential to the provision of the service in the least economic time.

Support processes are those that ensure that the core processes are being performed in the most cost-effective and efficient ways by monitoring the core processes and providing the necessary information and processing.

Foundation processes are those that set the vision, direction, constraints and business imperatives upon which the business will operate. The consistency and clarity of their outputs will have significant impact on the effectiveness of the supply chain.

CORE PROCESSES

The core processes identified are:

- order fulfilment
- purchase management
- contract management

The relationships between them are shown in Figure 22.7.

Order Fulfilment

Definition: From customer identifying a need, through to specifying the requirement, the issue/supply of that requirement, to delivery of and receipt of the goods or services by the customer.

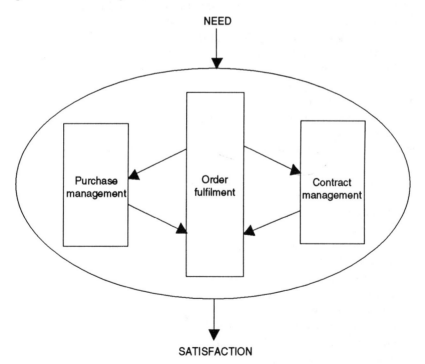

Figure 22.7   Core processes

This will be via:

Stock
Direct Supply (e.g. call-off contract)
New/Special Contract/Purchase

There will be a range of service levels available where appropriate. Process identified can be used for:

- Local purchase
- Orders from Central Warehouse
- New/special purchase
- Internal markets, supply

Main changes identified with benefits are:

- End user ordering
  - Empowerment
  - Cease manual orders
  - Cease hand-over of orders for authorisation
- Direct delivery receipt back to end user (mostly stocked items)
  - Cease via Div/Reg store to break bulk receipt
  - Cease part orders arriving (e.g. uniform)
- Reduce number of stores (reg/div)
  - Cease break bulk
  - Reduce inventory holding
- Single entry of data
  - Cease duplication of information input
  - Reduce cycle time
- Devolved authorisation of budgets and automatic authorisation of orders
  - Cease "hands-off" – release management time
  - Reduce cycle time
- Purchasing Section – change of role (expediters)
  - Improve control through MIS
  - Reduction in resource required (system to identify delays)
- Collection of product usage costs
  - Accurate management information
    = Reduction in inventory
    = Better forecasting
- Re-organisation of warehouse – workflows
  - small orders/packaging/attendance patterns
- Committed spend/actual spend
  - System will allow for better cost control

Purchase Management

Definition: To provide items from the most appropriate source with the best price to agreed service levels.

Main changes:

- Introduction of Product Group Teams – improve cost effectiveness by: Product Positioning work which will identify which items should be stocked: which purchased locally; which should be on call-off contract, etc.
- System will provide facility for automatic routing of order
    - Reduction in cycle time
    - Reduction in cost – "most effective source" used.

Contract Management

Definition: Placement of and management of call-off and one-off contracts.

- Reduce costs by better management of contracts

SUPPORT PROCESSES

The support processes identified are:

- Product positioning
- Supplier selection and management
- Demand forecasting
- Inventory management
- Payment/charging

The relationships between them are shown in Figure 22.8.

Product Positioning

Definition: The identification of the most appropriate (effective and efficient) way to purchase and supply goods and services: e.g. identify strategic items; those which should be stocked; those which should be purchased locally, and those for which call-off contracts are appropriate.

Supplier Selection and Management

Definition: Introduce develop and monitor supplier sources which reach minimum standard of performance as determined by the First Class Supplier Programme.

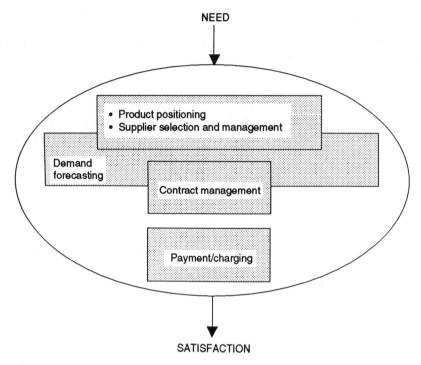

Figure 22.8 Support processes

Main changes

- Introduction of First Class Supplier Programme
  - = Reduce costs
  - = Improve quality/performance
- Strategic Coding – systems to support them
  - = Reduce time/cost ref use of effective control management

Demand Forecasting

Definition: Identify future requirements of goods and services: long term (2+ years); medium term (1+ year) and short term (2−3 months)

Main changes

Introduction of DF process
= Reduce costs (more accurate stocking)
= Reduce costs (supplier discounts)
= Customer Satisfaction (less stockouts)

Inventory Management

Definition: Control of stocking levels/issue of inventory (stock).

Main changes

- Ability to set stock management policy for the PO
  = Reduce costs
- Stock taking Group-wide/manage PO materials
  = Reduce costs (staff resource)
  = Less/no stock-outs
- Warehouse reorganisation (later study)
  = Reduce cycle time
  = Reduce costs

Payment/Charging

Definition: Payment to suppliers for goods/services received. Charge to Businesses for inter-business work in the supply chain.

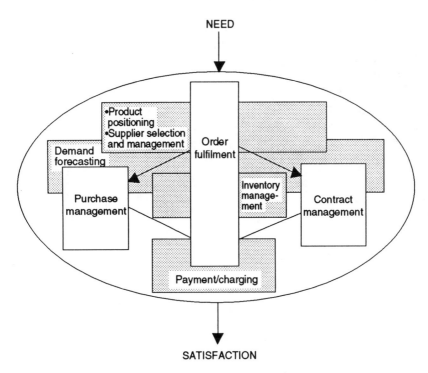

Figure 22.9 Relationship between Core & Support services

Main changes

- Abandonment of invoices → summary of usage with movement of funds
  = Reduce costs
- Payment on receipt or direct debit by supplier
  = Reduce costs

The relationships between the core and support processes are shown in Figure 22.9.

FOUNDATION PROCESSES

The foundation processes are:

- Business Planning
- Budgeting
- New Service Line Development

These underpin all business processes as shown in Figure 22.10.

The Supply Chain Review has concentrated on the core and support

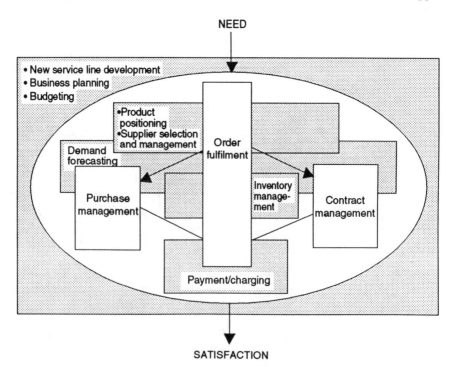

Figure 22.10 Foundation processes

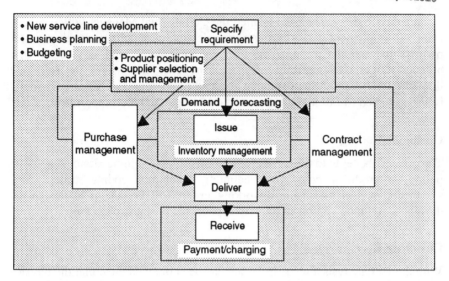

Figure 22.11   Overall business process model – with order fulfilment at the next level

processes to identify improvement areas, but recognises the need for changes to the foundation processes to highlight the important part that purchasing and logistics has to play in their successful outcome.

The main changes recommended for the foundation processes are early inclusion of purchasing professionals to ensure sufficient time is given to gain optimum provision of future goods and services required and best value for money (see Figure 22.11).

BUSINESS PROCESS IMPROVEMENT ASSUMPTIONS

The Business Process Improvement model, which follows, has been built on the basis of a number of key assumptions. These are documented below.

Product Group Team Role

The Product Group Teams (PGTs) are seen as having a key role in the supply chain management. They are assumed to have the twin and complementary roles of determining the logistic strategy; and also the day-to-day responsibility for ensuring the customer needs are met.

In the strategic role it is assumed the PGT Director (from the Businesses), the Commercial Manager and customer representative will determine the central/local balance, product positioning and other high-level issues.

On a day-to-day basis it is assumed the Commercial Manager with a support team will implement policy through the selection of suppliers, development of partnerships and the arrangements for sourcing goods and services in their product ranges. Responsibility for ensuring customer needs are fully met throughout the supply chain and that constant improvement is constantly sought is also assumed to fall to the Commercial Manager and the support team.

Customer Coding

The greatest benefits to the business, in terms of determining strategic sourcing policy for products, come from adopting a common coding strategy. It is assumed that a cross-Business working group will be set up to design and develop a common coding strategy to support the business processes.

Customer Receipt

With the BPI analysis a recurring issue has been the guarantee that the physical receipt of product to the final customer can be made within agreed service levels particularly at the customer's unit. It is assumed that in implementing the Business Processes that the mechanisms for ensuring final receipt of product have been resolved. The resolution of this issue will produce costs and benefits at customer unit level.

Distribution Network

It is central to the success of meeting customer needs that the changed processes will be served by an efficient and bespoke distribution network. The assumption that such a network is in place is inherent in these processes.

System/Process Interfaces

A critical success factor in the implementation of the business processes is the provision of interfaces between different parts of the business – for example, the definition, management and distribution of strategic codes to all parts of the business and the capture of orders by the central warehouse from the different parts of the business. It is assumed that in the short term business processes are established to manage these interfaces leading to these being fully automated once the systems are in place. It is also assumed that integrated and satisfactory change management is applied to these vital changes.

Warehouse Workflow Management

In the same way as an efficient distribution network (see assumption above) will need to be in place to support the supply chain processes, so it is necessary for the internal warehouse processes to be organised in such a way to support the speedy despatch of product to agreed delivery standards. It is assumed that these changes to workflow management will be implemented. It is assumed that warehouse and distribution process changes (including delivery at the operating unit direct to the customer) will be coordinated.

Business Sourcing Flexibility

It is assumed that call-off contracts negotiated on a national basis will be mandatory for use. However, we assume that the PGTs will ensure sufficient flexibility to allow local purchasing to conduct local buying to meet emergency requirements. In addition, the business should have the flexibility to raise local contracts for unique local needs, and will take note of objectives to support business in the community where applicable.

The business processes defined in the BPI imply no organisational implementation. The processes are designed in such a way as to allow their implementation at any level within the business. However, clearly inherent in some of the processes is an implication of changes to working methods.

Budgetary Approval

Budget authority and responsibility will be devolved to the lowest management position. In addition, it is assumed that the system should record expenditure against the Nominal Codes to which it is proper. The manager with the devolved budget should review and manage his budget against the codes where expenditure has been committed.

Chapter 23

Making the Valuable Difference: Successful BPR at National Vulcan

Ken Sinfield

(This article first appeared in *Focus on Change*, Issue 1, January 1994 and is reproduced by permission.)

"It's an ill wind that blows nobody any good" and it was certainly a biting blast of cold air that swept through National Vulcan Engineering Insurance Group Ltd in 1991. The first hint of the cold north-easterly came in 1990, when profits dropped to £6.1 million. The full force of the recessionary gale hit the company in 1991, however, when it was faced with a devastating loss of £6.3 million. This is the story of how that ill wind provided an opportunity to turn the business around. The company, facing a threat to its very survival, managed – through radical re-engineering – to regain its leading position in the engineering insurance sector within just one year. 1992 saw a profit of £3.4 million, reversing the previous year's downturn. The upward trend has continued in 1993, with a £5 million profit projected. Bearing in mind that all of this happened during the service sector's worst-ever recession, how was it achieved?

Even though many people have not heard of National Vulcan, its engineers are all over the country inspecting boilers, compressors, lifts and all types of mechanical and electrical equipment known as "plant". There is a statutory obligation to have this "plant" inspected once or twice a year. Once certified, the owners may also choose to have it insured against explosion, breakdown and other perils. National Vulcan provides both these services. Its engineers can be found anywhere, from the local garage to nine of the nation's thirteen nuclear power stations. That amounts to over 2000 on-site inspections every day, resulting in over 500 000 reports a year sent to customers. At the same time, National Vulcan provides insurance for many of the items inspected, issuing some 75 000 policies every year.

So Inspection and Insurance are the two key activities of the business. However, another function is to keep a detailed record of every item of plant inspected or insured. As there are over 2.5 million separate items to keep records of, this is no small task. All insurance policies and engineering inspections are based on this database, so it is critical that it be kept accurate and up to date.

THE CRISIS OF '91

The £6.3 million loss in 1991 was symptomatic of the overall malaise that had crept throughout the company over the decades. For over 130 years, National Vulcan enjoyed a pre-eminent position in its sector; as a result, rigidity and complacency had crept into every corner of the business. The one saving grace had always been, and continues to be, the technical excellence and dedication of the engineering inspectors. The main problems were back at the Head Office.

A customer satisfaction survey commissioned in 1991 made dismal reading. When presented to senior management, one comment was "I don't know what's wrong, we have not changed at all; the customer must have". Customers, even long-established major accounts, were beginning to leave National Vulcan.

In a way, National Vulcan had become a prisoner of its own history. Technical excellence and a captive market had developed a cosy lifestyle; staff expected (and got) jobs for life, were very inward-looking and had 55 different job grades. Any messengers of change were immediately shot. It was not long into 1991 before it became clear, despite that year's Business Plan forecasting a profit, that the company was in crisis and there is nothing like the prospect of death to focus the mind: 99.99% of the time wasted.

Although no-one knew exactly how bad things had become, it was nevertheless clear that reports, policies and plant database updates were taking months to process. In order to get a clearer picture of why this was so, the management took an accelerated walk through every "process step" that was required to process the simplest insurance policy. The tour took all morning. They witnessed dozens of strange procedural steps (reasons for which had long been forgotten) and had to pass through almost every department within National Vulcan. All this was for a mere £75 policy!

One encounter was with a senior engineer with files of paper piled so high that he was barely visible. When asked if he was struggling he replied, "Oh no, sir, I am doing very well. I used to have a six-month backlog; now it's only five months". When asked the key question as to what he actually did when processing the files, the answer gave birth to a new vision of how to organise work. He apparently only spent a couple of minutes making some key checks and then passed the file on for completion. Five months to add a few minutes of real value. Further investigation was definitely required!

The managers soon realised that, although the overall cycle time was taking months (typically three months), there was only about three days' worth of actual work going on; 97% of the time nothing was happening. Internal procedures and bureaucracy had built up so much over the years that the remaining 3% of the time when work was done, when analysed, was found to have only about three hours of activity that was worth doing at all. Three hours out of three months meant that useful work was only being performed for a mere 0.1% of the time!

The final step was to look at the three hours of work that was of value either to the customer or to the business and assess how much of it could be automated. They discovered that almost all the tasks could be handled by a computer, leaving only a few minutes of the most critical, value-added work for National Vulcan staff to do. It was the conversation with a customer, the risk assessment, the claim that "smells" wrong. This final, value-adding element was termed The Valuable Difference.

So, true value was being added for only minutes out of three months, or less than 0.01% effective; 99.99% of the time National Vulcan was processing a customer transaction, no real value was being added. When it was realised just how restricted everyone was in really making a Valuable Difference, a vision of a new National Vulcan was quickly developed; a vision of the incredible latent potential within every member of staff to spend almost all of their time making that Valuable Difference. People would be liberated from the tedium of mundane and bureaucratic administration and, instead, be transformed into Insurance Professionals.

OUTRAGEOUS TARGETS

Such an ambitious goal would require radical action, so some outrageous targets were set. Having witnessed the 0.01% phenomenon, targets were set with the full confidence that they really could be achieved. The two main targets were:

1. All customer transactions must be processed within 24 hours of receipt. This included policy issue, dispatching of inspection reports and plant database updates.

2. Only one pair of hands must be involved in the processing of those customer transactions, no matter where within the company they were received.

Since all transactions were currently taking months, and passing through dozens of hands, these targets sent shock waves throughout the company. The vision of The Valuable Difference meant that every time someone said, "But it just can't be done", the answer was always the same: "Then change the process so it can". Despite the shaking of heads, a solution was always found and these goals have now been achieved.

Other changes included not putting existing managers in charge of the new, customer-orientated processes, since they usually had the most to lose by radical change. Instead, staff with the most to gain were given responsibility for delivery. On some projects, this meant that managers ended up reporting to staff who were previously their juniors. This further reinforced the message that radical change was afoot!

THROWING OUT THE RULE BOOK

Perhaps the most important change was the use of Information Technology to liberate The Valuable Difference. It has become an industry showcase and has already won the company two top technology awards this year (*The Sunday Times*/Anderson Consulting "IT for Business Excellence"; and the *Computer Weekly* "IT Performance" awards). National Vulcan has developed, from scratch, three of the most sophisticated processing systems in the UK – one for each of the main business processes: Insurance, Plant Database and Reporting.

Incredibly, National Vulcan achieved all this in less than a year, using only small development teams of no more than ten people for each system. The secret was the absolute business imperative to achieve extremely well-defined results in a very short time period. This meant throwing out the rule book for all traditional approaches to IT development (which would have entailed hundreds of staff years of effort). Years of mainframe development were also thrown out. Instead, the company sought out a variety of innovative solutions to automate the software production process, giving the end users some of the most advanced facilities in the world.

LEGACY SYSTEMS

The overall objective was to replace the existing £2 million a year budget that was being spent on Sun Alliance IBM mainframe services with the three new systems that when complete would operate all within the same £2 million budget. The existing mainframe developments had taken three years to reach a pilot state and only covered 20% of the company's activity, and not very well either! The new systems would cover 95% of the business, employ the latest technologies and be very flexible in order to evolve with the changing business.

The development was initially going to require an extra several million pounds investment. As the parent company, Sun Alliance International, was about to announce the biggest ever loss by a private company in the UK, it was not a good time to be asking for money! However, the determination and confidence of the National Vulcan team won through and the risk was taken. The new IT systems now drive the three new, re-engineered business processes, each of which is a case study in itself.

INSURANCE PROCESS ALL ON ONE SCREEN

The Insurance Administration process had grown into a nightmare spread out over 24 branch offices. Branch salespeople were so busy with administration that they were rarely out of the office to meet customers. Branch administrators, on the other hand, had to deal with such complex customer administration problems that they would spend more time on-site with customers than in the branch office. A decision was made to centralise all administration into one Customer Service Unit at the Head Office in Manchester, and to merge all the branches into nine regional sales offices. This involved taking 17 of the best staff in the field, making them a "godfather" offer, and moving them and their families to Head Office in Manchester. At the same time, 120 extra staff were recruited from the Manchester area.

The outrageous target was to complete the entire operation in just three weeks. A great gamble was taken: to achieve the target it was necessary to stop all customer processing for the entire three weeks, hoping that the company had such backlogs that none of the customers would notice – and they did not!

This Insurance Administration process has achieved almost all its targets. Policies are now issued and cancelled within 24 hours, ten departments have been reduced to one and there are only two steps and two people left in the process that are not managed by the system. The system provides every function of the entire insurance administration process on single SUN Workstation screens. It employs the latest in ease-of-use features, including a full graphical user interface where the various insurance functions appear in windows on the screen and commands can be activated by clicking a mouse on icons and menus. The remarkable speed of development and continuing ease of maintenance has been achieved using INGRES development software, permitting a "fourth-generation" approach to automate much of the software production process and a "relational" approach to database management.

10 MILLION PIECES OF PAPER ELIMINATED

The Plant Database process consisted of manually locating and updating literally millions of files, each with dozens of pieces of paper. This mind-numbingly boring job achieved a pretty reasonable staff turnover. Around 30%, in fact. To map out that process took 13 pages of dense flowcharts. Now, the new process and system have eliminated the need for paper altogether, and almost all the need for people. The staff that are left now have interesting jobs, and turnover is down to just 2%.

Paper was eliminated, not by scanning it all into a Document Image Processing system as siren voices had encouraged, but by redesigning the process to remove the need for paper in the first place. Most of the updates and accesses are done directly from the other systems. Indeed, almost the entire business process has effectively become a "lights out office". This system runs on more traditional computer servers as there was not the intense need for a graphical user interface, but it is also driven by a powerful Application Builder and Relational Database called PACE.

HI-TECH AT HOME

Finally, the Reporting process has liberated National Vulcan's engineers from most of the tedium of filing reports. Of the 1100 staff employed by National Vulcan, 600 are engineers, of which 480 work from home and spend all day on-site inspecting plant. Every night they used to type up their reports on a form with seven carbons and copies behind it. Mistakes were interesting; National Vulcan must have been one of the UK's largest consumers of Snopake. All reports were sent off twice a week, by second-class post (not wanting to waste money), to Head Office. They would then be rechecked by senior engineers and often sent back for modification and the cycle repeated.

The new re-engineered process involved giving each engineer a Notebook PC with some very smart intelligent "forms" software on it, called FlexiForms (developed specially by Text Systems Ltd, an external company). The forms adapt themselves automatically, according to what data is input. This eliminates having to find the right form out of over 200 variants. Every night these are now sent over the phone, via a modem, to Head Office, where they are processed and reports dispatched to customers the next day; again, within 24 hours. The entire process and 2000 reports a day are now managed by a team of 12 professionals, rather than over 140 clerks as previously.

FOCUS ON THE VALUABLE DIFFERENCE

All this has been achieved in less than two years by ruthlessly focusing on that Valuable Difference. The result has been to put National Vulcan back in the number-one place as industry leader. The company returned to strong profitability and, while maintaining a no compulsory redundancy policy, has still reduced headcount from 1341 to 1100. This has been mainly through attrition, although many staff have found themselves working in higher-value areas as old jobs have disappeared. Engineers' Reporting productivity has doubled, per capita income has increased by 49.4% and cash flow has improved by 35%.

Staff are being transformed from administration clerks into Insurance Professionals by being given ownership of the entire customer process and more time to focus on Making The Valuable Difference. This means customers get more time and a better quality product and service from the company. Consequently, National Vulcan is now retaining its customers again, and is growing. Perhaps most telling is the fact that complaints fell steadily away to none by August 1992 and have remained there. Further, there has been industry recognition of the achievements. The Institute of Insurance Brokers recognised National Vulcan with the award "Best UK Engineering Insurer", less than a year ago. The message from National Vulcan, then, is to focus on the Valuable Difference, first, through understanding the current process and then by setting outrageous targets designed to liberate that Difference. National Vulcan has also shown how critical it is for top management to fully sponsor and personally champion this process.

As for that ill wind, it has not just done National Vulcan some considerable good, it was actually welcomed. The hard bite to that wind came from the recession. Without that edge, National Vulcan may never have had the impetus required to make such dramatic and radical changes. Which is why at National Vulcan people say, "Thank God for the recession!". The results are outlined below:

National Vulcan Engineering Insurance Group Ltd

- A subsidiary of Sun Alliance International Ltd
- 1100 employees (including 480 home-based field engineers)
- Turnover last year: £120 million
- 24 branch offices merged into nine regional sales offices and all administration centralised at Head Office
- 10 functional departments reduced to one
- All policies now issued within 24 hours (previously three months)
- 55 job grades down to seven grades
- 800 administrative staff reduced to 500 staff

Chapter 24

Cigna: Changing the Culture

Colin Armistead

Susan Kozik is a vice-president of Cigna a US insurance company, and a leading member of its internal re-engineering team. Since 1989 she has seen at close quarters the varying success of re-engineering in the insurer's 10 divisions. They all have projects either completed or under way, but the methods used have changed considerably in that time. In particular, the emphasis has been shifted to beginning cultural change a few months before the start of the re-engineering programme. "In some of the earlier cases we did not hold enough meetings of all staff in time to prepare them for the new language and thinking of re-engineering", Kozik says.

Without the other cultural initiatives such as team-based pay incentives, change tends to be rejected quickly when it does arrive says Kozik. It then takes far longer to reap any benefit from re-engineering. Cigna's experience with cultural change has been put to good use for two years in its UK arm, Cigna Employee Benefits. In 1991 four months before it started to introduce cross-department business processes in place of a functional hierarchy, staff began meeting Kozik's group twice a day to learn about re-engineering and team-work. Later teams were rolled out to work in the newly designed business processes. The meetings were used by staff to review work done and to set goals. Since then Cigna's UK operation which specialises in group health insurance, has turned six separate business functions into two separate processes based on pre- and post-sales activities. The time it takes to give a quote has been cut from 17 days to two, and staff who used to process between 35 and 40 claims a day are now working through 75 to 90 a day. As a result of this and a move from the south-east to a low-cost site in Greenock, Scotland, more than £1 million has been shaved off costs. The unit's underwriting loss of £2 million in 1992 was set to become a profit of £2 million in 1993.

It is not solely because cultural change came first that things have gone so well. Cigna has other ways to tackle managers who dig their heels in. First, all managers are interviewed by the re-engineering team before a decision to start change is taken. They are asked what they think about change and their attitudes are carefully recorded. Not everyone can be persuaded. Once the UK team had decided to go ahead, in spite of the expected resistance from particular people, it accomplished something novel for the parent company. "The easiest thing to do with senior managers who do not like re-engineering is to go round them" says Roger Dockett, managing director of the UK operation. "But we have actively sought to put people most resistant to change in some of the project's first positions of responsibility. We did lose about 5% of staff this way, but we have won over a lot more." The organisation has been flattened, eliminating four layers of management and basing everything on teams rather than functions.

Dockett says that two senior managers have had their jobs changed very early on. "At first they felt very threatened because decisions they were used to making every day were being taken by more junior staff. Now they realise that as leaders of the whole process they have more opportunity to influence the whole organisation".

Another way of increasing staff commitment would also raise a few eyebrows in the UK. The initial process design was fairly cursory, and in some cases non-existent. Cheerfully, Dockett says the abiding principle has been "do it, test it, fix it". The first time this was tried in the post-sales business two people, each from administration, claims and accounts, were taken from their desks and seated together around a different desk. Management's instruction was simply to carry on with the job. A few days later the group was processing far more claims.

Allowing a cross-functional team to design the process shows a measure of respect for junior staff that is not immediately apparent in other companies trying to re-engineer themselves. Kozik says that some of the US divisions of Cigna were scared to let more junior staff embrace changes in this way. "After our first programmes we learned you can trust teams. Management who tried to hand down changes were missing out on the most knowledgeable group of people. For smaller process changes we now allow staff to design new processes. For broader changes we use teams as a source of ideas." Both Kozik and Dockett say that, if staff are working in processes they have built, many cultural changes follow more naturally – such as ownership, process owner-ship, and team mindset. It is an effective way to change staff attitudes without stand-alone cultural seminars and training programmes.

Each client is assigned to a team which deals with every aspect of its business. Within the team the client company and all the employees covered by the scheme are given an individual who deals directly with their business and a direct-line telephone number straight to that person. Teams set their own daily work targets and measure themselves against those targets. Every morning each member of the team will tell the rest of the team what targets he or she is setting for the day, say in terms of the number of claims they expect to process, and next morning they report what they actually managed to do. "If someone isn't pulling their weight the other team members aren't going to carry them, because it reflects on them. It's all about not wanting to lose face."

Cigna has made 15% of individual salaries related to the performance of the team. That figure too was decided by more junior staff. Kozik says: "Too many top managers assume that staff do not want to risk their salary. Why not go out and ask them how much they want to risk?" By contrast, Cigna's first re-engineering project in the USA "did not discuss reward systems early enough", Kozik says. "We had introduced teams but not team goals. Whether teams will go the extra mile for the customer depends on monetary and non-monetary rewards." Kozik does not pretend that Cigna's re-engineering is the only approach to the subject. "You cannot clone re-engineering. This is not something you can learn from a book. It's about people and personalities."

The promise to customers is a range of payments if they fail, from £5 if there are delays in issuing settlement cheques to £100 if the company fails to send out a deposit request at least three weeks before the renewal date, a grace period which allows customers to seek quotes from other insurance groups.

The results have been tangible. In 1994 Cigna were the National Winners of the *Management Today* and Arthur Andersen Best Practices Awards for Service Excellence judged on corporate focus, market understanding, process alignment and shared values.

Source: Michaels, A. (1993) Culture vultures, *Financial Times* 23 July and Britain's Champions, *Management Today*, 1994.

Chapter 25

Reflections on a BPR Project

Colin Armistead, Graham Clark,
Paula Stanley and Philip Rowland

A re-engineering project for a company in the financial services sector aimed to improve revenue, customer service and efficiency through the use of technology. The message communicated to staff was that transformation was necessary for survival. The project got off to a shaky start when the company was without a CEO but once a new one was in place the project obtained the support of three directors and "it became easier because people saw it as an initiative we want to go for".

The project was facilitated initially with the help of consultants. Their approach included: a high-level redesign team meeting to determine "where the business was going", baselining existing processes, that is, to map existing processes in detail; to redesign the process with the human factors inputs; and finally to implement the new process. The execution was different! The lack of a CEO made the first stage difficult to complete. Before completing stage one the team went on to baseline existing processes by creating nine teams that represented their existing processes. All worked on-site for three days. The teams gathered data on service times for particular tasks and cycle times. Process mapping was carried out using a software package and 400 detailed activities were identified of which 60 were involved in correcting errors. This large number were aggregated into eight high level processes. However, many process overlaps were identified: "It basically was a nightmare that so many things were being done the same but in different departments with a different

name, with a different role title of the person that did it, it was amazing and ...
it had obviously been a long time since anyone had taken such a severe look at
the business."

Baseline teams were multi-functional, multi-grade, and different ages. Each
had core members and others were brought in as required, All core members
were part-time and predominantely technical specialists. Some individuals were
considered excellent at baselining but not as good at redesign. These people
were often used to validate redesigned processes. After being away on the
baselining activity, team members were expected to devote further time back in
their home "department". The activity of baselining took the organisation about
five months to complete.

The next stage involved a meeting with 30 or so senior managers from
around the business who identified what their core business processes should
be, thus linking them with their strategic vision for the company.

Redesign teams were created who worked full-time off-site to redesign the
business, bringing new ideas on the use of information technology and
information on customer values. Each team was led by a process champion
who was not necessarily a senior manager but "someone who would stand on
their soapbox and say why hasn't this been implemented". An HRM and a IT
specialist contributed to each team.

The methodology required the team to look at the parts of their processes
which added value and these which did not. However the teams decided to opt
for a "clean sheet" approach with facilitation from the consultants. Once they
had done this they were asked to ensure that the new processes would take the
existing and potential business.

The organisation is into the implementation stage having tested their ideas on
customers and it meets their internal rate of return for any project. The changes
proposed will increase their responsiveness to make changes for their
customers. The people who have been involved so far make a number of
comments about the process:

> "It was hard work. It was painful. It was awful ... The experience was brilliant,
> at the end of it I felt thoroughly elated and absolutely worn out."

This shows that some struggled with the concept of taking a process view of the
organisation. Others found it difficult to think freely. Generally it seemed to
take two or three days to get into the exercise. One aspect which concerned
some members of the teams was that they might be designing themselves or
colleagues out of a job:

> "I suddenly started to realise what it meant to the people. Then I had a sort of bit
> of nervous feeling about it, and really at that point I had a bit of soul searching
> and said to myself, well, there are no guarantees in any of this. I may not actually

have a job at the end of it, but there is no point trying to be negative or a blocker or whatever, because if you don't do it somebody else will."

The exercise also enables people to share a view of the organisation.

"Until you actually see the mess we're in and see where you actually fit in to all of that, that's when it hits you and you think, Oh my God, what have we been doing?"

Having the mix of team members also seemed to work:

"And the delightful thing that came out of it was that we actually started recognising the amount of potential that some of the kids have, and the amount of output from them was quite phenomenal and there's a sort of vibrancy – it was really key to the success of it, I think. It generated enthusiasm and so on. And also they weren't carrying any baggage with them."

Some people expressed scepticism about getting teams to map existing processes. A nomenclature developed of Nikeys, "Just say yes", then the Nancys "Just say no", and finally the Plain Clothes Nancys who appear cooperative but who in fact are not.

The move towards managing uncertainty was seen as a particularly difficult one by one team member. "A lot of people felt uncomfortable and … were walking around saying I can't understand what the hell we're doing here". Only towards the end of the team process did this become clear for some. Managing the new climate of uncertainty throughout the organisation was identified as an issue requiring attention.

Chapter 26

Apollo Fire Detectors

Colin Armistead

(This case was prepared by Professor Colin Armistead of the Business School at Bournemouth University. It is not meant to illustrate good or bad management practices. This case is produced by permission of Apollo Fire Detectors Ltd. Copyright 1995.)

Apollo Fire Detectors Limited are a wholly owned member of the Halma Group, a publicly quoted company. Apollo was formed in 1980 from a management buyout of part of the Wilkinson Match Company. In 1984 the company became part of the Halma Group whose companies are linked by interests in security, environmental control, fire and gas detection. Generally the Group is concerned with developing technology which has already been pioneered. In Apollo's case this relates to electronic and electromechanical assembly. The company employs 380 people and has a turnover in the region of £25 million and is organised according to Figure 26.1.

Apollo represents approximately 15% of the Halma Group's turnover and they have consistently met targets of 20% year-on-year growth in earnings together with returns on capital employed in excess of 40%.

The company sees itself competing on the basis of in-house design coupled with low-cost manufacturing. However, the company also perceives itself special in one regard:

> "In most industries when a product fails you have a complaint, in our industry if our product fails you have a potential loss of life or property. An example is a recent fire at the Sainsbury superstore in Chichester when no one was killed because the system did its job. No one sings our praises though. Saving life is our

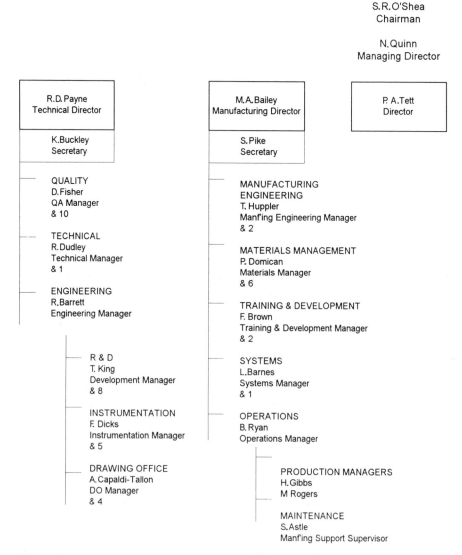

Figure 26.1 Organisation Chart for Apollo Fire Detectors Ltd

first priority and safeguarding property second, although we try to do both. Outside of the industry we are not a company which is well known."

The company has consistently increased its exports and has been the winner of three Queen's Awards for Export.

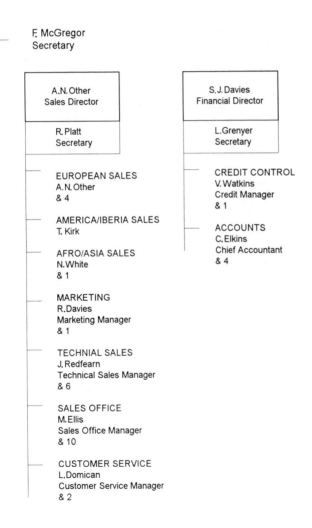

Figure 26.1 *Continued*

THE PRODUCTS AND MARKETS

Apollo sells a range of about 80 products of which about 60 are active. Variation in products can take the form either of badging for larger customers or differences to meet specific country approvals. The main products are fire detectors which monitor smoke either optically through smoke particles scattering light or where smoke enters an ionisation chamber and causes a drop in current or where changes in temperature are monitored. Two product lines, series 60 and XP95, make up 80% of the output. Typical prices for these products are £20 for the series 60 and £40 for the XP95 detector.

The earlier series 60 detectors are conventional alarms which are switched off until there is sufficient smoke to switch the alarm on. These detectors may be in a zone of 20 detectors on the floor of a building where in the event of fire it is only possible to tell that the fire is somewhere in the zone.

The newer XP95 addressable detectors are intelligent in that each detector is individually identified by a unique address. The detector will also send a signal proportional to the amount of smoke.

Apollo do not design, install or maintain systems. Their customers consequently are not the end users of the systems but rather systems houses who use the detectors as part of a system. Alternatively, the customer may be distributors who sell off the shelf and particularly overseas customers who then sell on a portfolio of products. Products are sold to 60–70 countries with 60% of the volume being for export.

Apollo have about 50% of the UK market and 12% of the world market for their products. They are number one in the UK and equal second in the world with Hochiki from Japan behind the world leader, Systems Sensor from the USA.

Apollo try not to sell on price but on technical aspects of the product and service levels. They try to respond quickly to requests from customers and present themselves as a "professional high-quality supplier". There is a tendency for the market to view the products as commodity items and therefore there is downward pressure on prices. "It's an electronics product and everyone knows what electronics prices do, don't they?" The company has seen prices decrease year on year. Apollo try to minimise this effect by negotiating financial arrangements as much as price.

MANUFACTURING

"Manufacturing is relatively straightforward. We have a limited number of lines and product variant is often putting on a label. We design for manufacture and have technically elegant designs". A high-volume product such as the series 60 ionisation detector has an output typically between 2000 and

2500 items a day or 500 000 to 600 000 a year. Over the last five to eight years there has been a move away from having a lot of people "sitting at benches stuffing components to the use of surface mounting technology". Currently the material content of the product costs are about four times the labour costs.

The detector products are relatively simple (see Figure 26.2), being made up in the case of the XP95 range of a base for securing the detector to a building, the base of the unit, a programming module, a holder for the detector, the detector, and a cover. The product design is critical for both the capability of the product in use and also for ease of manufacture for low-cost manufacturing. An example of this is that the screws which secure the printed circuit board of the detector also form the conducting pathway ...

Apollo have gone through two main phases to improve their manufacturing capability which has led to the present manufacturing system. The first phase in the last part of the 1980s was when they adopted a number of Japanese methods of manufacturing with the aim of streamlining manufacturing and cutting down throughput times and work in progress. They changed layout and introduced simple kanban systems. Lead times were reduced from 4–6 weeks to 1–2 weeks.

The second wave over the last four years has seen the introduction of continuous flow techniques where possible. As much of the product as possible is subjected to successive operations consecutively. The downside for Apollo is that some operations do not lend themselves to this approach. For example, a number of stages are time dependent including varnishing, test and calibration and electrical soak test. "My least favourite is soak where the product is made and has to be submitted to a soak test for 24 hours." In this phase of development, technology has been introduced to replace hand insertion with surface-mounting technology. This measure has been the main instrument for improvement, assisted by process engineering and process redesign. These measures have resulted in an improvement in labour productivity from about 70 detector heads per person per week to a figure of 120.

Customer lead times are currently quoted as 3 days but a 24-hour turn-round is often achieved. While they do not formally measure delivery reliability Apollo use a measure of "stock limited". If a customer is prepared to accept delivery of product and they fail to deliver it is deemed "stock limited". This measure applies even if a customer requests an early delivery on an order. A target of about 2% of all orders is set on the measure and is generally achieved.

Manufacturing is carried out in three units on the one site. The workforce comprises 200 permanent and 56 temporary workers who work a 38-hour week on an 8.30–4.30 day shift and a 20-hour week on a twilight shift between 6.00 pm and 10.00 pm.

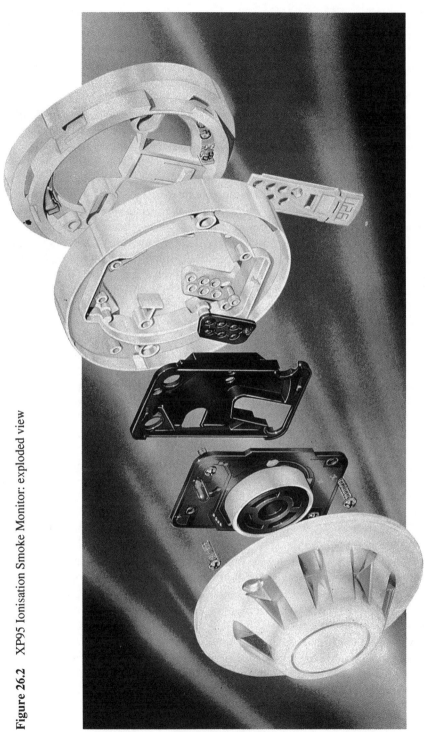

Figure 26.2 XP95 Ionisation Smoke Monitor: exploded view

The present factory is organised into cells mainly by type of product (Figure 26.3). The shopfloor is fairly crowded but the flow of material is clear within the cells. A typical assembly operation involving about six stages operates with cycle time of about 30 seconds. Work contents for typical series 60 and an XP95 detector are 12 minutes and 15 minutes respectively.

Operators in the cells are responsible for their own quality control and they fill in control charts. They also call off orders from suppliers to initiate delivery to the line or close to the line. Quality is supported by a Quality Assurance department which reports to the Technical Director. The section has four quality control staff and six quality assurance engineers. Accreditation to ISO 9000 Part 2 was achieved in the late 1980s. The company also has its products approved by external agencies, in particular markets this acts as a barrier for entry to potential competitors.

Production is against forecast although some customers' orders will be included in the figures supplied from sales. There is very little reliance currently on software systems for production planning. An existing system is elderly and most planning is carried out on spreadsheets. There is a project to replace the business control system and sales management, sales order

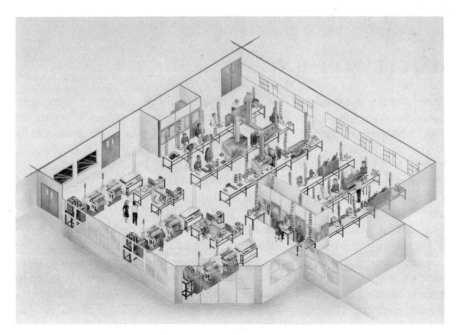

Figure 26.3   Production layout of Apollo Fire Detectors Ltd

processes and sales information systems have been implemented. Eventually the manufacturing systems will be replaced.

SUPPLIERS

Suppliers are very important as Apollo are essentially designers and assemblers. They have worked with their suppliers to develop ship-to-line techniques. Where possible, they negotiate with a supplier once a year to place blanket orders for a year's worth of product. The product is then called off by the shopfloor workers. Apollo have concentrated on products like moulding where there are physical considerations. They may be making millions of detectors but do not want three months' supply at a time to store. The same applies to electronic components which are of high value relatively or with screws and washers which have weight dimensions.

Apollo have been trying to develop confidence in their suppliers' ability to provide product at the right quality and quantity at the right time. They have recently introduced a system of vendor assessment. The number of suppliers has been reduced from 200–300 to about 80, about half of whom are used for any quantity of supplies. This reduction has been achieved, for example, by using distributors for electrical items rather than going to the manufacturers, thereby gaining from the focus.

STAFF DEVELOPMENT

Manufacturing management structure is undergoing change. Apollo have looked to develop their junior managers/supervisors formally with an assessment programme for the individual. They are instituting a development programme which is specifically geared towards achievement of a particular level of NVQs (National Vocational Qualifications). These awards have been offered across the whole of the shopfloor to the direct workforce at Level 1 and 2 in electronics manufacture. So far, after eighteen months about 15% of the people eligible have achieved the award.

In addition, Apollo are developing supervisors/managers in a Level 3 NVQ in supervisory management. This move includes a definite statement to recognise these staff as members of the management team and try to select this grade on the basis of merit. Previously the case was that staff were judged to be potentially good supervisors because they were good workers. The consequences were often too many square pegs in round holes. This scheme is new, and so far no one has completed the award programme to Level 3. These initiatives are seen as part of a general desire on the part of the manufacturing management to involve people at all levels in the company in improving performance.

THE FUTURE

Apollo see the need to make sure that new developments take the techniques which have been learned and develop them further. They are still looking for costs which are less than are currently being achieved. Also market expectations are increasing for more features on existing products and for new products, for instance to cope with more stringent environments such as those found in the petrochemical industry. There is a perceived potential for developing customers' business so that their business grows and Apollo have the opportunity to develop complementary products. These developments will probably require an expansion of the company's design capabilities.

The company will move to a new manufacturing site within a year where it will be possible to have all the existing production under one roof. They are trying to make the best of this opportunity by reviewing their manufacturing processes and are using simulation techniques as one way of assessing options.

The company has been very successful during its relatively short life but now it is embarking on a major development. The successful management of the change will determine the future of the company and its present management.

Managing a Re-engineering Project

Philip Rowland and Colin Armistead

WHAT WILL YOU FIND IN THIS APPENDIX?

Running a process re-engineering project is not easy and this appendix is intended to help those currently involved. In this appendix you will find:

- An outline of the basic steps in a re-engineering project
- A checklist of questions to consider during a project

INTRODUCTION

While re-engineering is firmly focused on processes and the redesign of these to bring about significant improvements in performance, actually undertaking a re-engineering programme is fundamentally about *change management*. Having the best redesign on paper but being unable to implement it is almost useless. Change is not synonymous with improvement, and it is unfortunate that some organisations go through tremendously disruptive and painful change with little real improvement to show for it. Effective change management never loses sight of the objectives of change and ensures that the project remains focused on them, acting swiftly to remove obstacles as they occur.

There is no guaranteed formula for managing a re-engineering project and it is important that organisations manage such projects in a way that suits them and their situation. Having said that, there are some general guidelines which we believe it is appropriate to outline as an appendix to this book which should serve to provoke thought and debate on how a specific project should be run.

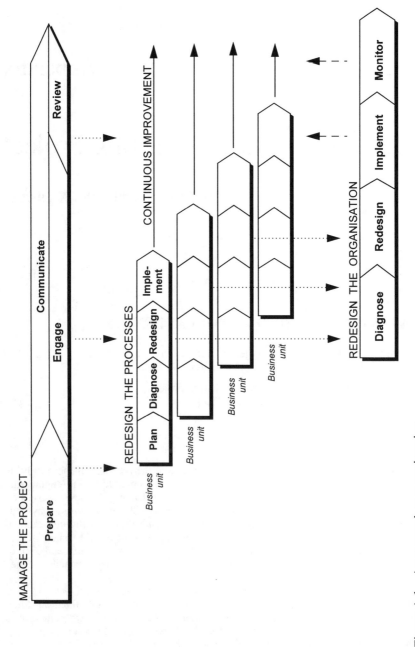

Figure A.1 An approach to re-engineering

AN APPROACH TO RE-ENGINEERING

Figure A.1 outlines an approach to re-engineering which would apply to a large organisation. In general, whatever the size of the organisation it is necessary to go through the basic steps, although the management of the project may be considerably simpler in a small organisation. We have not shown timescales on Figure A.1 as these vary. However, as a general rule of thumb the redesign of processes should be completed within 12 months with each area achieving significant improvements within that period and further improvements in subsequent years.

There are three main elements to the re-engineering project:

1. *Managing the project*   Overseeing the re-engineering project across the organisation – providing strong and visible leadership, communicating continually and consistently
2. *Redesigning the processes*   Designing and implementing new processes, including the roles of people and technology, to improve performance significantly in a number of business units
3. *Redesigning the organisation*   Changing the structure and policies of the organisation to underpin the new process operations

plus the desire that afterwards the skills and experiences in improvement will be applied on an on-going basis:

4. *Continuous improvement*   Continue to improve performance and build improvement skills learned during the re-engineering project while a period of relative stability allows the changes to be refined and finalised

MANAGING THE PROJECT

Senior management play a key role in setting up re-engineering projects and overseeing their progress across the organisation (Figure A.2).

1. Preparation

Projects should support the strategy of the organisation and this requires clarity of direction to which all teams can align their efforts.

1.1 Context

● Is the strategic direction of the organisation and the challenges facing it in delivering this strategy clear?

Figure A.2   Basic steps in managing a BPR project

- Are the major processes of the organisation understood at a high level, with perspectives from different groups such as staff, customers and suppliers adding further insights?
- Are the key leverage points within the process identified?
- Are those processes which directly impact the delivery of the strategy identified?

1.2 Setting ambitious aspirations

- How will the organisation know if it has succeeded?
- Are targets specific, measurable and clearly related to the strategic goals of the organisation?

1.3 Resources and project structure

- Is the *sponsor* of the project senior enough? For major organisation-wide initiatives this means the CEO or COO.
- Is the *re-engineering leader*, the person responsible for the project's success, senior enough and able to exert a high degree of influence over the major organisational constituents of the project?
- Is the *steering group*, comprising the sponsor, re-engineering leader and other senior executives, functioning well as a team and acting decisively in support of the project?
- Is there a *re-engineering support team* to act as coaches to project teams? This team also acts as a school for managers who will later lead projects by putting them together with other managers who have experienced the project in their areas.
- Are the brightest and best staff assigned to the re-engineering effort? If not it is unlikely to deliver real success. The assignment of staff is usually the first tangible signal to the organisation of senior management's commitment to the project. What signals are you sending?

1.4 Approach

- Is the approach to re-engineering understood?
- Are roles clearly identified including outside parties such as customers, suppliers and advisors (e.g. academics and consultants)?

1.5 Early human resources plan

- Are the likely human resources implications of the project identified including the scale of any job cuts?
- Is the succession plan in place for key staff?

2. Communication

Change programmes nearly always generate a great degree of anxiety and fear. This is exacerbated by two natural tendencies. First, management often "duck" talking about issues such as the problems facing the organisation and the scale of any jobs cuts. This may be driven by a desire not to demotivate people or a feeling that they should have all the answers – even at the early stages of the project. Second, people tend to subconsciously "filter" what they are told and this leads to a growing suspicion of senior management's motives and a feeling of not being told the full story. The only way to overcome these problems is to "overcommunicate" – repeatedly and in as many ways as possible tell people what is going on and continually reinforce the need for rapid progress.

Senior management can do little to allay people's fears and insecurities about job cuts which may indeed be about to come true. What they can do by confronting these issues, in an open and honest way, is harness this nervous energy by giving people something to apply it to – the redesign effort. A compelling message of need and inevitability with an approach which gets everyone working hard towards the objective will enable staff to progress the project to a successful conclusion for the organisation. The *quid pro quo* is that management maintain their integrity in communicating with staff and continue to talk to them even though it may be difficult.

2.1 Approach to communication

- Are the "groundrules" for communication established and agreed (e.g. integrity, two-way, timely, continuous)?
- Are issues dealt with proactively (rather than waiting until they surface)?
- Are there opportunities for all staff to raise issues and questions?
- Are management visible and supportive (are they "walking the talk")?
- Are management consistent in their messages (both formal and informal)?
- Is the role of the unions in the project clearly thought through with a communication plan established?

2.2 At the start

- Is the need for change very clear?
- Are the consequences of not changing also clear?
- Is the determination of management to drive the changes through evident?
- Is the project calendar known?

2.3 On-going

- Is the need for change continually reinforced?
- Is progress communicated constantly?
- Are staff kept up to date with progress on HR issues, particularly job changes, job cuts, redundancy packages etc?
- Are early "wins" celebrated?
- Are mistakes and failures acknowledged and the learning identified?

3. Engagement

Management must become fully engaged in the project and this means getting involved in a level of detail which many will find uncomfortable: many will find either God or the Devil in the details, depending on their experience of getting truly engaged. Management must remain "in touch" with the project, encouraging open and honest debate of the issues. This is difficult at a time when people at all levels will be concerned about their jobs and the senior team's behaviour will set the tone for the project at a very early stage.

3.1 Pilot and roll-out areas

- Are pilots being used to test new processes (or is everything being risked on a big-bang approach)?
- Are the right pilot areas selected (e.g. potential for demonstrable impact, representative of the business, sufficient material, high likelihood of success)?
- Is the roll-out plan aggressive in timing while also being sufficiently realistic? Goals generally should be "out of reach, but not out of sight".

3.2 Support, challenge and ownership

- Does the re-engineering leader and other senior management actively support, challenge and own the project?
- Are issues dealt with in a timely, decisive manner with roadblocks removed and the momentum of the project maintained?
- Is the project clearly a top priority in the minds of senior management (do they spend time on it, participate, hold regular reviews, make themselves accessible to teams on the project)?

4. Review

The opportunity to learn from the re-engineering project and create a lasting improvement culture should be taken when the disruptive redesign projects give way to a "bedding down" of the new ways of working.

4.1 Learning

- Are improvements to the re-engineering approach identified and implemented?
- Are any unresolved issues identified and a team assigned to work on them?

4.2 Continuous improvement

- Are targets for on-going improvements set and progress monitored?
- Are the skills in improvement (analysis, idea development and implementation) actively employed day to day (rather than being forgotten)?

REDESIGNING THE PROCESSES

The substance of the task in re-engineering is in designing a new organisation which delivers better products or services faster, more efficiently and more flexibly (Figure A.3).

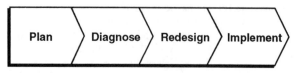

Figure A.3 Basic steps in redesigning processes

1. Planning

Plans should address which processes are to be re-engineered and who will play the key roles in delivering success.

1.1 Project definition

- Are "order of magnitude" targets clear?
- Are accountabilities clear?
- Does the project's scale and scope match its ambitions (i.e. is the project considering all aspects of the operation and doing so across the business unit)?

1.2 Training and building re-engineering teams

- Is training effective at developing skills and team building?
- Are games and simulations used in training?
- Are benchmarking visits to other organisations used to inform teams and encourage new thinking? Do the right people go?

2. Diagnosis

The re-engineering team should rapidly define the core processes driving value in their business and assess any performance gaps in these processes.

2.1 Definition of process boundaries

- Are the boundaries of the project clear and understood by everyone?
- Are any constraints on the team minimised?
- Is a holistic perspective of processes being taken?
- Is the focus of the redesign effort maintained (project "creep" should be avoided at all costs)?

2.2 Evaluation of existing process performance

- Are the later effects of early stages in the process clearly understood?
- Are the real inputs and outputs of the process understood?
- Does management recognise the differences in what happens to what they thought happens? Are insights genuinely being gained or is the exercise superficial?
- Are insights from benchmarking being rapidly shared throughout the organisation?

2.3 Momentum

- Are teams maintaining momentum or are they getting "bogged down"? Watch out for this in process mapping.

3. Redesign

Ideas for new ways of working should be developed and those selected as holding potential be tested by experiments and simulations.

3.1 Idea development

- Are inherent assumptions about the business being challenged?
- Are people thinking creatively about what the ideal world would look like?
- Is a "clean sheet" approach being taken to foster ideas?
- Are areas of obvious waste and underperformance identified?
- Is the potential of technology being fully exploited?
- Are all staff involved?

3.2 Experimentation

- Are teams pushing hard enough to make new ideas work as experiments or simulations?
- Are results being evaluated with sufficient rigour?
- Is the balance of insiders and outsiders from the process being redesigned correctly?

3.3 Design refinement

- Are ideas tested as experiments being sufficiently refined?
- Are all aspects of the new process operation being considered, particularly people and technology?
- Are new process designs being thoroughly reviewed for improvement opportunities? Are activities being eliminated, simplified, integrated and automated as appropriate?

4. Implementation

Turning ideas into working systems is the key challenge in re-engineering.

4.1 Planning and preparation

- Are all aspects of the changes considered (tasks, locations, layout, systems, team structures and objectives)?
- Are the organisational implications of the new processes understood?
- Does training address changes in skills and behaviours?

4.2 Roll-out

- Are management determined to push implementation forward?
- Is the calendar for roll-out clear and achievable?
- Are problems dealt with quickly and efficiently?
- Are changes in jobs and job cuts handled sensitively and with respect?
- Do management communicate effectively with staff?

REDESIGNING THE ORGANISATION

The redesign of processes will have thrown up a number of issues relating to the wider organisation. As the process designs are approved it will be important for management to recognise the further change tasks these will create. Further problem areas are likely to arise during implementation in the leading areas which will experience the tension of operating ahead of the underpinning changes (Figure A.4).

1. Diagnosis

The new requirements for the organisation must be well understood if improvements are to be long-lasting.

1.1 New process requirements

- Are new *responsibilities* and *accountabilities* understood?
- Are *financial systems* being overhauled?
- Are requirements of *information technology* clear?
- Do the *values* and *beliefs* of the organisation need realignment?
- Are changes to *recruitment*, *development* and *training* considered?
- Are required changes to *incentives* understood?
- Are all changes in organisational *relationships* understood (e.g. customers, suppliers)?

1.2 Priorities

- Are the priorities for change understood – what must happen and when?
- Are lead times for changes understood? This may mean delaying some aspects of the proposed process changes until certain elements are in place.

2. Redesign

The redesign of the organisation is often most taxing for senior management as their status, reputations and livelihoods will be affected. This is the same discomfort as others in the organisation will have felt in redesigning processes, and how management responds to this challenge will determine the wider organisational view of the success of the project and the attitude of management. Potentially each area outlined above in Section 1.1, "New process requirements", will require redesign. In addition, the following should be considered.

2.1 Realignment

- Will functional expertise be maintained in critical areas (e.g. marketing)?
- What will career progression be based on in future?
- What will characterise career progression and development?

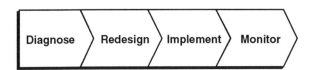

Figure A.4 Basic steps in redesigning the organisation

2.2 Politics

- Is the political agenda of the senior management overriding key changes?
- Is the *sponsor* of the project acting decisively on major issues?

3. Implementation

Some changes in the organisation can be made relatively quickly while others, particularly behaviours, can take a very long time and can only be fully implemented through consistent and strong leadership acting as an example.

3.1 Consequences

- Have all the consequences of changes been thought through (e.g. what undesirable behaviours may result from changes in incentives)?
- Are all staff recognised as "victims" not just those losing their jobs?

3.2 Communications

- Are staff kept up to date about changes?
- Are changes explained clearly and in a way that is relevant to staff?
- Are external communications being well managed?

4. Monitoring

Once again it is the "staying power" of senior management in finishing the job which is often key to achieving an outstanding project. Changes in the organisation, particularly cultural ones, will take a long time and management cannot afford to "revert" to old ways if they wish others to change. Management must monitor the changes and act swiftly to correct problems without compromising the overall integrity of the new organisational design.

Bibliography and References

BIBLIOGRAPHY

There are a large number of books dealing with BPR. Many are contained in the References below but we would highlight some of the earlier books as being important for an understanding of the development of the area:

Hammer, M. and Champy, J. (1993) *Re-engineering the Corporation: A Manifesto for Business Revolution*. Nicholas Brealey Publishing, London.
Davenport, T.H. (1993) *Process Innovation: Re-engineering Work Through Information Technology*. Harvard Business School Press, Boston.
Rummler, G. and Brache, A. (1990) *Improving Performance: How to Manage the White Space on the Organisation Chart*. Jossey-Bass, San Francisco, California.
Harrington, H.J. (1991) *Business Process Improvement*. McGraw-Hill, New York 1991.

REFERENCES

Allen, B.R. and Boynton, A.C. (1992) Information architecture: in search of efficient flexibility, *MIS Quarterly*.
Ames, B.C. (1970) Rappings vs Substance in Industrial Marketing *Harvard Business Review*, July–August.
Ansoff, H.I. (1965) *Corporate Strategy*. Penguin, Harmondsworth.
Ansoff, I. (1984) *Implanting Strategic Management*. Prentice Hall, New York.
Argyris, C. (1990) *Overcoming Organisational Defenses*. Allyn and Bacon.
Armistead, C.G. (1990) Service operations management and strategy: framework for matching the service operations task and the service delivery system. *International Journal of Service Industry Management*, **1**, No. 2.
Armistead, C.G. (1995) Untangling the intangibles: managing by service processes, Inaugural Lecture, Bournemouth University.
Armistead, C.G. and Clark, G. (1994) *Service Management Audit*. Strategic Direction Publishers, Zurich.

Armistead, C.G. and Mapes, J. (1993) Impact of supply chain integration on operating performance. *Logistics Information Management*, **6**, No. 3.

Armistead, C.G., Clark, G. and Stanley, P. (1994) Managing service recovery, in P. Kunst & J. Lemmik (eds.), *Quality Management in Services II*, Van Gorcum, Assen Masstricht.

Barker, R. (1993) Value-adding performance measurement: a time-based approach, *International Journal of Production Management*, **13**, No. 5.

Barnes, J., Burton, F., Hawker, I. and Lyons, M.H. (1994) Scenario modelling of demand for future telecommunication services, International System Dynamics Conference (Business Decision Making), 11–22.

Beier, F.J. (1973) Information systems and the life cycle of logistics departments, *International Journal of Physical Distribution*, **3**, No. 3.

Billesbach, T.J. (1991) Study of the implementation of just-in-time in the United States, *Production & Inventory Management Journal*, **32**, Issue 3, 3rd quarter, 1–4.

Bjorn Andersen, N. and Cavaye, A. (1994) Re-engineering the role of IS professionals, in *Proceedings of IFIP TC8 Open Conference on Business Process Re-engineering: Information System Opportunities and Challenges*, Gold Coast Queensland, Australia, 8–11 May, 17–26.

Bowman, C. (1990) *The Essence of Strategic Management*. Prentice Hall, London.

Bowman, C. and Faulkner, D. (1994) Measuring product advantage using competitive benchmarking and customer perceptions, *Long Range Planning*, **27**, No. 1, 119–32.

Bradley, K. (1993) *PRINCE: a Practical Guide*. Butterworth-Heinemann, Oxford.

Brady, J. and Davis, I. (1993) Marketing's mid life crisis, *The McKinsey Quarterly*, **2**, 17–28.

Bridge, W. (1994) The end of the job, *Fortune*, 19 September, 62ff.

Brophy, J.T. and Monger, R.F. (1989) Competitive capacity from an integrated IS infrastructure, *Information Strategy: The Executive's Journal*, **5**, 2, 26–33.

Brown, S. (1993) Post modern marketing? *European Journal of Marketing*, **27**, No. 4, 19–34.

Brownlie, D., Saren, M., Whittington, R. and Wensley, R. (1994) The new marketing myopia, *European Journal of Marketing*, **28**, No. 3, 6–2.

Butler Cox Foundation (1991) *The Role of Information Technology in Transforming the Business*. Research Report 79, London, January.

Byrne, S.J. and Roberts, L. (1994) Efficient parts supply: information flows, International System Dynamics Conference (Production & Operations Management), 11–19.

Cabinet Office Efficiency Unit (1988) *Improving Management in Government: the Next Steps*. Ibbs Report, HMSO.

CCTA, *Market Testing IS/IT* (booklets available from the Library, CCTA, Rosebery Court, Norwich, NR7 0HS).

CCTA (1989) *Strategic Planning for Information Systems*. CCTA Information Systems Guides, A2, Wiley, Chichester.

CCTA (1991) *Appraisal and Evaluation of IS Strategies*. March, HMSO.

CCTA (1994a) *An Introduction to Programme Management & Guide to Programme Management*. HMSO.

CCTA (1994b) *BPR in the Public Sector*. May, HMSO.

Cecil, J. and Goldstein, M. (1990) Sustaining competitive advantage from IT, *The McKinsey Quarterly*, **4**, 74–89.

Chandler, A.D. (1962) *Strategy and Structure*. MIT Press, Cambridge, MA.

Chandler, A.D. (1977) *The Visible Hand*. Harvard University Press, Cambridge, MA.

Checkland, P.B. (1981) *Systems Thinking, Systems Practice*. Wiley, Chichester.

Christopher, M. (1993) Logistics and customer relationships, *Proceedings of the First International Colloquium on Relationship Marketing*, Monash University, Melbourne, Australia.

Clark, K.B. and Fujimoto, T. (1990) The power of product integrity, *Harvard Business Review*, November/December, 107.

Clark, K.B. and Fujimoto, T. (1991) *Product Development Performance*. Harvard Business School Press, Boston, MA.

Collins Dictionary of the English Language, 2nd edn (1986).

Cranfield Centre for Logistics and Transportation Logistics (1994) *Futures in Europe – A Delphi Study* (Executive Report), February.

Crosby, P. (1979) *Quality is Free: The Art of Making Quality Certain*. Mentor Books, London.

CSC Index (1994) *The State of Re-engineering*. CSC Index, London.

Currie, W. (1994) The Strategic Management of Large Scale IT Projects in the Financial Services Sector, *New Technology Work and Employment*, **9**, No. 1, 19–29.

Dair, I. (1993) Building a new organisation for nature conservation, *Long Range Planning*, **26**, No. 1.

Davenport, T.H. (1993a) Need radical improvement and continuous improvement? Integrate process re-engineering and TQM, *Planning Review*, No. 3, 6–12.

Davenport, T.H. (1993b) *Process Innovation: Re-engineering Work Through Information Technology*. Harvard Business School Press, Boston, MA.

Davenport, T.H. (1993c) *Process Innovation*. Harvard Business School Press, Boston, MA.

Davenport, T.H. and Short, J. (1990) The new industrial engineering: information technology and business process redesign, *Sloan Management Review*, Summer, 11–27.

Davidow, W.H. and Malone, M.S. (1992) *The Virtual Corporation*. HarperCollins, New York.

Davis, A. (1994) Application of system dynamics to re-engineering career plans, International System Dynamics Conference (Business Decision Making), 31–39.

De Jonquières, G. (1993) A clean break with tradition, *Financial Times*, 12 July.

Deming, W.E. (1986) *Out of Crisis*. Cambridge University Press, New York.

Development Dimensions International (DDI) Scherer, J. & Associates (1994) *Re-engineering Forum*. PEPI Sixth International Conference Brochure, Atlanta, GA.

Doman, A., Glucksman, M., Mass, N. and Sasportes, M. (1994) The dynamics of managing a life insurance company, International System Dynamics Conference (Business Decision Making), 40–52.

Done, K. (1994) £9.4 m aid to halt Jaguar move abroad, *Financial Times*, 30 March.

Doppler, K. and Lauterburg, Ch. (1994) *Change management. Den Unternehmenswandel gestalten*. Frankfurt am Main.

Drucker, P. (1974) *Management: Tasks, Responsibilities, Practices*. Heinemann, London.

Drucker, P. (1993) *Post Capitalist Society*. Harper Business, New York.

Earl, M. (1989) *Management Strategies for Information Technology*. Prentice-Hall, Hemel Hempstead.

Earl, M. (1992) Putting IT in its place: a polemic for the nineties, *Journal of Information Technology*, **7**, 100–108.

Earl, M. (1993) Experiences in strategic information systems planning, *MIS Quarterly*, March.

Easton, G.S. (1993) The state of US Total Quality Management: A Baldridge examiner's perspective, *California Management Review*, **35**, Issue 3, Spring, 32–54.

Economist (1992) White collar computers. 1 August.

Economist (1994a) Between two worlds (a survey of manufacturing technology). 5 March.

Economist (1994b) Re-engineering reviewed, 2 July, 80.

Economist (1995) How to turn junk mail into a goldmine – or perhaps not, 1 April, 82.

Edwards, C. and Peppard, J. (1994) Business process redesign: Hype, hope or hypocrisy, *Journal of Information Technology*, **9**, 251–266.

Edwards, C., Burke, G., Davis, M. and Peppard, J. (1995) On-going research.

Evans, G.N. and Naim, M.M. (1994) The dynamics of capacity constrained supply chains, International System Dynamics Conference (Production & Operations Management), 28–39.

Feeney, D. and Ives, B. (1991) In search of sustainability – reaping long term advantage from investments in information technology, *Journal of Management Information Systems*, **7**, 1, Summer, 27–46.

Flynn, D.J. and Goleniewska, E. (1993) A survey of the use of strategic information systems planning approaches in UK organisations, *Journal of Strategic Information Systems*, **2**, 4, 292–319.

Forrester, J.W. (1961) *Industrial Dynamics*. MIT Press, Boston, MA.

Forrester, J.W. (1992) Policies, decisions, and information sources for modeling, *European Journal of Operational Research*, **59**(1), 42–63. This and other key papers previously published in a special edition of the *European Journal of Operational Research* **59**(1) in 1992 are reprinted with other material in *Modeling for Learning Organizations* (Morecroft and Sterman, 1994).

Galliers, R.D. and Sutherland, A.R. (1991) Information systems management and strategy formulation: the "stages of growth" model revisited, *Journal of Information Systems*, **1**, 89–114.

Galliers, R.D. (1992) Strategic information systems planning: myths, realities and guidelines for successful implementation, *European Journal of Information Systems*, **1**, 1, 55–64.

Galliers, R.D., Pattison, E.M. and Reponen, T. (1994) Strategic information systems planning workshops: lessons from three cases, *International Journal of Information Management*, **14**, 51–66.

Gavin, D.A. (1995) *Leveraging Processes for Strategic Advantage*, Harvard Business Review, September–October 77–90.

George, M., Freeling, A. and Court, D. (1994) Re-inventing the marketing organisation, *McKinsey Quarterly*, No. 4.

Ghosal, S. and Barlett, C.A. (1995) Changing the role of top management: beyond structure to process, *Harvard Business Review*, January–February, 87–96.

Gleick, J. (1988) *Chaos: Making a New Science*. Heinemann, London.

Gore, A. (1993) From red tape to results: creating a government that works better and costs less, in *The National Performance Review*, Times Books, Random House, New York.

Graham, A.K., Morecroft, J.D.W., Senge, P.M. and Sterman, J.D. (1991) Model-supported case studies for management education, *European Journal of Operations Research*, **59**, 151–166.

Granovetter, M. (1985) Economic action and social structure: the problem of embeddedness, *American Journal of Sociology*, **91** (3), 481–510.

Grant, R.M. (1991) The resource-based theory of competitive advantage: implications for strategy formulation, *California Management Review*, Spring, 114–35.

Grint, K. (1995) Utopian re-engineering, in G. Barke and J. Peppard (eds), *Examining Business Process Re-engineering: Current Perspectives and Research Directions.* Kogan Page, London, pp. 192–216.

Grover, V., Tang, J.T.C. and Fiedler, K.D. (1993) Information technology enabled business process redesign: an integrated framework, *Omega*, 21, 4, 433–47.

Hall, G., Rosenthal, J. and Wade, J. (1993) How to make re-engineering really work, *Harvard Business Review*, November–December, 119–31.

Hall, R.I. (1976) A system pathology of an organisation: the rise and fall of the old *Saturday Evening Post, Administrative Science Quarterly*, 21, 185–211.

Hall, R.I. (1994) Organizational learning and adapting trajectories found in a system dynamics based business game, International System Dynamics Conference (Business Decision Making), 73–82.

Hammer, M. (1990) Re-engineering work: don't automate, obliterate, *Harvard Business Review*, July/August, 104–12.

Hammer, M. (1994) Succeeding at re-engineering or in the footstep of Leonid Kravchuk, Presentation at SGO, Herbsttagung, Zürich.

Hammer, M. and Champy, J. (1993) *Re-engineering the Corporation: A Manifesto for Business Revolution.* Nicholas Brealey Publishing, London.

Hammer, M. and Stanton, A. (1995) *The Re-engineering Revolution: A Handbook.* HarperCollins, New York.

Handy, C.B. (1985) *Understanding Organisations*, Penguin Books, London, p. 13.

Handy, C.B. (1989) *The Age of Unreason.* Century Hutchinson, London.

Harrison, A. (1992) *Just-in-Time Manufacturing in Perspective.* Prentice Hall, Hemel Hempstead.

Harvard Business School (1986) Baxter Healthcare Corporation: ASAP Express, Harvard Business School, 9-186-005 (April 1986), 9-188-080 (February 1991).

Hayes, R.H. and Wheelwright, S.C. (1979) Link manufacturing processes and product life cycles, *Harvard Business Review*, January–February, 133–42.

Heller, R. (1994) In pursuit of paragons, *Management Today*, May.

Henderson, B.D. (1989) The origin of strategy, *Harvard Business Review*, November–December, 139–43.

Henderson, J. and Sifonis, J.G. (1986) Middle out strategic planning: the value of IS planning to business planning, in *Proceedings of the 1986 NYU Symposium on Strategic Uses of Information Technology*, New York, 21–23 May.

Henderson, J.C. and Venkatraman, N. (1993) Strategic alignment: leveraging information technology for transforming organisations, *IBM Systems Journal*, 32, 1, 4–16.

Heskett, J.L. (1986) *Managing in the Service Economy.* Harvard Business School Press, Boston, MA.

Heygate, R. (1993) Memo to a CEO: avoiding the mainframe trap in redesign, *The McKinsey Quarterly*, Autumn, 79–86.

Hill, T.J. (1985) *Manufacturing Strategy: The Strategic Management of the Manufacturing Function.* Macmillan, Basingstoke.

Hinterhuber, H.H. (1995) Business process management: the European approach, *Business Change & Re-engineering*, 2, No. 4, 63–73.

Hitchcock, D. (1994) *The Work Redesign Team Handbook. A Step-by-Step Guide to Creating Self-Directed Teams.* Quality Resources, New York.

HM Treasury (1993) *The Private Finance Initiative.* TRSY J08112ONJ, HMSO.

Hocking, A.C. and Lee, P.S. (1994) Systems thinking and business process re-design: a case for combining techniques, International System Dynamics Conference (Problem-Solving Methodologies), 90–103.

Hooley, G.J. and Lynch, J.E. (1985) Marketing lessons from the UK's high flying companies, *Journal of Marketing Management*, **1**, 65–74.

Hopper, M.D. (1990) Rattling SABRE – new ways to compete on information, *Harvard Business Review*, May–June, 118–25.

Houlder, V. (1995) EDI: What benefit is it? *Financial Times*, 27 March, 13.

Hsieh, T.Y. (1992) The road to renewal, *The McKinsey Quarterly*, No. 3, 28–36.

Hsu, M. and Howard, M. (1994) Work-flow and legacy systems, *Byte*, July, 109–16.

Hunt, S.D. (1994) On re-thinking marketing: our discipline, our practice, our methods, *European Journal of Marketing*, **28**, No. 3, 13–25.

Hunt, V.D. (1994) *Re-engineering. Leveraging the Power of Integrated Product Development*. Essex Junction/VT.

IIR Institute for International Research (ed.) (1993) *Implementing Business Process Re-engineering. Achieving Breakthrough in Performance*. Congress Orlando, FLA.

IS Analyzer (1993) The role of IS in business process re-engineering, August.

Johansson, H.J., McHugh, P., Pendlebury, A.J. and Wheeler, W.A. (1993) *Business Process Re-Engineering*. Wiley, Chichester.

Johnson, G. (1992) Managing strategic change – strategy, culture and action, *Long Range Planning*, **25**, No. 1, 28–36.

Johnson, G. and Scholes, K. (1993) *Exploring Corporate Strategy*, Prentice Hall, Hemel Hempstead.

Juran, J.M. (1975) *Quality Control Handbook*, 3rd edn, McGraw-Hill, New York.

Kaplan, R.S. (1992) The balance scorecard – measures that drive performance, *Harvard Business Review*, January–February, 71–9.

Katz, A.S. (1993) Eight TQM pitfalls, *Journal for Quality & Participation*, **16**, Issue 4, July/August, 24–7.

Keough, M. and Doman, A. (1992) The CEO as designer: an interview with Jay. W. Forrester, *McKinsey Quarterly*, **2**, 3–30.

Ketkar, M. (1994) Management of the IT infrastructure, Working Paper, Information Systems Research Centre, Cranfield School of Management, Bedford.

King, S. (1985) Has marketing failed or was it never really tried? *Journal of Marketing Management*, **1**, 1–18.

Kotler, P. (1980) *Marketing Management*, 4th edn, Englewood Cliffs, NJ, Prentice Hall.

Kanst, P. and Lemmik, J. (1994) *Quality Management in Services II*. Van Gorcum, Assen Maastricht.

La Roche, U. (1994) A basic business loop as starting template for customized business-process-engineering models, International System Dynamics Conference (Change Management), 39–45.

Lambert, R. and Peppard, J. (1993) IT and new organisational forms: destination but no road map, *Journal of Strategic Information Systems*, **2**, 3, 180–205.

Lamming, R. (1993) *Beyond Partnership: Strategies for Innovation & Lean Supply*. Prentice Hall, Hemel Hempstead.

Laurence, C. (1994) Computer gets to the bottom of fitting jeans, *Daily Telegraph*. 9 November.

Lawrence, P.R. and Lorsch, J.W. (1967) *Organisation and Environment*. Irwin, Homewood, IL.

Lederer, A.L. and Sethi, V. (1988) The implementation of strategic information systems planning methodologies, *MIS Quarterly*, **12**, 3, 445–61.

Levitt, T. (1976) The industrialisation of service, *Harvard Business Review*, September–October, 63–74.

Lorenz, C. (1994) Ringing the changes brings mixed results, *Financial Times*, 24 June, 14.

Losee, S. (1994) Mr Cozzette buys a computer, *Fortune*, 18 April.

Lynch, J.E. (1991) The repositioning of brand management, *Proceedings of 24th Annual Conference of the Marketing Education Group of Great Britain*, Cardiff Business School, July, Vol. 2, pp. 670–81.

Lynch, J.E. (1994a) What is marketing? in N. Hart (ed.), *Effective Industrial Marketing*. Kogan Page, London, pp. 19–32.

Lynch, J.E. (1994b) Only connect: the role of marketing and strategic management in the modern organisation, *Journal of Marketing Management*, **10**, No. 6, 527–42.

MacKenzie, B. (1994) Business process re-engineering, *Management Extra* (The Association of MBAs), February.

Mazur, L. (1995) Called to account, *Marketing Business*, April, 23–6.

McDonald, M. (1994) Marketing – A mid-life crisis? *Marketing Business*, May, 10–4.

Meirs, D. (1994) *Process Product Watch*: Volumes 1–3. Enix Limited, Richmond, Surrey.

Miles, R. and Snow, C. (1987) Network organisations: new concepts and new forms, *Calfornia Management Review*, Spring.

Mintzberg, H. (1987) Crafting strategy, *Harvard Business Review*, July–August, 65–75.

Mintzberg, H. and Waters, J. (1982) Emergent strategy, *Strategic Management Journal*, **6**, 3.

Mintzberg, H. (1983) *Structures in Fives: Designing Effective Organisations*. Prentice Hall, Englewood Cliffs, NJ.

Mitchell, A. (1993) The transformation of marketing, *Marketing Business*, November, 9–14.

Mitchell, A. (1994) Marketing's new model army, *Management Today*, March, 42–9.

Morecroft, J.D.W. and Sterman, J.D. (eds.) (1994) *Modeling for Learning Organisations*. Productivity Press, Portland, OR.

Morris, D. and Brandon, J. (1994) *Revolution im Unternehmen. Re-engineering für die Zukunft*, Landshut am Lech.

Mumford, E. (1987) Socio-technical design: evolving theory and practice, in Bjerknes, Hen and King (eds), *Computers and Democracy*, Avery, New York.

Mumford, E. (1995) Creating chaos or constructive change: Business process re-engineering versus socio-technical design? in G. Barke and J. Peppard (eds), *Examining Business Process Re-engineering: Current Perspectives and Research Directions*. Kogan Page, London, pp. 192–216.

Murray, J.A. (1994) The challenge to marketing education, 14th Annual Marketing Teachers' Conference, Trinity College, Dublin, May.

Neely, A. (1993) *Performance Measurement System Design – Theory and Practice*. Cambridge Manufacturing Group Internal Report, Cambridge University.

Niederman, F., Brancheau, J. and Wetherbe, J.C. (1991) Information systems management issues for the 1990's, *MIS Quarterly*, **15**, 4, 475–95.

Nolan, R.L. (1979) Managing the crisis in data processing, *Harvard Business Review*, March–April.

Nolan, R.L. and Gibson, C.F. (1974) Managing the four stages of EDP growth, *Harvard Business Review*, January–February.

Northcote, S.H. and Trevelyan, C.E. (1954) *The Organisation of the Permanent Civil Service*. HMSO.

Oakland, J.S. (1989) *Total Quality Management*. Heinemann Professional, Oxford.

Obeng, E. and Crainer, S. (1994) *Making Re-engineering Happen*. Pitman, London.

Ohmae, K. (1987) *The Mind of the Strategist: Art of Japanese Management*, Penguin, Harmondsworth.

Olstroff, F. and Smith, D. (1992) Redesigning the corporation: the horizontal organisation, *The McKinsey Quarterly*, No. 1, 149–68.

Orgland, M.Y. (1994) *Designing and Implementing Holistic Change Programs in Business Process Re-engineering*. Doctoral Program, St Gallen, p. 15.

Osborne, D. and Gaebler, T. (1992) *Reinventing Government*. Addison-Wesley, Reading, MA.

P-E Centre for Management Research (1993) *The role of IT in business re-engineering*.

Paich, M. and Sterman, J.D. (1993) Boom, bust, and failures to learn in experimental markets, *Management Science*, **39**(12), 1439–58.

Parasuraman, A., Zeithaml, V.A. and Berry, L.L. (1986) *Servqual: A Multiple Item Scale for Measuring Consumer Perceptions of Service Quality*. Marketing Science Institute, Cambridge, MA.

Parker, M.M. and Benson, R.S. (1988) *Information Economics – Linking Business Performance to Information Technology*. Prentice Hall, Englewood Cliffs, NJ.

Parnaby, J. (1988) A systems approach to the implementation of JIT methodologies in Lucas Industries, *International Journal of Production Research*, **26**, No. 3, 483–92.

Peppard, J. and Preece, I. (1995) The content, context and process of business process re-engineering, in G. Burke and J. Peppard (eds), *Examining Business Process Re-engineering: Current Perspectives and Research Directions*. Kogan Page, London, pp. 157–85.

Peppard, J. and Rowland, P. (1995) *The Essence of Business Process Re-engineering*, Prentice Hall, Hemel Hempstead.

Peteraf, M. (1993) The cornerstones of competitive advantage: a resource-based view, *Strategic Management Journal*, **14**, 179–91.

Pettigrew, A. (1985) *The Awakening Giant: Continuity and Change in ICI*. Blackwell, Oxford.

Porter, M. (1980) *Competitive Strategy*. Free Press, New York.

Porter, M. (1985) *Competitive Advantage*. Free Press, New York.

Poulsen, P.T. (1993) *LEGO – en virksomhed og dens sjael*, translated from *The Paradoxes of Process*. Copenhagen.

Prahalad, C.K. and Hamel, G. (1990) The core competence of the corporation, *Harvard Business Review*, May–June, 71–91.

Prahalad, C.K and Hamel, G. (1994) Strategy as a field of study: why search for a new paradigm? *Strategic Management Journal*, **15**, 5–16.

Price Waterhouse (1993a) *Information Technology Review 1993/94*. London, p. 25.

Price Waterhouse (1993b) *Price Waterhouse IT Survey*. London.

Pugh, D.S. and Hickson, D.J. (1989) *Writers on Organisations*, 4th edn, Penguin Books, London, pp. 186–7.

Pyburn, P. (1991) Redefining the role of information technology, *Business Quarterly*, Winter, 89–94.

Quinn, J.B. (1992) *Intelligent Enterprise*. Free Press, New York.

Quinn, J.B. and Hilmer, F.G. (1994) Strategic outsourcing, *Sloan Management Review*, Summer, 43–55.

Quinn, J.B. and Bailey, M. (1995) Information Technology: increasing productivity in services, *Academy of Management Executive*, **8**, No. 3, 28–48.

Rai, A. and Paper, D. (1994) Successful re-engineering through IT investment, *Information Strategy: The Executive's Journal*, **10**, 4, 15–20.

Reed, R. and DeFillipini, R.J. (1990) Causal ambiguity, barriers to imitation and sustainable competitive advantage, *Academy of Management Review*, **15**, No. 1, 88–102.

Richardson, G.P. (1991) *Feedback Thought in Social Science and Systems Theory*. University of Pennsylvania Press, Philadelphia.

Rockart, J. and Short, J. (1989) IT in the 1990s: managing organisation interdependencies, *Sloan Management Review*, **30**, 2, 7–17.

Rummler, G. and Brache, A. (1990) *Improving Performance: How to Manage the White Space on the Organisation Chart*. Jossey-Bass, San Francisco, CA.

Sasser, W.E., Olsen, R.P. and Wycoff, D.D. (1978) *Management of Service Operations*. Allyn & Bacon, Boston, MA.

Sauer, C. (1993) Why information systems fail: A case study approach, Alfred Waller, Henley on Thames.

Schaffer, D.S. (1993) Why total quality programs miss the mark, *Journal for Quality & Participation*, **16**, Issue 5, September, 18–27.

Schary, P. (1994) Organising for logistics, in J. Cooper (ed.), *Logistics and Distribution Planning: Strategies for Management*, 2nd edn. Kogan Page, London.

Scherr, A. (1993) A new approach to business processes, *IBM Systems Journal*, **32**, 1, 80–98.

Scholz, R. (1994) *Geschäftsprozessoptimierung. Crossfunktionale Rationalisierung oder strukturelle Reorganisation*. Bergisch Gladbach.

Schonberger, R.J. (1987) *World Class Manufacturing Casebook: Implementing JIT and TQC*. Free Press, New York.

Schonberger, R.J. (1989) *Building a Chain of Customers: Linking Business Functions to Create the World Class Company*. Free Press, New York.

Schonberger, R.J. and Knod, E.M. (1991) *Operations Management: Improving Customer Service*, 4th edn. Irwin, Homewood, IL.

Scott Morton, M. (1991) *The Corporation of the 1990s: Information Technology and Organisational Transformation*. Oxford University Press, New York.

Segal-Horn, S. (1995) Core competence and international strategy in service multinational, in C. Armistead and R. Teare (eds), *Services Management: New Directions and Perspectives*. Cassell, London.

Senge, P.M. (1990) *The Fifth Discipline: The Art and Practice of the Learning Organisation*. Doubleday/Currency, New York.

Senge, P. and Sterman, J.D. (1992) Systems thinking and organisational learning: acting locally and thinking globally in the organization of the future, *European Journal of Operational Research*, **59**(1), 137–50.

Servatius, H.-G. (1994) *Business Process Re-engineering. Von erstarrten Strukturen zu fliessenden Prozessen*. Stuttgart.

Shingo, S. (1989) *The Toyota Production System*, translated by Andrew Dillon, Productivity Press, 1989.

Shrivastava, P. (1986) Is strategic management ideological? *Journal of Management*, **12**(3), 363–77.

Siegel, B. (1991) Organising for a successful CE process, *Industrial Engineering*, **23**, No. 12, 15–9.

Skinner, W.M. (1969) Manufacturing – the missing link in manufacturing strategy, *Harvard Business Review*, September–October, 136–45.

Skinner, W. (1974) The focused factory, *Harvard Business Review*, May–June, p. 113.

Slack, N., Chambers S., Harrison, A., Johnston, R. and Harland, C. (1995) *Operations Management*. Pitman Publishing, London.

Sloan, A.P. (1963) *My Years With General Motors*. Sidgwick & Jackson, London.

Stalk, G. and Hout, T.M. (1990) *Competing against Time: How Time-based Competition is Reshaping Global Markets*. Free Press, New York.

Stalk, G., Evans, P. and Schulman, L.E. (1990) Competing on capabilities: the new rules of corporate strategy, *Harvard Business Review*, March/April, 57–69.

Stephens, C.S., Mitra, A., Ford, F.N. and Ledbetter, W.N. (1995) The CIO's dilemma: participating in strategic planning, *Information Strategy: The Executive's Journal*, Spring, 13–7.

Sterman, J.D. (1989) Modeling managerial behaviour: misperceptions of feedback in a dynamic decision making experiment, *Management Science*, **35**(3), 321–39.

Stevens, M. (1994) Getting the processes right, *Marketing Business*, May, 18–22.

Sullivan, C.H. (1985) Systems planning in the information age, *Sloan Management Review*, Winter.

Suzaki, K. (1994) *Die ungenutzten Potentiale. Neues Management im Produktionsbereich*. Munich.

Talwar, R. (1994) Business re-engineering – a strategy driven approach, *Long Range Planning*, **26**, 6, 22–40.

Tapscott, D. and Caston, A. (1993) *Paradigm Shift: The New Promise of Information Technology*. McGraw-Hill, New York.

Taylor, F.W. (1967) *Principles of Scientific Management*. Harper and Row, New York.

Teng, J.T.C., Grover, V. and Fiedler, K.D. (1995) Re-designing business processes using information technology, *Long Range Planning*, **7**, 1, 95–106.

Thomas, J. (1993) *Business Process Reengineering: Reinventing the Business Enterprise*. MBA thesis, Warwick University.

Thompson, J.D. (1967) *Organisations in Action*. McGraw-Hill, New York.

Thurlby, R. and Chang, J. (1994) The application of system dynamics to the re-engineering of value processes, International System Dynamics Conference (Change Management), 59–68.

Todd, P.A., McKeen, J.D. and Gallupe, R.B. (1995) The evolution of IS job skills: a content analysis of IS job advertisements from 1970–1990, *MIS Quarterly*, March, 1–27.

Tong, I. (1994) Using workflow to understand our business, in *Proceedings of Unicom Conference, Improving Business Performance Through Effective Use of IT*, 7–9 June, pp. 319–26.

Towers, S. (1994) *Business Process Reengineering. A Practical Handbook for Executives*. GB, Cheltenham.

UK Government (White Paper) (1991) The Citizen's Charter, Cm 1597, HMSO.

UK Government (White Paper) (1994) The Civil Service: Continuity and Change, Cm 2627, HMSO.

UK Government (White Paper) (1994–95) Statistical supplement, in Financial Statement and Budget Report, Cm 2519, HMSO.

van Ackere, A., Larsen, E.R. and Morecroft, J.D.W. (1993) Systems thinking and business process redesign: an application of the beer game, *European Management Journal*, **11**(4), 412–23.

Venkatraman, N. and Loh, L. (1993) The shifting logic of the IS organisation: from technical portfolio to relationship portfolio, *Information Strategy: The Executive Journal*, Winter.

Venkatraman, N. and Short, J. (1993) Beyond business process redesign: redefining Baxter's business network, *Sloan Management Review*, Fall, 7–21.

Venkatraman, N. (1991) IT induced business re-configuration in M.S. Scott Morton (ed.), *The Corporation of the 1990s: Information Technology and Organisational Transformation*. Oxford University Press, New York.

Venkatraman, N. (1994) IT-enabled business transformation: from automation to business scope redefinition, *Sloan Management Review*. Winter, 73–87.

Voss, C.A., Russell, V. and Twigg, D. (1991) Implementation issues in simultaneous engineering, *International Journal of Technology Management*, **6**, No. 3, 293–302.

Ward, J., Griffiths, P. and Whitmore, P. (1990) *Strategic Planning For Information Systems*. Wiley, Chichester.

Ward, J. and Peppard, J. (1996) The IT/business relationship: a troubled marriage in need of guidance, *Journal of Strategic Information Systems*, **15**, No. 1.

Waterman, H.R., Peters, T.J. and Phillips, J.R. (1980) Structure is not organisation, *Business Horizons*, June.

Weber, M. (1947) *The Theory of Social and Economic Organisation*. Free Press, New York.

Webster, F.E. Jr (1992) The changing role of marketing in the corporation, *Journal of Marketing*, **56**, October, 1–17.

Weil, P. (1993) The role and value of IT infrastructure: some empirical evidence, in R.D. Banker, R.J. Kaufman and M.A. Mahmood (eds), *Strategic Information Technology Management: Perspectives on Organisational Growth and Competitive Advantage*. Idea Group Publishing, Harrisbury, PA, pp. 547–72.

Wernerfelt, B. (1984) A resource-based view of the firm, *Strategic Management Journal*, **5**, 2, 171–80.

Whittington, R. (1993) *What is Strategy – and Does it Matter?* Routledge, London.

Wiesbord, M.R. (1989) The flying starship factory, *Industry Week*, 3 April.

Wiseman, C. (1985) *Strategy and Computers*. Dow Jones-Irwin, Homewood, IL.

Wolstenholme, E.F. (1990) *System Enquiry*. Wiley, Chichester.

Womack, J.P. and Jones, T.D. (1993) *The Machine that Changed the World*. HarperCollins, London.

Womack, J.P. and Jones, D.T. (1994) From lean production to the lean enterprise, *Harvard Business Review*, March/April.

Woodward, J. (1965) *Industrial Organisation: Theory and Practice*. Oxford University Press, Oxford.

Index